Space in Modern Egyptian Fiction

Edinburgh Studies in Modern Arabic Literature
Series Editor: Rasheed El-Enany

Writing Beirut: Mappings of the City in the Modern Arabic Novel
Samira Aghacy

Autobiographical Identities in Contemporary Arab Literature
Valerie Anishchenkova

The Iraqi Novel: Key Writers, Key Texts
Fabio Caiani and Catherine Cobham

Sufism in the Contemporary Arabic Novel
Ziad Elmarsafy

Gender, Nation, and the Arabic Novel: Egypt 1892–2008
Hoda Elsadda

The Unmaking of the Arab Intellectual: Prophecy, Exile and the Nation
Zeina G. Halabi

Post-War Anglophone Lebanese Fiction: Home Matters in the Diaspora
Syrine Hout

Prophetic Translation: The Making of Modern Egyptian Literature
Maya I. Kesrouany

Nasser in the Egyptian Imaginary
Omar Khalifah

Conspiracy in Modern Egyptian Literature
Benjamin Koerber

War and Occupation in Iraqi Fiction
Ikram Masmoudi

Literary Autobiography and Arab National Struggles
Tahia Abdel Nasser

The Arab Nahḍah*: The Making of the Intellectual and Humanist Movement*
Abdulrazzak Patel

Blogging from Egypt: Digital Literature, 2005–2016
Teresa Pepe

Space in Modern Egyptian Fiction
Yasmine Ramadan

Occidentalism: Literary Representations of the Maghrebi Experience of the East–West Encounter
Zahia Smail Salhi

Sonallah Ibrahim: Rebel with a Pen
Paul Starkey

Minorities in the Contemporary Egyptian Novel
Mary Youssef

edinburghuniversitypress.com/series/smal

Space in Modern Egyptian Fiction

Yasmine Ramadan

EDINBURGH
University Press

Edinburgh University Press is one of the leading university presses in the UK. We publish academic books and journals in our selected subject areas across the humanities and social sciences, combining cutting-edge scholarship with high editorial and production values to produce academic works of lasting importance. For more information visit our website: edinburghuniversitypress.com

© Yasmine Ramadan, 2020, 2021

Edinburgh University Press Ltd
The Tun – Holyrood Road
12 (2f) Jackson's Entry
Edinburgh EH8 8PJ

First published in hardback by Edinburgh University Press 2020

Typeset in 11/15 Adobe Garamond by
Servis Filmsetting Ltd, Stockport, Cheshire, and

A CIP record for this book is available from the British Library

ISBN 978 1 4744 2764 7 (hardback)
ISBN 978 1 4744 2765 4 (paperback)
ISBN 978 1 4744 2766 1 (webready PDF)
ISBN 978 1 4744 2767 8 (epub)

The right of Yasmine Ramadan to be identified as author of this work has been asserted in accordance with the Copyright, Designs and Patents Act 1988 and the Copyright and Related Rights Regulations 2003 (SI No. 2498).

Contents

Series Editor's Foreword	vi
Note on Transliteration	ix
Acknowledgements	x
Introduction: Space and the Sixties	1
1 Cairo: Urban Space, Surveillance and the State	31
2 Of Other Cities	73
3 Re-imagining the Rural: The Mystical and the Mythical	116
4 The Politics and Economics of Exile	154
5 Beyond the Sixties	184
Appendix	195
Bibliography	205
Index	227

Series Editor's Foreword

Edinburgh Studies in Modern Arabic Literature is a new and unique series that will, it is hoped, fill in a glaring gap in scholarship in the field of modern Arabic literature. Its dedication to Arabic literature in the modern period (that is, from the nineteenth century onwards) is what makes it unique among series undertaken by academic publishers in the English-speaking world. Individual books on modern Arabic literature in general or aspects of it have been and continue to be published sporadically. Series on Islamic studies and Arab/Islamic thought and civilisation are not in short supply either in the academic world, but these are far removed from the study of Arabic literature qua literature, that is, imaginative, creative literature as we understand the term when, for instance, we speak of English literature or French literature. Even series labelled 'Arabic/Middle Eastern Literature' make no period distinction, extending their purview from the sixth century to the present, and often including non-Arabic literatures of the region. This series aims to redress the situation by focusing on the Arabic literature and criticism of today, stretching its interest to the earliest beginnings of Arab modernity in the nineteenth century.

The need for such a dedicated series, and generally for the redoubling of scholarly endeavour in researching and introducing modern Arabic literature to the Western reader, has never been stronger. Among activities and events heightening public, let alone academic, interest in all things Arab, and not least Arabic literature, are the significant growth in the last decades of the translation of contemporary Arab authors from all genres, especially fiction, into English; the higher profile of Arabic literature internationally since the award of the Nobel Prize in Literature to Naguib Mahfouz in 1988; the growing number of Arab authors living in the Western diaspora and writing both in English and Arabic; the adoption of such authors and others by mainstream, high-circulation publishers, as opposed to the academic publishers of the past; the establishment of prestigious prizes, such as the International Prize for Arabic Fiction (IPAF; the Arabic Booker), run by the Man Booker Foundation, which brings huge publicity to the shortlist and winner every year, as well as translation contracts into English and other languages; and, very recently, the events of the Arab Spring. It is therefore part of the ambition of this series that it will increasingly address a wider reading public beyond its natural territory of students and researchers in Arabic and world literature. Nor indeed is the academic readership of the series expected to be confined to specialists in literature in the light of the growing trend for interdisciplinarity, which increasingly sees scholars crossing field boundaries in their research tools and coming up with findings that equally cross discipline borders in their appeal.

There is no exaggerating the importance of the so-called '*jīl al-sittīnāt*' or the sixties generation of last century in modern Egyptian literature, the focus of the present study. The 'sixties generation' refers to a 'group' of different writers of different genres, but predominantly novelists and dramatists, who started their creative career in the prime of youth in the 1960s. Perhaps 'group' is not an accurate description: they did not form a school or have a manifesto of a political, social or even artistic nature. They were very different writers who worked individually but who came to maturity under Nasser in the heyday of his power, and who were soon to witness his decline and, with his defeat in the war with Israel in 1967 and premature death in 1970, the demise of everything he had stood for: the dream of pan-Arabism and the establishment of a modern, progressive, independent and socially just Egyptian state. Their writing styles, aesthetics, philosophical interests, sociopolitical concerns, settings (urban/rural/international), widely varying, had in common those heady years in Egypt's modern history and were influenced by their spirit in one way or another. Ironically, while that decade was one of huge national disillusionment and decline, it was conversely one of blossoming talent and artistic thriving not only in fiction but also in the theatre, poetry and the arts generally in a manner that has not been since repeated on such a phenomenal scale and that has caused it often to be referred to in literary histories as a 'golden age'. Much has been written about the period and its many important figures, including a recent monograph in this series, viz. Paul Starkey's *Sonallah Ibrahim: Rebel with a Pen*. But much more still needs to be written; the wealth and variety of the output of that generation, whose writing careers peaked under Nasser's successors, Sadat and Mubarak, still beckons invitingly to slow scholarly endeavour. With all of them now in their twilight years, if not already dead, and their oeuvre complete, the time is ripe for assessment and reassessment of individuals, or clusters of individuals; for comparisons; for reappraisal of the literature and society of the period through their work; and for reading continuity of and departure from their achievement in current literary trends. The volume to hand with its focus on space, an approach not much attempted in studies of the period's output, is a welcome step in that direction.

Professor Rasheed El-Enany, Series Editor,
Emeritus Professor of Modern Arabic Literature,
University of Exeter

Note on Transliteration

I have followed the IJMES system for transliterating from Arabic to English. *Ayn* (ʿ) and *hamza* (ʾ) are shown throughout. Personal names appear in their most common English form, such as Gamal Abdel Nasser, Anwar Sadat and Husni Mubarak. Names of authors whose works are widely available in English translation appear as they do in the conventional English spelling (for example, Sonallah Ibrahim and Abd al-Hakim Qasim).

Acknowledgements

This project began when I was a graduate student at Columbia University. I start by thanking Muhsin al-Musawi for his help, productive observations and suggestions. My gratitude also to Roger Allen, Gil Anidjar, Brent Edwards and Timothy Mitchell for their advice and insight, and in making this a much better project than it otherwise would have been. I am grateful to Noha Radwan who helped guide me particularly when this book was still just an idea. Special appreciation is due to my professors at The American University in Cairo. It is through the teaching and writing of Samia Mehrez and Ferial Ghazoul that I discovered my love of Arabic literature many years ago.

My thanks also to the writers and intellectuals in Cairo, many of whom I was fortunate enough to meet, and others whom I wish I could have met: Ibrahim Abdel Meguid, Yahya Taher Abdullah, Radwa Ashour, Ibrahim Aslan, Muhammad al-Bisati, Gamal al-Ghitani, Sonallah Ibrahim, Edwar al-Kharrat, Bahaa Taher, Yusuf al-Qaid and Abd al-Hakim Qasim. Their political and intellectual commitment and struggles was a source of continuous inspiration.

I would like to thank Rasheed El-Enany, the editor of this series, for his help, direction and enthusiasm at every stage of this process. My sincere appreciation to Nicola Ramsey, Adela Rauchova, Eddie Clark and Kirsty Woods at Edinburgh University Press who were a pleasure to work with. The introduction is based on an earlier article, 'The Emergence of the Sixties Generation in Egypt and the Anxiety of Categorization', *Journal of Arabic Literature*, Volume 43, Issue 2–3 (2012), pp. 409–30. I thank Koninklijke Brill NV for permission to republish.

I was incredibly lucky to spend two years (2012–14) as an Andrew W.

Mellon Postdoctoral Fellow at Wellesley College. Special thanks to Rachid Aadnani, Lidwien Kapteijns and Louise Marlow in the Middle Eastern Studies Program who made teaching and research at Wellesley a true pleasure. My thanks to Carol Dougherty at the Newhouse Center for the Humanities for creating such an enriching experience and to the fellows for being incredible interlocuters: Marié Abe, Erika Boeckeler, Eugenie Brinkema, Beth DeSombre, Claire Fontijn, Kate Grandjean, Laura Grattan, Nikki Greene, Eugene Marshall, Patricia Melzer, Jessie Morgan-Owens, David Olsen, Sonia Sabnis, Kristel Smentek, Duncan White and Kristin Williams. The friendship, humour and support of Alex Orquiza, Elizabeth Falconi and Sima Shakhsari made my time at Wellesley all the more memorable.

At the University of Iowa, I would like to thank the College of Liberal Arts and Sciences for the Old Gold Summer Award that funded portions of this research, and the Flexible Load Assignment that allowed me to complete this book. I am grateful to Russell Ganim, Cinzia Blum, Rosemarie Scullion, Roland Racevskis and Michel Laronde who ensured that the department was a place for junior faculty to thrive. My thanks to the members of the Circulating Cultures Group at the Obermann Center for Advanced Studies. Not only did our interdisciplinary discussions influence my thinking in a myriad of ways, but I was also fortunate to workshop portions of this book with the group: Claire Fox, Laura Graham, Elke Heckner, Julie Hochstrasser, Jennifer Sessions, Yasemin Mohammad, Beatrice Mkenda, Kathleen Newman and Ariana Ruiz. Special thanks to Anny Curtius who first invited me to the group and who has since become a trusted colleague and friend. I am infinitely thankful for the community of friends who have made Iowa City one of many homes: Aron Aji, Asma Ben Romdhane, Emile Destruel-Johnson, Heather Bingham, Mark Bingham, Anna Blaedel, Elana Buch, Andy High, Mary High, Ken Hill, Lexy Ihrig, Kirsten Kumpf Baele, Alexei Lalagos, Hajer Larbi, Amira Rammah, David Supp-Montgomerie, Jenna Supp-Montgomorie, Emily Wentzell, Adam Yack and Marina Zaloznaya.

I cannot fully express my gratitude to the friends across the globe whose care and understanding sustained me throughout this journey. Jenn Derr as always provided me with unwavering love, advice and encouragement. I am so very lucky that she welcomed me into her life and never looked back. Kristin Soraya Batmanghelichi gave generously of her time, love, wit and guidance. I continue to be so grateful that our paths crossed as we prepared for our orals many years ago. May Ahmar, Hala al-Hoshan, Elizabeth Johnston, Tsolin Nalbantian and Nader K. Uthman made New York home and graduate school a much more enjoyable and rewarding experience. I cannot thank them enough for their friendship over the years. Special thanks to Tsolin for being a much-needed virtual writing partner this past year. Engy al-Barkouki and Walid el-Hamamsy made summers writing in Cairo not only bearable but very fun. Sarah Rifky continues to offer love, advice and laughter as our paths cross in Boston, New York and Cairo.

I owe my family endless gratitude. My parents Ali Ramadan and Mona Aboulnasr have been the source of unfaltering love and support. I am indebted to them for opening up the world of Arabic language and culture to me, and for continuing to make Cairo very much my home. Without my mother's determination, patience and tireless effort in teaching me Arabic I would never have written this book. Dina Ramadan, my sister and friend, has been a companion on this journey for many years and in many places. I am grateful for her emotional and intellectual support. I am so glad that we undertook this journey together.

Without Ari Ariel's friendship, love and encouragement this book would not have been possible. I am grateful to him for the time and effort he spent reading and editing chapters, and for the many conversations we had about my ideas. I thank him for challenging my assumptions and helping me see things from different perspectives. And of course, he always makes sure I am very well fed!

Introduction: Space and the Sixties

The present epoch will perhaps be above all the epoch of space.
                            Michel Foucault, 'Of Other Spaces'[1]

I blame the old generation and invite the new generation to refuse to reconcile and to begin the dialogue with the word 'No!'
                    Ahmad Hashim al-Sharif, *al-Hilal*, August 1970

Representations of the city, country, landscape, and the nation conceal a complex network of social relations and historical processes that impact how readers imagine the world inside and outside the novel.
                            Eric Bulson, *Novels, Maps, Modernity*[2]

In the 1960s, a group of young writers exploded onto the scene, transforming Egypt's literary landscape. They would come to be known as *jīl al-sittīnāt* (the sixties generation), a movement whose impact would be felt for decades.[3] Emerging at a time of great instability in Egypt, the members of this generation broke with the realist tradition of their predecessors and significantly altered the dominant aesthetic trends in Egyptian fiction. Their disillusionment with the postcolonial project resulted in new literary styles and a new aesthetics of space that significantly altered the representation of urban, rural and exilic space in the modern Egyptian novel. The countryside, no longer the idealised space of the nation, became a space of alienation and degradation. And yet, neither the Cairene metropolis nor cosmopolitan Alexandria took its place as the romanticised centre of national unity. Moreover, the transgression of borders to the exilic spaces of Europe and the Gulf further unsettled understandings of national and regional belonging.

At the heart of *Space in Modern Egyptian Fiction* is an argument about the disappearance of an idealised nation in the Egyptian novel. Each of the chapters is thus mindful of the intersection between nationalism, literature and space. The representation of the various spaces of, and outside, the nation reflects disappointment with the increasingly repressive regimes that followed independence. The writers in question, once supportive of Gamal Abdel Nasser's political and ideological direction, struggled to contend with the transformations of post-revolutionary Egypt, critiquing the ideology of Egyptian nationalism, and calling into question the policies of state socialism and Arab nationalism that were the hallmarks of the regime. This was exacerbated in the decades that followed; Anwar Sadat's reversal of his predecessor's direction meant further alienation for members of the intellectual community. The political and economic policies of Husni Mubarak continued to elicit virulent criticism from the writers of this generation. Given such shifts this book asks significant questions about the imagining and reimagining of the Egyptian nation, the novel's role as a site of opposition and dissent, and the literary articulation of individual and collective agency.

This study is inspired by scholarship that applies a sociological approach to the study of modern Arabic literature. Pioneered by Richard Jacquemond, Elisabeth Kendall and Samia Mehrez, and drawing on the work of Pierre Bourdieu, this work presents the field of cultural production as a space of contestation, 'the site of struggles in which what is at stake is the power to impose the dominant definition of the writer and therefore to limit the population of those entitled to take part in the struggle to define the writer'.[4] Here this struggle is specifically related to the formulation of the category of literary generation; the anxiety over categorisation reveals how power and authority are negotiated in the cultural field in Egypt.[5] The formulation of the group as a generation is thus understood as a strategic undertaking that showcased its aesthetic innovations *and* as a means to gain access to, and prominence in, the field. Jacquemond, Kendall and Mehrez all draw upon literary history and sociology to explore the dynamics, negotiations and constraints that shape the field of cultural production in Egypt. In doing so they focus upon the textual production of the sixties generation to varying degrees; Mehrez's work offers perhaps the most sustained engagement with the literary texts themselves. Here, I build upon this scholarship and combine a sociological approach to literature with close readings of literary texts. In this way *Space in Modern Egyptian Fiction* brings together the space of the cultural field and readings of space in literature.[6]

My analysis of the sixties generation centres on the work of eleven novelists and short story writers: Yahya Taher Abdullah, Ibrahim Abdel Meguid, Radwa Ashour, Ibrahim Aslan, Muhammad al-Bisati, Gamal al-Ghitani, Sonallah Ibrahim, Edwar al-Kharrat, Yusuf al-Qaid, Abd al-Hakim Qasim and Bahaa Taher. While each chapter focuses on a set number of works, the group's predecessors, contemporaries and successors populate the larger narrative of the book to provide a full picture of the transformation of the literary sphere. The decision to select novels that cover the period 1966–2012 is deliberate and is intended to promote the consideration of the literary production of this generation beyond the boundaries of a single decade. This expansive reading takes into consideration the social, political and economic changes that impacted their writing in the decades after their appearance on the scene. In this way I offer a sustained chronicling of the emergence and consecration of this generation of writers.

My understanding of these writers in relationship to the socio-economic and political positions from which they emerged, builds upon Edwar al-Kharrat's *al-Hassasiyya al-Jadida: Maqalat fi al-Zahira al-Qasasiyya* (1993) and Muhammad Badawi's *al-Riwaya al-Haditha fi Misr: Dirasa fi al-Tashkil wa-l-Aydiyulujiyya* (1993), two seminal works that categorise the literary contributions of this generation according to aesthetic innovation. Both critics show the ways in which these writers turned away from the realist paradigms that had dominated literary production in earlier decades and that had come to be associated with the establishment of the postcolonial nation state. Instead they employed new aesthetic techniques, fracturing the time and space of the realist narrative. This new fiction focused on the subjective, and the merging of dreams and reality, depicting a world in which the individual was increasingly alienated. Some writers drew upon the mythic, historical or folkloric tradition to undermine notions of linearity and progress. Others employed a form of hyper-realism that captured the banal details of everyday existence. The sixties writers produced novels that blended autobiography and fiction, often drawing on journalism and history, and experimenting with the narrative form. In examining the aesthetic innovations of this generation, I also connect them to the thematic concerns. By focusing on the analysis of space in the literary works of this generation I bring the political, economic and social changes of postcolonial period Egypt to bear on the aesthetic innovations for which these writers have become known.

A New Generation: Setting the Scene

> I repeat: the new generation is truly new.
> Naguib Mahfouz, *al-Hilal*, August 1970

In late 1969, the journal *al-Taliᶜa* (1965–77) dedicated a number of issues to the emerging literary generation in Egypt. The feature 'Hakadha Yatakallamu al-Udabaʾ al-Shabab' (This is how the Young Writers Speak) became a reoccurring feature in the journal, sparking intense debates and controversies among writers, critics and intellectuals, of all ages.[7] The writings sought to understand what this new '*jīl*' (generation) of writers in the 1960s represented, who they were, and what role they aspired to play in the fraught political, economic and cultural arena of late 60s Egypt.

The attention given to the writers and their work on the pages of cultural and literary periodicals shows that there was little doubt, even at the time, that something momentous was taking place within the cultural sphere in Egypt. *Al-Taliᶜa* was not alone in the attention it paid to the emerging writers; *al-Hilal*, *al-Masaʾ* and *al-Majalla* all published editions in the late 1960s and early 1970s that focused on this burst of innovation.[8] Here were a younger group of writers whose literary production exhibited new aesthetic innovations worthy of critical attention. *Jīl al-sittīnāt* (the sixties generation), the term now most associated with the writers of this group, is broadly understood as designating writers who began writing in the decade of the 1960s and who were driving the new literary innovations of the time. Its most prominent members include Yahya Taher Abdullah, Ibrahim Abdel Meguid, Muhammad Ibrahim Abu Sinna, Radwa Ashour, Ibrahim Aslan, Muhammad al-Bisati, Amal Dunqul, Gamal al-Ghitani, Sonallah Ibrahim, Edwar al-Kharrat, Raʾuf Musᶜad, Yusuf al-Qaid, Abd al-Hakim Qasim, Muhammad Hafiz Rajab, Bahaa Taher and Majid Tubya. The absence of women writers (notable exceptions being Radwa Ashour and Salwa Bakr) is immediately apparent and is reflective of the significant gender bias within the literary and cultural field. It is not an overstatement to say that the sixties generation comes to be formulated as an almost entirely male group. Critics in the field have however been involved in the work of refocusing attention on women writers from different literary generations.[9]

The sixties generation emerged during a turbulent moment in Egypt's history; the promise of a democratic, independent, postcolonial nation state, pursued with such optimism in the fifties, had given way to a much more foreboding reality. Sabry Hafez calls the 1960s 'a decade of confusion' which witnessed the expansion of Nasser's state socialism alongside intensified suppression of all political opposition and dissent.[10] Nasser's policies of land reclamation, industrialisation and the construction of the Aswan Dam were accompanied by a climate of increased surveillance, imprisonment and numerous crackdowns on writers and intellectuals. Persecution began as early as 1954 with the expulsions that took place at Cairo University and largely targeted members of the Muslim Brotherhood, communists and leftists. Imprisonments continued throughout the decade, reaching their height between 1959 and 1964.[11] It was also the decade of Egypt's embroilment in the war in Yemen and the catastrophic defeat by Israel in 1967 that led to the loss of the Sinai Peninsula.[12]

This defeat compounded the feelings of loss and disappointment that had plagued many writers throughout the decade of the 1960s. The defeat was intensely debated by both writers and critics who questioned whether it was a significant break, a natural development given the events of the decade, or a crisis that was predicted by writers and intellectuals.[13] It was certainly front and centre of the discussions; for example, *al-Taliʿa* asked the writers' position on what they called 'the question of Israeli aggression'.[14] Writers explained that though they did not write about the events of 1967 explicitly these events 'permeated' their work.[15] For many this was yet another example of the failure of the international struggle for freedom, equality and justice, and an additional burden that was placed upon the shoulders of this generation.[16] Yet, significantly, while many of the writers of this generation had been producing work since the beginning of the decade, they were only labelled as a group following 1967.[17]

Faced with this bleak reality, writers who had enthusiastically supported Nasser's policies, particularly those calling for social and economic justice, struggled to contend with what was undeniably an authoritarian regime, albeit one that propelled Egypt to the centre of the Arab world. The *infitāḥ* (Open Door) policies initiated by Sadat in the decade that followed benefited the political and economic elites, at the expense of the majority of the population, and thus served to heighten the sense of disillusionment, spelling the death of the socialist dream in Egypt. Sadat dismantled the cultural edifice established by Nasser, terminating the state's support for the arts and further exacerbating the disenchantment felt in the cultural sphere. Sadat's 'Corrective Revolution,' begun in 1971, targeted his political opponents and further marginalised members of the artistic community, forcing many writers into exile. His policies redirected Egypt's interest away from the Arab world and towards the United States, increasing the antagonism between the regime and intellectuals. This reached its height with Sadat's visit to Jerusalem in 1977 and the signing of the Camp David Accords with Israel the following year.

With the coming to power of Mubarak in 1981 there was a reversal of the cultural policies of the state, with greater emphasis placed upon establishing links between intellectuals and the institutions of power; in fact, many of the writers of this generation were recognised by the state, and awarded accordingly, during this period. This policy did not of course prevent numerous confrontations from erupting over the years between the writers and government officials, surrounding issues of corruption, censorship, domestic and foreign policy, and the exercise of state power. Mubarak's unpopularity was exacerbated by the issue of presidential succession in what many believed was a strategy for his son, Gamal Mubarak, to succeed as President.

Within this socio-economic and political context, and given the growing and continued sense that the success of the postcolonial project in Egypt was in jeopardy, the writers of the sixties generation struggled to represent the new social and political reality that confronted them. The members of what Ghali Shukri labelled as '*jīl al-taḥaddī*' (the generation of confrontation) would continue to wage the war for social justice, democracy and freedom in their works for decades after their emergence on the literary scene.[18]

Defining a Generation

Despite the ongoing debates over terminology, I utilise the label sixties generation in recognition of its continued usage and dominance in the cultural field in Egypt – the robust discussions for alternative labels notwithstanding.[19] In doing so I recognise my own role in this continued drive to categorise and classify, to distinguish one literary generation from the next. As W. J. van de Akker and G. J. Dorleijin explain 'generations are constructs that are used by the primary literary field of writers and critics to get a grip on their contemporary literary world'.[20]

In what follows I offer an examination of the formation of the sixties generation, a literary movement that emerged at a time of great instability in Egypt and whose members significantly altered the dominant aesthetic trends in Egyptian fiction. I base this upon the debates that took place on the pages of the cultural journals at the time of the writers' appearance and on significant critical interventions in the years since the group's emergence. I have already outlined the political and socio-economic context of which they were both a part and an expression. I now proceed to show how the convergence of issues of age as innovation, aesthetics, and influence and inspiration helped define the sixties generation. Finally, I maintain that it was strategically beneficial for the writers to band together. Here I draw upon the work of Jacquemond and Kendall, who both delineate the cultural sphere in Egypt according to the theoretical framework presented by Pierre Bourdieu.[21] Bourdieu defines the field of cultural production as a 'field of forces . . . a field of struggles tending to transform or conserve this field of forces' in which individuals, institutions or groups are in constant contestation over positions of authority, positions which in effect decide 'the legitimate definition of literary or artistic production'.[22] What was a strategy to showcase the importance of their aesthetic innovations was also a way to argue for their significance as a new generation of writers. As Jacquemond notes 'the rallying of a group of works and authors under the banner of a "generation", even one with imprecise boundaries, is part of a collective strategy for access and the conquest of symbolic power, within a strongly hierarchical field'.[23] It thus becomes a sign of prominence and standing within the field in the years following the group's emergence on the cultural scene. And while the writers did share a broad artistic vision, such a strategy was also possible as a result of shared biographical and ideological profiles.

Age as Innovation

At the time of the group's emergence in the late 1960s, great emphasis was placed upon their youth. A case in point is *al-Taliʿa*'s use of the term '*al-udabāʾ al-shabāb*' (the young writers) in its title, which cast the debate in terms of the writers' ages (eighteen to thirty-five) and pointed to their youth as *the* source of innovation.[24] The oppositional binary of old and young was central to the discussion surrounding the emergence of this group. Literary critics regularly used the idea of '*ṣirāʿ al-ajyāl*' (a generational struggle) in framing this debate; questions were asked about whether this was an antagonistic struggle, or a sign of the health and vitality of the literary sphere and a necessary part of the path towards literary innovation.[25] Youth was often emphasised by the writers themselves as a positive attribute, which meant that the responsibility for innovation and experimentation lay with them. It also meant that they understood the contemporary situation in a way that their predecessors could not and were better equipped to explore new aesthetic forms to capture the changing world in which they lived.[26] This sense of responsibility for innovation was at the heart of the now famous manifesto which Sonallah Ibrahim published in 1966 (along with Kamal Qalash, Raʾuf Musʿad and Abd al-Hakim Qasim) on the back cover of his first novel *Tilka-l-Raʾiha* (*The Smell of It*). In it the writers articulated the idea that it was their responsibility, as a new generation, to break the existing boundaries in literature and art:

> If this novel in your hands doesn't please you, it is not our fault, but rather that of the cultural and artistic atmosphere in which we live, which through the years has been controlled by traditional works and superficial, naive, phenomena. To break the prevailing artistic environment which has solidified and hardened, we have chosen this form of sincere and sometimes painful writing . . . it is an art concerned overwhelmingly with the attempt to express the spirit of an age and the experience of a generation.[27]

And yet, their youth was also used against them, as a sign of inexperience, and a means for older, more established writers and critics to challenge the significance of the emerging writers' literary production.[28] A common metaphor was that of reproduction, which framed the struggle as one of the biological anxiety that drives the young to revolt against their fathers.[29]

While the issue of youth was front and centre of the discussion at the time, coming to represent the potential for innovation (or inexperience), the sixties generation should not be limited to a biological or historical category; it does not refer merely to a single decade, nor does it apply only to writers of a certain age. That the designation came to be associated with writers that began writing and publishing in the decade of the 1960s inevitably meant that this group was largely composed of younger writers at the beginning of their careers, and not with more established figures. Exceptions exist: Abdel Meguid and Ashour started publishing after the 60s. Al-Kharrat, who began writing in the 1940s and whose work was experimental even then, came to be recognised as one of the principal members and founders of the movement, bolstering his own standing in the cultural field in Egypt.

Aesthetics

What captured the attention of literary and cultural critics in the 1960s was the explosion of aesthetic innovation appearing in narrative fiction. Much of the discussion surrounded the short story in particular; many of the writers in question began their literary careers as short-story writers, producing novels a number of years after their emergence on the literary scene.[30] This could be attributed to the difficulties in publication and the existence of cultural journals more suited to the short story, or to a sense that the form of the short story was particularly appealing in light of the drive for experimentation and innovation.[31] Whatever the reason, what was increasingly apparent was the rejection of realism (and social realism specifically) and its literary techniques as an acceptable mode of representation in the current context.

What Yusuf al-Sharuni referred to as 'a revolution against realism' was one of the most discussed markers of the new literature.[32] This is not surprising given the way social realism had dominated literary production in the previous decade and had come to be associated with the literature of the Nasserist period. Ghalib Halasa highlights a number of traits fundamental to this revolt: an immersion in the subjective, the use of indirect discourse, the absence of a virtuous hero, the focus upon the flaws of a character, the breakdown of linear narrative, an excessive romanticism, and evidence of a wide variety of intellectual influences.[33] Writers were praised for the innovation and experimentation that challenged a vision of reality tied to the social realist literary project, which had championed the postcolonial nation state in the years following the Egyptian Revolution. This challenge was also a refusal of a social reality that had grown ever more oppressive, and that had increasingly revealed the failures of Nasser's postcolonial project.[34]

The first period in literary production (from the beginning of the twentieth century to the end of colonial rule) was marked by a concern for the realism of the literary text, and an understanding that literature was a representation of reality in a way that was recognisable to the reader.[35] The second period (that began in the 60s) saw writers redefining the relationship between literature and reality, such that the latter became an inspiration for the former but was not necessarily mimetically reproduced in it.[36] As Hafez explains:

> The second phase of literary development substituted metaphoric rules of reference for the metonymic ones, thus liberating the literary text from slavish adherence to the logic and order of social reality and allowing for occasional flights into fantasy, the dissolution of time, a wider gap between the world of art and that of reality, and a higher degree of textual autonomy.[37]

Perhaps the best critical articulation and analysis of the aesthetic interventions of this generation is to be found in al-Kharrat's work *al-Hassasiyya al-Jadida: Maqalat fi al-Zahira al-Qasasiyya* published in 1993, which attempted a categorisation of the different aesthetic trends within the larger movement.[38] This idea of a 'sensibility' represents al-Kharrat's attempt to bring together the social, historical and aesthetic, revealing the way that the interplay between these different forces was responsible for the explosion of innovation that took place in the 1960s and continued in the decades that followed.[39] Al-Kharrat identifies five main aesthetic trends which make up this 'new sensibility', providing detailed literary analysis of the work of the writers of this movement, and stressing that no author need be designated to one single category.

The first of the five trends that al-Kharrat describes is '*Tayyār al-Tashyī*'' (The Wave of Objectification/Reification) in which characters appear like objects, representing only themselves. In these works, the authors employ an objective language, bare and stripped down, void of emotion, much like the vision they represent. This vision of the world is both a refusal of it, with all its oppression and injustice, and also a deep engagement with it. These writers match the severity of the world with an aesthetic severity, while also suggesting the possibilities of other realities, other worlds. The work of Bahaa Taher, Ibrahim Aslan, Muhammad al-Bisati and Jamil ʿAtiyya all fall within this category.[40]

The second trend is '*al-Tayyār al-Dākhilī*' (The Wave of Interiority) which in many ways is on the other end of the spectrum to '*Tayyār al-Tashyīʾ*'. Here the focus is on the interior world of the characters, presented in a language that is bursting with emotion and sensation. Conventional dialogue is not important, replaced instead with internal monologues or the stirrings of the imagination. Time follows the logic of dreams. Internal and external worlds intermingle in a vision of obscurity and confusion. Few writers have dedicated themselves entirely to this wave, though notable among them is Muhammad Hafiz Rajab and the Syrian writer Haydar Haydar.[41]

The third wave identified by al-Kharrat is that of '*Tayyār Istīḥāʾ al-Turāth al-ʿArabī al-Taqlīdī, al-Tārīkhī aw al-Shaʿbī*' (The Wave that Draws on the Traditional, Historical or Popular Heritage). Here the writers draw on folklore and popular stories, depending on the collective memory of the people. The most notable writers in this case are Gamal al-Ghitani, Yahya Taher Abdullah and Abd al-Hakim Qasim, though both Muhsin Yunis and Yusuf Abu Riyya have also drawn on a similar tradition.[42]

'*Al-Tayyār al-Wāqiʿī al-Siḥrī*' (The Wave of Magical Realism) is the fourth wave within *al-Hassāsiyya al-Jadīda*. Here the boundaries between the objective world of the senses and that of the imagination fall away. The work of Ibrahim ʿIsa, Ibrahim Abdel Meguid and al-Kharrat himself fall into this category.[43] The fifth and final wave is that of '*al-Tayyār al-Wāqiʿī al-Jadīd*' (The Neo-Realist Wave), which brings together writers such as Sulayman Fayyad, Sonallah Ibrahim, Salwa Bakr, Khayri Shalabi and ʿAlaʾ al-Dib. This wave is the purification of the conventional realist form, using it in such a way as to express the opposition to existing forms of power. Writers employ a variety of modernist techniques, among them the use of documentary language, political discourse and the story within a story.[44] Al-Kharrat's categories are largely in line with much of the discussions about aesthetic innovation that were taking place in the 1960s and early 1970s.

Not surprisingly, the different aesthetic directions within the movement grew clearer with the increased literary production of the group. What was clear, even in the early days of the group's emergence, was the importance of literary and philosophical influences from local, regional and global sources.

Influence and Inspiration

The move away from the social realist tradition was closely connected with the traits of '*ightirāb*' (alienation) that were becoming increasingly noticeable in this literature, and which speak to the influence of writers such as Jean-Paul Sartre and Albert Camus upon this emerging generation. As Kendall notes however, the position of these writers was somewhat different than their European counterparts: 'their alienation did not seek to sever ties to life, but to reject old ties while striving for new ones . . . it was the basic image of normal men crushed in an intolerable world . . . not simply escapism and death'.[45] The growing sense that literature could not necessarily mirror reality, and that this reality was in fact much more fractured than the social realists had conveyed in their work, produced fiction in which the alienated individual – in both a literal and metaphorical sense – occupied an ever more arbitrary world.[46] Citing the work of Majid Tubya, Hafez provides a useful description of the relationship between departure from the realist tradition and the increasing sense of alienation present in the literary works. He notes that these stories 'depend on the point of fantasy, the separation from reality and the rejection of this reality in a relentless attempt to unite with it and originate from it'.[47] Furthermore, the various techniques employed by writers reveal 'the individual's loss of security and balance, and the feeling of alienation from a reality full of deception in which any true connection is impossible'.[48]

There was also a great deal of discussion surrounding the sources of influence and inspiration which these new writers were drawing upon. Yusuf al-Sharuni, Edwar al-Kharrat, Fuʾad al-Tikirli and Naguib Mahfouz (in his post-*Trilogy* novels) were the most cited Arab writers – al-Kharrat is strikingly positioned as both an inspiration and a member of this generation.[49] These writers were seen as displaying the earliest manifestations of this innovative movement in their work, beginning their careers as early as the 1940s. It was in these works that the shift away from social realism could be first detected: the breakdown of linear narrative; the turn towards literary expressionism;

the fracturing of time and space; the focus on the subjective; the use of stream of consciousness; and the merging of the worlds of dreams and reality.[50] Critics also noted the end of the influence of Guy de Maupassant and Anton Chekov, both of whom had served as significant sources of inspiration for the writers of the realist tradition.[51] Instead, the similarities in style to Ernest Hemingway, J. D. Salinger, Saul Bellow and the intellectual influence of Albert Camus were discussed as more relevant points of comparison for the work of the emerging generation.[52] Hemingway's influence could be seen in the use of short sentences, the absence of an idealised hero, and in that the external world became the way to understand the internal world of the characters, who often suffered emotional or physical wounds in their constant confrontations with death.[53] Camus offered writers a way to articulate their visions in a world in which they felt increasingly alienated, overcome with a sense of the futility and absurdity of life.[54]

The influences cited, and the concerns that brought the writers together, illuminate the local, regional and global dimensions of this generation.[55] This was a group of writers who, from the beginning, recognised the commonalities they shared with their counterparts in the Arab and international domain; common causes extended beyond national or even regional borders, uniting Arab writers and artists with their partners in the United States, Europe, Latin America and Africa. The literary, political and philosophical inspirations include such thinkers as T. S. Eliot, Jean-Paul Sartre, Fyodor Dostoevsky, Vladimir Lenin and Che Guevara.[56] The ongoing war in Vietnam, the struggles of African Americans in the United States and the student movements in France were all linked in the mind of these writers with their own struggles against capitalism, Israeli aggression and US neo-colonial ventures in the region.[57]

This ongoing struggle to innovate, experiment and find better ways to represent an ever-changing reality was connected to a larger battle in the name of socialism, democracy and freedom. The battle was social and political as well as artistic and aesthetic. The writers acknowledged that literature and art played a vital role in the ongoing fight for liberty and equality in the postcolonial age. Here we see the '*iltizām*' (commitment) inherited from the previous decade.[58] But as Jacquemond notes, it was reformulated to allow for a different utilisation of the Sartrian notion:

Sartre could be appropriated not only by the supporters of a literature that was in the service of the great national and social causes – and, as the case may be, in the service of the political party that claimed to incarnate them (commitment in the instrumental sense) – but also by the avant-gardes, which foregrounded instead the critical and liberating function of literature (commitment as liberation for the writer and for the reader).[59]

Literature was thus to be used both in the collective fight for socio-economic and political liberation, the 'great national and social causes' of the age *and* in the individual quest for freedom to be attained through reading and writing.

Strategy

That the writers of the sixties generation shared aesthetics directions, and were preoccupied with similar regional and global issues, is not the whole story. As I suggested in the opening of this chapter, it was largely advantageous both at the time of the group's emergence and in the years that followed that they band together. In a literary field that remains predominantly generational, discussions about the emerging group, what they should be called, and their significance, were as much about categorisation as they were about the negotiation of power and authority in what Bourdieu has called 'the field of cultural production'.[60] The angst about whether or not this group constituted a generation, and what defined a generation, what I have termed elsewhere 'the anxiety over categorization', was part of a larger struggle over legitimacy.[61] The emergence of a new generation of writers posed a threat to the established figures in the field, raising questions about whether or not aesthetic innovation was strictly the domain of the young. As Bourdieu states 'the opposition, within the sub-field of restricted production [is] between the consecrated avant-garde and the avant-garde, the established figures and the new comers, i.e. between *artistic generations*, often only a few years apart, between the "young" and the "old"'.[62] This meant that appearing as a cohesive, innovative group was strategically beneficial to the emerging writers, providing them with access to the cultural field.

This strategy of banding together was also related to a broader critique of cultural institutions and publishing houses, particularly to what was referred to as '*azmat al-nashr*' (the crisis of publishing).[63] We are told by the poet

Hasan Muhsib in *al-Taliʿa*, for example, that the publishing houses Dar al-Maʿarif and Dar al-Hilal rarely published any new authors.[64] This crisis in publishing led many writers to seek venues outside of Egypt, namely in Lebanon; Zuhayr al-Shayib regretfully notes how his work was welcomed by literary journals in Lebanon in a way that it was not in Egypt.[65] It was not just the young writers who made note of this crisis, but literary giants such as Mahfouz also recognised the problems that plagued the publishing world, but explained that this was due to the inability of the publishers to cater to the growing number of writers in the field.[66] These concerns are of course difficult to verify, but Stagh's work on publishing statistics during this period lends credibility to Muhsib's claims. In evaluating the publications during this time Stagh concludes, 'publishers gave more scope to new writers during the fifties, especially in the period 1955–60, than they did in the sixties, 1961–7'.[67] She also traces what she calls the 'flight to Beirut' which began in the 1950s but increased significantly in the decades of the 60s and 70s.[68]

This was at least partly the impetus for the establishment of the innovative, independent journal *Gallery 68* (*Jaliri 68*).[69] Although it ran for only eight issues *Gallery 68* made an impact on the literary scene, publishing an impressive number of young writers, many of whom would become the most prominent members of the generation.[70] In its first issue, dated May/June 1968, the Editor-in-chief Ahmad Mursi states that 'if it succeeds in revealing the truth about that which moves the wings of the writers, poets, and artists of the members of "*jīl al-yawm*" (today's generation) then it would have lived up to the promise it made to itself to participate in the battle for freedom and reconstruction'.[71] As evidenced by Muhammad al-Bisati's appraisal of the journal published in November 1968, some felt that *Gallery 68* was failing in its goal of being a 'platform for the new generation', publishing too many older established writers.[72] Given this criticism, *Gallery 68* then was as much about propagating a different vision of literary innovation as it was about providing a legitimate forum for emerging writers to publish their work, and a means to address the problems of the publishing world.[73]

As an independent journal it is also an example of one of the ways the members of the sixties generation attempted to create space for themselves outside of Nasser's control. As Muhmmad Badawi illustrates in his work, the sixties writers did not become a part of Nasser's cultural apparatus nor did they benefit from it financially.[74] He argues that antagonism towards the establishment was an attempt on the part of the younger generation to redefine its role as writers and intellectuals: they simultaneously rejected the state's attempt to dictate the function of the intellectual and tried to separate themselves from those enmeshed in the cultural apparatus of the state.[75]

This and other ideological positions were shared by many members of the sixties generation.[76] The majority of the group were leftists in their political leanings and strongly supportive of Nasser's state socialism. While some like Aslan never joined a political party, al-Ghitani, Ibrahim, Qasim, Ashour and al-Kharrat were all involved with the Egyptian Communist Party. As a result of this membership, and other political activity, a large number of them faced periods of imprisonment beginning in the 1950s; these include al-Ghitani, Ibrahim, Qasim and al-Kharrat. The commonalities also extend to a shared biographical experience; many of the writers of this group came from the lower and lower-middle classes and, as identified by Badawi, are part of the group of bureaucrats and technocrats.[77] Like the majority of writers in Egypt they mostly pursued their literary careers alongside an alternative profession – Ibrahim and Abdullah stand out as examples of professional writers, who devoted themselves exclusively to their art. They are not predominantly from Cairo (Ibrahim and Ashour are notable exceptions), though almost without exception they moved to the capital early in their lives to pursue their careers as writers. Instead, we see writers from al-Karnak (Abdullah), Sharqiyya (al-Bisati), al-Jayahna (al-Ghitani), Alexandria (al-Kharrat and Abdel Meguid), al-Bihira (al-Qaid) and Tanta (Qasim and Aslan). While Taher was born in Giza he is clearly influenced by the Upper Egypt of his origins. Not only did this impact their choice of fictional geographies, as will be discussed throughout the chapters of this book, but it meant that they came from places that were not the political, economic or cultural centres of Egypt. This also explains the spatial turn in their work, that reimagines Cairo, Alexandria, rural Egypt, and beyond.

Spatial Representations

According to Eric Bulson,

> spatial representations in novels *are* ideological, they are influenced by the culture, history, economy, and politics of a particular time and place, they

reflect ways of seeing the world and the scores of individuals who live, and have lived, and will live in it.[78]

The focus upon spatial representations that motivates this book is driven by the broader 'spatial turn' that has taken place in the humanities and the social sciences in the last few decades. As Foucault famously stated in 1967, space was to replace time as the central concern of the twentieth century:

> The great obsession of the nineteenth century was, as we know, history: with its themes of development and of suspension, of crisis and cycle, themes of the ever-accumulating past, with its great preponderance of dead men and the menacing glaciation of the world. The nineteenth century found its essential mythological resources in the second principle of thermodynamics. The present epoch will perhaps be above all the epoch of space.[79]

Alerting us to the way time has been privileged over space, Foucault's assertion has had a profound impact upon literary and cultural studies. Much of his own work has focused upon the relationship between time and space; *Madness and Civilization* (1961), *The History of Sexuality* (1976) and *Discipline and Punish* (1975) all demonstrate Foucault's preoccupation with the spatial, and its relationship to regimes of power and knowledge. His analysis of the ways power is negotiated between the individual and the state is fundamental to the readings of fiction in this book. The members of the sixties generation experience state discipline as a political technology, exercised through surveillance, maintaining control at the level of the body itself and of the body in space. Nevertheless, they struggled to fulfil their roles as writers and intellectuals.

Power is not to be understood as all encompassing, but rather as a repressive and productive force.[80] And thus opportunities for resistance and dissent emerge. Here I draw upon Lefebvre's articulation of the relationship between mental, physical and social space to read the fiction of the sixties generation as a form of resistance.[81] In *The Production of Space* (1974), Lefebvre argues that social space does not precede human presence, but rather is a product of it.[82] This is a result of the interaction of the three spheres: spatial practice – the routes and networks of daily reality, the social practices of the individual as they pertain to the everyday, and as they serve to connect him/her to society and its space; representations of space – space as it is conceptualised and planned, the space conceived by urban planners and architects, associated with the authoritarian and repressive power of the state; and representational spaces – the metaphorical and symbolical ways we understand and experience physical space, and also the space of art itself.[83] It is

> space as directly *lived* through its associated images and symbols, and hence the space of 'inhabitants' and 'users' but also of artists and perhaps of those, such as a few writers and philosophers, who *describe* and aspire to do no more than describe. This is the dominant – and hence passively experienced space which the imagination seeks to change and appropriate.[84]

Lefebvre draws our attention to the difficulties inherent in the endeavour to interpret representational space, stating that 'the problem is that any search for space in literary texts will find it everywhere and in every guise: enclosed, described, projected, dreamt of, speculated about'.[85] And yet literary texts, as representational spaces, play a crucial role in his theory of the formation of social space and the ways in which it is perceived, conceived and lived by the subject, revealing the connections between spatial practice, and the spaces of authority and confrontation. And hence this endeavour, as tricky as it may be, is necessary. It is as representational spaces, aesthetic forms that provide opportunities for the consideration of state power and possibilities of opposition and dissent, that I situate the novels of this generation.

This focus upon space is not to dismiss the importance of the relationship between time and space. As Foucault states

> it is necessary to notice that the space which today appears to form the horizon of our concerns, our theory, our systems, is not an innovation; space itself has a history in Western experience and it is not possible to disregard the fatal intersection of time with space.[86]

The importance of time and its relationship to space, particularly as it manifests in literature, is the focus of Mikhail Bakhtin's discussion in his essay 'Forms of Time and of the Chronotope in the Novel: Notes Towards a Historical Poetics'. Bakhtin explains the use of the term chronotope as addressing the inseparability of time and space in literary analysis: 'We will give the name *chronotope* (literally, "time space") to the intrinsic connectedness of temporal and spatial relationships that are artistically expressed in literature.'[87] Focusing specifically upon Greek literature, Bakhtin argues that changes in the representation of time and space are connected to tranformations that occur in our experience of time and space beyond the world of the novel. This is not unlike the argument David Harvey puts forth with regards to the shift from modernism to postmodernism and the role of capitalism in the production of space. Harvey concludes that global capitalism has so altered the way in which we experience time and space that this has led to the 'compression of our spatial and temporal worlds'.[88] The term 'time-space compression' that he employs thus encapsulates the 'processes that so revolutionize the objective qualities of space and time that we are forced to alter, sometimes in quite radical ways, how we represent the world to ourselves'.[89] It is not my intention here to suggest that the transformation from modernity to post-modernity that Harvey describes can be mapped directly onto the Egyptian context. Rather, I argue that in keeping with Foucault, Bakhtin and Harvey, the analysis at the heart of *Space in Modern Egyptian Fiction* maintains the inseparability of time and space in narrative representation, to show how the changes that took place in Egypt, beginning in the decade of the 1960s, meant that writers were compelled to find new ways to represent time and space in their novels, to better represent their changing experience of reality.

The relationship between representations of time, space and the novel are central to Benedict Anderson's theory of imagined community. Anderson famously argues that the novel and the newspaper 'provided the technical means for "re-presenting" the kind of imagined community that is the nation'.[90] The capacity of the novel to serve such a function is largely based upon its ability to present the progression of time in a linear fashion:

> What has come to take the place of the medieval conception of simultaneity-along-time is, to borrow again from Benjamin, an idea of 'homogenous, empty time', in which simultaneity is, as it were, transverse, cross-time, marked not by prefiguring and fulfillment, but by temporal coincidence, and measured by clock and calendar.[91]

Anderson explains simultaneity-along-time as 'simultaneity of past and future in an instantaneous present'.[92] This idea of Messianic time, as Anderson refers to it, came to be replaced by the measuring of time by clock and calendar. The sense that the characters of a novel are advancing through history is one of the hallmarks of the realist novel. It is also what connects the movement of time in the novel to that of the imagined community of the nation; 'the idea of a sociological organism moving calendrically through homogenous, empty time is a precise analogue of the idea of the nation, which also is conceived as a solid community moving steadily down (or up) history'.[93] The dissolution of linear time is well-documented with regards to the work of the sixties generation; scholars such as Sabry Hafez, Edwar al-Kharrat, Samah Selim (who also draws upon Anderson's work) and Muhammad Badawi cite it as a hallmark of the group's writing. In fracturing the time (and space) of the realist paradigm that had dominated the literary production that preceded them, the sixties generation called into question the postcolonial Egyptian nation state with which it was associated.

This turn to a reflection upon the importance of the production of space has also found resonance within the literary critical sphere. Franco Moretti has argued that we must focus upon 'the study of space in literature' and 'literature in space'.[94] In *Atlas of the European Novel 1800–1900*, Moretti proposes the use of maps as 'analytical tools: that dissect the text in an unusual way, bringing to light relations that would otherwise remain hidden'.[95] His work has been fundamental in alerting critics to the importance of thinking about what can be gained from readings of novels that privilege space.[96] Furthermore, if as Moretti has argued (following Benedict Anderson) the novel acts as the 'symbolic form' that readers needed to 'make sense of the nation-state', I ask what are the ways in which writers manipulate this form (and here I refer specifically to the form of the realist novel) to raise questions about the unity of the nation state.[97] The question that Moretti poses at the end of his work thus frames much of the analysis in the chapters that follow. He notes that the 'paradigm shift' that has occurred in the history of the novel, away from the realism of the European novel and towards the Russian novel of ideas and Latin American magic realism, has been accompanied by a shift in space. This narrative shift is, according to Moretti, related to a geographic shift, such that 'the new model is the product of a new space'.[98] Here I ask: what are the transformations that took place in Egyptian society that led to a shift in the representation of space within the novel, and what are the new forms and aesthetics that emerged to represent these spaces?

This attention to the spatial is well represented in the literary critical material on Arabic literature. The urban, and particularly the city of Cairo, as represented in modern and contemporary Egyptian literature is the subject of significant works by Sabry Hafez, Husayn Hammuda, Dina Hishmat, Samia Mehrez and Mara Naaman.[99] The move beyond Cairo, to the city of Alexandria, has been undertaken by Hala Halim, Duaa Muhammad Salameh and Deborah Starr.[100] The rural is investigated in scholarship by Abdel Muhsin Taha Badr and Samah Selim.[101] This project, *Space in Modern Egyptian Fiction*, born of this 'spatial turn' in Arabic literary criticism, seeks to bring together the examination of urban, rural and exilic spaces within a single work to provide a broader and more complex understanding of the socio-economic and political changes that took place in Egypt during a pivotal moment in contemporary history, and their influence on the literary production of this generation. Within this context I address the multitude of geographical spaces that figure within the literary imagination, and the ways in which they are imagined and reimagined, thereby contributing to an articulation and critique of the ideology of Egyptian nationalism in the postcolonial period.

Conclusion: Space and the Sixties

The novelists selected as the focus of the following chapters all became 'consecrated' members of the sixties generation.[102] Consecration is here understood as the recognition of the writers as important players within the cultural sphere, by their taking up significant positions as editors of newspapers, literary journals and periodicals. It is reflected in the continued publication of their work, its critical reception, its translation into foreign languages, and in the conferral of awards and accolades.[103] Emerging at a time of great uncertainty and instability, the writers of the sixties generation positioned themselves as a departure from their predecessors, ready to spearhead an innovative movement that turned away from realism and embraced new literary aesthetics. Drawing inspiration from across the globe, the writers understood themselves to be part of the struggle for freedom, equality and justice in the postcolonial world, a struggle shared by their counterparts in

Europe, Latin America, the United States and Africa. While they shared a broad artistic vision, biographical, political and ideological similarities, the group's formation as a generation was salient as a means to gain access and standing in the field of cultural production in Egypt.

The works chosen by the 'consecrated' members of this generation all register a significant transformation in the representation of urban, rural and exilic space. This generation's disillusionment with the postcolonial project resulted in the disappearance of the idealised space of the Egyptian nation from the literary landscape, and the emergence of a new aesthetics of space. Untangling the connections between literary realism, narrative and national identity, the writers of the sixties generation undermined the time and space of the realist novel. The representations of space in these works of fiction belie the group's disappointment with the postcolonial project in Egypt and its ongoing struggle in the face of the increasingly repressive power of the state. The critique of the successive regimes of Nasser, Sadat and Mubarak is embedded in the depictions of the urban centres of Cairo and Alexandria, in the villages of the Delta and the South, and in the exilic spaces of Europe and the Gulf. The readings of the novels of the sixties generation in the chapters that follow, foreground the political, economic and social changes in postcolonial Egypt, and connect these changes to the aesthetic innovation for which these writers have become known.

Chapter 1 focuses on changes in the representation of the urban space of Cairo. I examine Sonallah Ibrahim's *Tilka-l-Raʾiha* (*The Smell of It*, 1966), Gamal al-Ghitani's *Waqaʾiʿ Harat al-Zaʿfarani* (*The Zafarani Files*, 1976), Ibrahim Aslan's *Malik al-Hazin* (*The Heron*, 1981) and Radwa Ashour's *Faraj* (*Blue Lorries*, 2008), reading the novels in opposition to the realist narratives of earlier decades. The shift away from depictions of the urban metropolis as the site of national struggle, or of the alley as the cross section of Egyptian society, is accompanied by a new representational aesthetics. Through the presentation of the city as the space of incarceration, the reimagination of the alley as a fantastic space, and the turn towards the previously ignored neighbourhood of Imbaba, these writers showcase new literary techniques – aspects of magical realism, elements of the fantastic and a turn to hyper-realism – in order to represent the transformation of the urban space of Cairo into one of surveillance and control.

Chapter 2 expands the urban literary landscape beyond the boundaries of Cairo, to the coastal city of Alexandria. Largely absent from the literary landscape throughout the twentieth century, the writers of this generation place Alexandria front and centre in their fiction. The work of two natives of the city, Edwar al-Kharrat and Ibrahim Abdel Meguid, who both produced 'Alexandrian Trilogies' provides the impetus for this chapter. Both writers present Alexandria not only as the possible alternative for the Cairene exile (as in Naguib Mahfouz's novels al-*Summan wa-l-Kharif*, 1962, and *Miramar*, 1967) but as a city with a complicated past and present. In works that blend autobiography and fiction, realism and the fantastic, the two novelists contend with the city's colonial, cosmopolitan and post-revolutionary contexts, calling into question Cairo's position of dominance.

Chapter 3 centres on works by Abd al-Hakim Qasim, Yahya Taher Abdullah and Yusuf al-Qaid. Here we move to the villages of the Delta and Upper Egypt, the latter appearing in Egyptian novels for the first time. I situate these novels in opposition to the social realist works of the previous generation, with their concentration upon the countryside as the space of revolutionary struggle and political mobilisation. The rural here is transformed into a space of suffering and degradation, in which the villagers struggle to contend with the difficulties of their daily lives. The village is thus represented as mystical and mythical space, with the writers employing literary techniques from fantastic literature and magical realism, as well as the folkloric tradition, in order to represent the ongoing marginalisation of the Egyptian village and its separation from the rest of the nation. I situate the reading of these novels within the broader socio-economic context of the period, particularly Nasser's agricultural reforms of the 1950s, in order to show that disillusionment with the Nasserist policies in the countryside was reflected in the literary output of the generation, which grappled to come to terms with the continued marginalisation and exclusion of the Egyptian village.

The fourth chapter moves beyond the boundaries of the Egyptian nation state, to Europe and the Gulf, to explore the space of political and economic dislocation, and brings together the work of Bahaa Taher and Muhammad al-Bisati. While Arabic narratives from the beginning of the twentieth century showed a movement outside of Egypt largely for the purposes of education, the novels in this chapter depict Europe as the space of political exile, and the Arab Gulf as the site of economic exploitation. In both cases, the novels under examination raise questions about the unity of the Egyptian nation state in an age when political, social and economic flows extend beyond the boundaries of the nation. The two works engage not only with the issue of national identity and belonging, but also with that of regional affiliation; the experience of economic and political dislocation illuminates the failure of Nasser's Arab nationalist dream, and its dissolution under the regimes of Sadat and Mubarak in the following decades.

I conclude with a discussion of the continued importance of the sixties generation and its impact upon contemporary writers in the field. This serves to relate the historical experience of the sixties generation to the present day. Recent changes in Egypt and the Arab world provide the impetus to return to the work of the sixties generation. They too were a generation contending with the aftermath of revolutionary change, the realities of the failings of democratic projects, and the role of artists and intellectuals in confronting the injustices of the state. *Space in Modern Egyptian Fiction* sheds light on a pivotal moment in modern Egypt's history and on a group of writers who transformed the literary landscape and whose relevance in the cultural field continues up to and beyond the events of the Arab Spring.

Notes

1. Foucault, 'Of Other Spaces', p. 22.
2. Bulson, *Novels, Maps, and Modernity*, pp. 19–20.
3. Among the most prominent members of the sixties generation are Yahya Taher Abdullah, Ibrahim Abdel Meguid, Muhammad Ibrahim Abu Sinna, Radwa Ashour, Ibrahim Aslan, Muhammad al-Bisati, Amal Dunqul, Gamal al-Ghitani, Sonallah Ibrahim, Edwar al-Kharrat, Raʾuf Musʿad, Muhammad Hafiz Rajab, Bahaa Taher, Majid Tubya, Yusuf al-Qaid and Abd al-Hakim Qasim.
4. Bourdieu, *The Field of Cultural Production*, p. 42.
5. I discuss these debates in more detail in Ramadan, 'The Emergence of the Sixties Generation in Egypt and the Anxiety of Categorization', pp. 409–30.
6. This is inspired by Franco Moretti's call to pursue 'the study of space in literature' and 'literature in space', although my formulation here is somewhat altered. Moretti, *Atlas of the European Novel*, p. 3.
7. For an extensive discussion of *al-Taliʿa*'s feature, see Ramadan, 'The Emergence

of the Sixties Generation in Egypt and the Anxiety of Categorization', pp. 409–30.
8. *Al-Hilal*'s edition in August 1969 was dedicated to the short story and showcased many 'young writers'. In September and October 1970, it ran a segment entitled 'al-Jil al-Qasasi al-Jadid Yatakallam' ('The New Narrative Generation Speaks') reminiscent of *al-Taliᶜa*'s feature. *Al-Masaʾ* and *al-Majalla* both ran a series of articles in the late 1960s that also focused on the issue of the emergence of a new generation as it related to the short story.
9. See for example Jacquemond, *Conscience of the Nation*, pp. 184–91; Ashour *et al.*, *Arab Women Writers*; and Elsadda, *Gender, Nation, and the Arabic Novel*.
10. Hafez, 'The Egyptian Novel in the Sixties', p. 171.
11. See Stagh, *The Limits of Freedom of Speech*; Jacquemond, *Conscience of the Nation*; and Mehrez, *Egyptian Writers Between History and Fiction*.
12. Hafez, 'The Egyptian Novel in the Sixties', p. 171.
13. This position was expressed by Ghali Shukri, for example, who insisted that 1967 was not a decisive break but instead a 'crowning' of events that had preceded that year. It was as such part of the 'historical progression of events'. See 'al-Basma al-Akhira fi Adab al-Sittinat', p. 234. See also Shukri, 'al-Adab al-Misri baᶜd al-Khamis min Yunyu'.
14. 'Hakadha Yatakallamu al-Udabaʾ al-Shabab', pp. 14–15.
15. Najib, 'Hakadha Yatakallamu al-Udabaʾ al-Shabab', p. 44.
16. See Abdel Baqi, 'Hakadha Yatakallamu al-Udabaʾ al-Shabab', pp. 31–2; Qasim, 'Hakadha Yatakallamu al-Udabaʾ al-Shabab', pp. 20–2; al-Ghitani, 'Hakadha Yatakallamu al-Udabaʾ al-Shabab', p. 54; and Faris, 'Qabl an Yughriq al-Nahr al-Jamiᶜ', pp. 109–11.
17. Jacquemond, *Conscience of the Nation*, p. 8. While many critics agree on this point, the exact moment of designation is difficult to verify.
18. Shukri, 'al-Adab al-Misri baᶜd al-Khamis min Yunyu', p. 108. Among the examples he gives of '*jil al-taḥaddi*' are Sonallah Ibrahim and Gamal al-Ghitani, both of whom write of the failures of the regime in the years before the defeat.
19. The literary critical material from the time is replete with discussions of what term to use to describe this generation. Critics suggested '*ruʾya*' (vision), '*mawja*' (wave), '*ḥaraka*' (movement) and '*itijāh*' (direction). This would continue in the decades that followed. See al-Kharrat, *al-Hassasiyya al-Jadida*; Badawi, *al-Riwaya al-Haditha fi Misr*; Shukri, 'Jil Jadid am Ruʾya'; and Ramadan, 'The Emergence of the Sixties Generation in Egypt and the Anxiety of Categorization'.

20. Van de Akker and Dorleijin, 'Talkin' 'Bout Two Generations', p. 18.
21. Jacquemond, *Conscience of the Nation*, pp. 5–9; and Kendall, *Literature, Journalism and the Avant-Garde*, pp. 110–39.
22. Bourdieu, *The Field of Cultural Production*, pp. 30, 46.
23. Jacquemond, *Conscience of the Nation*, pp. 171–2.
24. The journal's editorial team, having realised this problem, published an amendment in the following issue, stating that although their label of '*jīl jadīd*' (new generation) was not intended to contain within it a specific age limit, they did realise that most of the innovative work was being produced by younger writers, hence the choice of the eighteen to thirty-five age range. They did not, however, include testimonies by older writers even in later issues. See [unattributed], 'Kalim min *al-Taliᶜa*', p. 95.
25. See, for example, Shukri, 'Thaqafat 68', p. 87; and Barakat, 'al-Qissa al-Qasira bayn Jilayn', pp. 188–200. It was also the title of Shukri's book, *Siraᶜ al-Ajyal fi al-Adab al-Muᶜasir* (The Generational Struggle in Contemporary Literature). Jalal al-ᶜAshri's book *Jil waraʾ Jil* (One Generation After Another) had the subtitle '*al-Ajyal: Liqaʾ am Siraᶜ?*' (The Generations: A Meeting or a Struggle?). See al-ᶜAshri, *Jil waraʾ Jil*, p. 7.
26. See Dunqul, 'Hakadha Yatakallamu al-Udabaʾ al-Shabab', p. 18; Qasim, 'Hakadha Yatakallamu al-Udabaʾ al-Shabab', p. 21; and Ashour, 'Hakadha Yatakallamu al-Udabaʾ al-Shabab', p. 17.
27. Ibrahim, 'The Experience of a Generation', p. 22.
28. See al-Qalamawi, 'Zahirat al-ᶜAqqad lan Tatakarrar', p. 68; and ᶜAwad, 'Hadha al-Jil: Iᶜsar Haqiqi am Zawbaᶜa fi Finjan?', p. 69.
29. ᶜAwad, 'Hadha al-Jil: Iᶜsar Haqiqi am Zawbaᶜa fi Finjan?', p. 69; and al-ᶜAshri, *Jil waraʾ Jil*, p. 18.
30. Sonallah Ibrahim is one of the exceptions to this trend.
31. This question was asked in the journals at the time. See, for example, Shukri, 'Jiluna wa-l-Riwaya', pp. 84–96, and 'Thaqafat 68', pp. 75–87; ᶜAyyad, 'al-Qissa al-Misriyya al-Qasira', pp. 94–7; and Hafez, 'Mustaqbal al-Uqsusa al-Misriyya', pp. 6–16.
32. Al-Sharuni, 'Hiwar Hawl Azmat al-Qissa al-Qasira', pp. 131, 133.
33. Halasa, 'al-Kibar wa-l-Sighar', p. 43; and Hafez 'Majmuᶜat 1969 al-Qasasiyya', p. 74. The breakdown of the boundaries between the past, present and future was also discussed by Abdel Hamid Ibrahim in an article that appeared in *al-Masaʾ*. Ibrahim, 'Adab al-Shabab fi Masarahu al-Sahih', p. 6.
34. This refusal is discussed in greater detail, for example, in relationship to the

work of Ibrahim Aslan. See al-Kharrat, 'Ibrahim Aslan wa Qinaᶜ al-Rafd', pp. 78–83.
35. Hafez, 'The Transformation of Reality and the Arabic Novel's Aesthetic Response', pp. 100–4.
36. Ibid. p. 104.
37. Ibid. p. 99.
38. This idea was developed by critics who referred to the aesthetic developments that appeared in the 60s and continued in the decades that followed as 'post-Mahfouzian'. See, for example, al-Musawi, *Infirat al-ᶜAqd al-Muqaddas*.
39. I borrow the translation of '*hassāsiyya*' as 'sensibility' from Kendall. Al-Kharrat began using the term in the late 1960s. In his exploration of the 'new sensibility' or what he terms the 'post-Mahfouzian' novel, al-Musawi shows that al-Kharrat borrowed his formulation from the work of Leslie Fiedler, Irving Howe and Susan Sontag, a point which interestingly is not mentioned by al-Kharrat in his work. Al-Musawi, *Infirat al-ᶜAqd al-Muqaddas*, pp. 76–8.
40. Al-Kharrat, *al-Hassasiyya al-Jadida*, pp. 15–17.
41. Ibid. pp. 17–18.
42. Ibid. pp. 18–19.
43. Ibid. p. 19.
44. Ibid. pp. 19–20.
45. Kendall, *Literature, Journalism and the Avant-Garde*, p. 151. Kendall also cites Sami Khashaba who notes that Egyptian writers of this period read translations of existentialist literature much more than existentialist philosophy, thereby accounting for the strong human presence in their work. See also al-Musawi, *al-Nukhba al-Fikriyya wa-l-Inshiqaq*; and Jabra, 'Modern Arabic Literature and the West', pp. 87–91.
46. Hafez, 'Majmuᶜat 1968 al-Qasasiyya', p. 68.
47. Ibid. p. 68.
48. Ibid. p. 68.
49. See, for example, the testimonials in *al-Taliᶜa*. See also Hafez, 'al-Uqsussa al-Misriyya wa-l-Hadatha', pp. 83–90; and al-ᶜAshri, *Jil waraʾ Jil*.
50. Abu ᶜAwf, 'Muqaddima fi al-Qissa al-Misriyya al-Qasira', p. 186; and ᶜAwad, 'Hadha al-Jil: Iᶜsar Haqiqi am Zawbaᶜa fi Finjan?', p. 70.
51. Shukri, 'al-Basma al-Akhira fi Adab al-Sittinat', p. 235. See also Fathi, 'Malamih Mushtarika fi al-Intaj al-Qasasi al-Jadid', p. 111.
52. See, for example, Abu ᶜAwf, 'al-Bahth ᶜan Tariq Jadid li-l-Qissa al-Misriyya

al-Qasira', p. 82; Halasa, 'al-Adab al-Jadid: Malamih wa Ittijahat'; and Haqqi, *Fajr al-Qissa al-Misriyya maʿa Sitt Dirasat Ukhra ʿan Nafs al-Marhala*.

53. See Halasa, 'al-Adab al-Jadid: Malamih wa Ittijahat', p. 118, and 'al-Kibar wa-l-Sighar', pp. 43–51; and Hafez, 'Majmuʿat 1968 al-Qasasiyya', p. 65.
54. See Halasa, 'al-Adab al-Jadid: Malamih wa Ittijahat', pp. 115–25. In this article Halasa recognises the influence of Camus most clearly in Bahaa Taher's *al-Khutuba*.
55. For example, even though the journal *Gallery 68* did not specifically reference the student movements in Paris of the same year, it is quite likely that the title was intended to make this connection.
56. See the various testimonies in 'Hakadha Yatakallamu al-Udabaʾ al-Shabab', pp. 13–91.
57. See the testimonies given by Abdel Baqi and Qasim in 'Hakadha Yatakallamu al-Udabaʾ al-Shabab', pp. 20–3 and 32; and Faris, 'Qabl an Yughriq al-Nahr al-Jamiʿ', pp. 109–11.
58. See, for example, Ashour, 'Hakadha Yatakallamu al-Udabaʾ al-Shabab', p. 18. The term *'iltizām'* (commitment) was in use amongst socialist circles in the 1950s. It was however first coined by Taha Hussein in the 1940s, in his attempt to translate the Sartrian notion of *'littérature engagée'*. For more, see Klemm, 'Different Notions of Commitment (*Iltizam*) and Committed Literature (*Al-Adab al-Multazim*) in the Literary Circles of the Mashriq'; and Di-Capua, 'Arab Existentialism'.
59. Jacquemond, *Conscience of the Nation*, p. 99.
60. Bourdieu, *The Field of Cultural Production*. Critics in the field of Arabic literature largely agree that this remains the case. See, for example, Jacquemond, *Conscience of the Nation*, pp. 168–70; Kendall, *Literature, Journalism and the Avant-Garde*, pp. 2–3; Badawi, *al-Riwaya al-Haditha fi Misr*; Shukri, *Siraʿ al-Ajyal fi al-Adab al-Muʿasir*; and al-ʿAshri, *Jil waraʾ Jil*.
61. Ramadan, 'The Emergence of the Sixties Generation in Egypt and the Anxiety over Categorization', p. 412.
62. Bourdieu, *The Field of Cultural Production*, p. 53.
63. See, for example, the testimonies in 'Hakadha Yatakallamu al-Udabaʾ al-Shabab', pp. 13–88; the testimonies in 'Hiwar Hawl Azmat al-Qissa al-Qasira', pp. 122–38; and ʿAdas, 'Azmat Nashr am Azmat Intaj', pp. 8–10.
64. Muhsib, 'Hakadha Yatakallamu al-Udabaʾ al-Shabab', p. 25.
65. Al-Shayib, 'Hakadha Yatakallamu al-Udabaʾ al-Shabab', p. 47.
66. Mahfouz, 'Hiwar Hawl Azmat al-Qissa al-Qasira', p. 124. Rushdi attributed

this to the fact that journals and newspapers had stopped printing literature. See Rushdi, 'Hiwar Hawl Azmat al-Qissa al-Qasira', p. 133.
67. Stagh, *The Limits of Freedom of Speech*, p. 51.
68. Ibid. pp. 88–113.
69. For a thorough discussion of the journal, see Kendall, *Literature, Journalism and the Avant-Garde*, pp. 110–39.
70. For a complete list of the authors published by *Gallery 68*, see Surur, 'Kashaf Majallat Gallery 68'.
71. Mursi, 'Tasdir', p. 2.
72. Al-Bisati, 'al-Tajdid ... wa Majallat 68', p. 6. Al-Bisati himself had been published in the June 1968 edition of the journal. His short story '*Ibtisamat al-Madina al-Rumadiyya*' was published alongside a critical study by Ghalib Halasa of the collection *al-Kibar wa-l-Sighar* of which it was a part.
73. Approximately a third of the writers interviewed for *al-Taliʿa* had published work in *Gallery 68* by the time *al-Taliʿa*'s feature appeared at the end of 1969. Kendall, *Literature, Journalism and the Avant-Garde*, p.154. Examples include Abd al-Hakim Qasim, Majid Tubya, Ahmad Hashim al-Sharif, Amal Dunqul, Muhammad Ibrahim Mabruk, Gamal al-Ghitani and Mahir Shafiq Mabruk. Some had also been published in *al-Majalla* and *al-Qissa*.
74. Badawi, *al-Riwaya al-Haditha fi Misr*, pp. 224–5.
75. Ibid. pp. 228–35.
76. For more a more detailed exploration of the biographies of the writers featured in this book, see the Appendix.
77. Badawi, *al-Riwaya al-Haditha fi Misr*, p. 255.
78. Bulson, *Novels, Maps, Modernity*, p. 11.
79. Foucault, 'Of Other Spaces', p. 22.
80. Foucault, *The History of Sexuality*, p. 93.
81. In the work of Edward Soja, we find a similar triad to that of Lefebvre, this time in the form of First, Second and Thirdspace, which resonate with the perceived, the conceived and the lived. Like Lefebvre's representational space, Soja's Thirdspace provides the opportunity for resistance and difference: 'If Firstspace is explored primarily through its readable texts and contexts, and Secondspace through its prevailing representational discourses, then Thirdspace must be additionally guided by some form of potentially emancipatory *praxis*, the translation of knowledge into action in a conscious – and consciously spatial – effort to improve the world in some significant way.' Soja, *Thirdspace*, p. 22.

82. Lefebvre, *The Production of Space*, pp. 22–7.
83. Ibid. pp. 33–46.
84. Ibid. p. 39.
85. Ibid. p. 15.
86. Foucault, 'Of Other Spaces', p. 22.
87. Bakhtin, 'Forms of Time and of the Chronotope in the Novel', p. 84.
88. Harvey, *The Condition of Postmodernity*, p. 240.
89. Ibid. p. 240.
90. Anderson, *Imagined Communities*, p. 25.
91. Ibid. p. 24.
92. Ibid. p. 24.
93. Ibid. p. 26.
94. Moretti, *Atlas of the European Novel*, p. 3.
95. Ibid. p. 3.
96. In his work Moretti draws upon earlier attempts within the literary field to consider the significance of the spatial. In particular, he highlights the work of Pierre Bourdieu in mapping the social space of Gustave Flaubert's *L'Education Sentimentale*. Moretti, *Atlas of the European Novel*, pp. 110–13.
97. Ibid. p. 20.
98. Ibid. p. 196.
99. See Hafez, 'Jamaliyyat al-Riwaya al-Jadida al-Qatiʿa al-Maʿrifiyya wa-l-Nazʿa al-Mudadda li-l-Ghinaʾiyya', and 'The New Egyptian Novel'; Hammuda, *al-Riwaya wa-l-Madina*; Hishmat, *al-Qahira fi al-Adab al-Misri al-Hadith wa-l-Muʿasir*; Mehrez, 'From the Hara to the ʿImara', *The Literary Atlas of Cairo* and *The Literary Life of Cairo*; and Naaman, *Urban Space in Contemporary Egyptian Literature*.
100. Halim, *Alexandrian Cosmopolitanism*; Salameh, *Nom de Lieu*; and Starr, *Remembering Cosmopolitan Egypt*.
101. Badr, *al-Riwaʾi wa-l-Ard*; and Selim, *The Novel and the Rural Imaginary in Egypt*.
102. Bourdieu, *The Field of Cultural Production*, p. 42. I expand on this discussion in Chapter 5.
103. This is explored further in Chapter 5 and the Appendix.

1

Cairo: Urban Space, Surveillance and the State

Masr is Egypt, and *Masr* is also what Egyptians call Cairo. On Tuesday 1 February, I watched a man surveying the scene in Tahrir with a big smile: the sun was shining and people were everywhere, old and young, rich and poor, they talked and walked and sang and played and joked and chanted. Then he said it out loud: 'Ya Masr, it's been a long time. We have missed you.'

Ahdaf Soueif, *Cairo*[1]

To think of Egypt is, for many, to think of Cairo. As the momentous events of late 2010 unfolded, Egyptian novelist and journalist Ahdaf Soueif wrote what would become a memoir of Cairo. The story of a nation and a people transformed by revolutionary struggle is here a story of the city. Soueif's Cairo is at once a rendering of the real city, the materiality of the urban metropolis, through the lived reality of its habitants, but also an imagined city that encompasses and transcends the Cairo of her experiences. In writing this urban narrative, Soueif follows a long Arabic literary tradition from at least the end of the nineteenth century, in which Cairo is at the heart of Egyptian literary production.[2]

Throughout the first half of the twentieth century, Egyptian writers drew on this urban setting and on the experience of its inhabitants in the development of two relatively new literary genres: the novel and the short story. Cairo was the backdrop against which writers depicted the nation's struggle against British colonialism, the possibilities of national independence, and the people's confrontation with a rapidly changing world. From the earliest prose narratives, such as Muhammad al-Muwaylihi's *Hadith ᶜ Isa Ibn Hisham* (*A Period of Time*, 1907), Cairo dominated literary production in Egypt.

These early works focused upon the old quarters of Islamic Cairo: the neighbourhood of Sayyida Zaynab captured by Yahya Haqqi's greatly celebrated novella *Qindil Umm Hashim* (*The Lamp of Umm Hashim*, 1944) and the alleys of Jamaliyya immortalised by the novels of Naguib Mahfouz.

It is Mahfouz who comes to be the foremost chronicler of Cairo; *Zuqaq al-Midaqq* (*Midaq Alley*, 1947), *Khan al-Khalili* (1945) and *al-Thulathiyya* (*The Cairo Trilogy*, 1956–7), Mahfouz's realist novels par excellence, follow the lives of Egypt's middle class in narratives in which Cairo's alleys and streets, its architecture and edifices, are as important as its people. Nowhere is this more poignantly captured than in the opening of *Midaq Alley*, which introduces us to the space of the *ḥāra* (alley), so ubiquitous in Mahfouz's early works. This novel tells of the trials of the inhabitants of the alley, living in the turmoil of colonial Cairo. Yet their alley is also a portal to the past, 'a relic of bygone times' that 'once shone like a brilliant star in the firmament of Old Cairo'.[3] The descriptions of the alley establish continuity with the past, and foreground the sights, smells and sounds that characterise it. This is a world that boasts of Cairo's rich history, as far back as the Fatimids, even while it struggles with the changes of the contemporary moment. The alley is the nation writ large, representing as Mehrez explains, 'Egyptian society at different historical junctures and the various transformations that beset it'.[4] It is in these early novels that the trope of the alley as nation is born.

The writers of the sixties generation present a very different Cairo in their works. Gone is the realist depiction of the city as the site of national struggle, or of the alley as the cross section of Cairene society.[5] Instead new representations abound, of new urban spaces such as the working-class neighbourhood of Imbaba, or of old spaces in new ways: the alley as a fantastical space or of Cairo as a prison. Writers transformed the aesthetic landscape, shattering the space and time of the realist narrative in their continued attempts to capture the new social and political reality of the post-revolutionary period.

This chapter focuses on four novels from the writers of this generation: Sonallah Ibrahim's *Tilka-l-Raʾiha* (*The Smell of It*, 1966), Gamal al-Ghitani's *Waqaʾiʿ Harat al-Zaʿfarani* (*The Zafarani Files*, 1976), Ibrahim Aslan's *Malik al-Hazin* (*The Heron*, 1981) and Radwa Ashour's *Faraj* (*Blue Lorries*, 2008).[6] Structurally, each of these novelists employs the metonymic and the metaphoric in the mapping of urban space; through individual itinerary;

a portrait of an alley; a portrait of a neighbourhood; and the rendering of the city as jail. In doing so, they simultaneously present searing critiques of the state under Nasser, Sadat and Mubarak, revealing how the regimes use techniques of violence, repression and surveillance to monitor and control the urban population of Cairo. The struggle for power in these novels becomes a struggle over space, with writers confronting and negotiating the limitations placed upon them as intellectuals.[7]

Each of these works is a literary expression of surveillance that disrupts, undermines and challenges the project of state surveillance, and signals the political role of the Egyptian literati, as it was understood by the sixties generation. As Mehrez argues, writers within the Egyptian literary sphere consider themselves the 'conscience of the nation, responsible for articulating its collective disillusionments and for voicing its silenced realities'.[8] This is a role not unlike the one Edward Said famously articulated with regards to the public intellectual as one who 'is endowed with a faculty for representing, embodying, articulating a message, a view, an attitude, philosophy or opinion to, as well as for, a public'.[9] The struggle to fulfil their roles as writers and intellectuals thus emerges as a central concern of these urban narratives.[10] Unable to successfully fulfil these creative and intellectual roles, or to mobilise individual or collective political action, the writers contend with the limitations of their agency. As such these novels are allegories of the writer's vocation representing the struggles of the author to realise his/her function as a public intellectual in postcolonial Egypt.

Individual Itinerary in Sonallah Ibrahim's Cairo

The Smell of It, Ibrahim's semi-autobiographical work, presents a Cairo that bears little resemblance to the city of revolutionary struggle.[11] Employing an innovative form of hyper-realism that focuses on the banal details of the everyday, Ibrahim produces a space of surveillance and control, a city that imprisons its citizens in a world where linear time has been replaced with a never-ending circularity. Written in the aftermath of Ibrahim's release from prison in 1964, the novel follows a nameless, newly released prisoner as he contends with the parole regulations that control his new life.[12]

Early in the Nasserist regime, Islamists, communists and leftists in Egypt found themselves in a contentious position vis-à-vis the state. Arrests began as early as 1954, when Nasser targeted Cairo University, and would continue in waves throughout the following decade. These attacks reached their height in 1959, when all suspected members of the Communist Party were arrested, and only released in 1964, when the Party was officially dissolved. Persecution went hand in hand with the establishment of a state monopoly over cultural, intellectual and educational institutions, which forged an uneasy alliance between the intellectuals and the state.[13] Ibrahim was arrested in 1959, spending the next five years in the famous Kharja internment camp, and facing strict parole regulations upon his release. *The Smell of It* is based largely on his experience.[14]

Despite the protagonist's recent discharge, his daily life is not so different from his time in prison. Days are dull and repetitive; everyday he walks the streets of Cairo, rides the metro, and inevitably returns home in time for the daily visits of his parole officer. The protagonist is isolated and disconnected, alienated from the world around him. In this respect he is not dissimilar to the protagonists that populate many of Ibrahim's novels: those of *Najmat Aghustus* (*August Star*, 1974), *al-Lajna* (*The Committee*, 1981), *Sharaf* (Honor, 1997), *Zaat* (*Zaat*, 1992), and even the 2011 *Thalj* (Ice).[15] Remaining completely detached he notes how 'this was the moment I had continually dreamed of throughout those past years. I searched within myself for some unusual sensation, of pleasure or joy or excitement, but found none.'[16]

This alienation manifests itself in the protagonist's movements through and experiences of the streets of Cairo. Movement dominates much of the novel through the creation of an individual itinerary. Leaving his apartment in Heliopolis, a newer suburb of Cairo, the protagonist travels daily to visit family and friends around the city. Heliopolis represents the changing geography and expansion of Cairo and separates the protagonist from the city of his past, the more familiar downtown Cairo, which serves as the backdrop to many of his recollections. Built in the early part of the twentieth century by the Belgium businessman Baron Empain, Heliopolis was intended to house the well-to-do European and native population. One of the earliest examples of the satellite cities created to alleviate the city's housing problem, the suburb's population continued to grow throughout the century, driven by the exodus of the upper and middle classes out of downtown Cairo.[17] Ibrahim has resided in this neighbourhood for many years, thus the spatial biography of the author impinges upon the text.

The protagonist's movement from point A to B, from his home in Heliopolis to those he is visiting, is the principal action of the text, which is significant given that remarkably little else happens. This itinerary recalls Michel de Certeau's understanding of the 'tour' as a description that 'organises movements', wherein space is moved through and not just seen.[18] De Certeau opposes the 'tour' to the 'map', the latter being a 'tableau' based on seeing rather than moving; the distinction then is between 'the itinerary (a discursive series of operations) and the map (a plane projection totalizing observations)'.[19] The descriptions of the protagonist's movement are stripped down, succinct, and lacking emotion – a hallmark of Ibrahim's innovative prose.

In a description of his walk around downtown Cairo, which continues for four pages, we are told *exactly* which streets he took and which squares he crossed:

> I got up and left the cafe. I walked to the bridge and boarded a bus. I got off at the beginning of Soliman Street. I sat down in the first cafe I came to. I drank a coffee, then lit a cigarette. I got up and walked to Tewfik Street, then I branched off into Tewfikiyya and stood in front of the Cairo Cinema. It was showing a comedy. I went off in the direction of Fouad Street, which I crossed. I turned down into Sherif Street. I continued walking, crossed Adly Street, then Sarwat Street, and went off in the direction of Soliman Street, and continued on until I reached the Square. Water from the sewers overflowed the street. Pumps were set up everywhere, pumping the water out from the shops into the street. The smell was unbearable . . . I crossed the street and went back in the direction of the Square, then I plunged down into Kasr El-Nil Street until I reached the cinema there . . . I left the cinema and once again walked in the direction of the Square, and back into Soliman Street. This time I walked on the opposite side to the one I had come by. When I reached the Metro Cinema I found that it too was showing a comedy. I passed by it. I stood in front of the Americaine Cafe, undecided. The Rivoli Cinema was on my left and there was a vast crowd in front of it. The cinemas of Emad El-Din Street came to my mind. I crossed

the street and continued walking up Fouad Street to Emad El-Din; I turned into it, walking on the left-hand side.[20]

The itinerary produced in this lengthy description does not serve to acquaint the reader with Cairo's downtown streets but instead contributes to a sense of *disorientation*. This is familiarisation to the point of exhaustion. The protagonist is perhaps the 'anti-flaneur', unable to experience joy from his excursions, and yet obsessively tracking his own movement to exercise control in a world in which he has none. This is one of the ways Ibrahim disrupts the project of state surveillance, and the form of the map associated with it, a form that 'colonizes space'.[21] Instead, Ibrahim's protagonist is an example of de Certeau's 'tour describers', and it is the act of walking that here produces the urban space of Cairo.[22] It is the dweller, the pedestrian (and by extension the reader) as consumer and producer that occupies centre stage. And within this lengthy description, the reader cannot ignore the repeated reference to the comedic films playing in the movie theatres, allusions to alternate realities that mirror the social farce the protagonist is experiencing. Movie theatres will once again feature prominently in the urban landscape of Ibrahim Abdel Meguid's novels discussed in Chapter 2.

The brevity of the statements and the jarring punctuation, exemplified in the passage above, no doubt shocked both readers and critics at the time, who were accustomed to long descriptive passages of narrative prose. The protagonist's movements are recounted in a disengaged, dispassionate manner, that critics have termed Ibrahim's hyper-realism or neo-realism. According to al-Kharrat, Ibrahim's work is an example of what he terms '*al-tayyār al-wāqiʿī al-jadīd*' (the neo-realist trend), focusing on the base and banal details of everyday life and purifying the traditional form so as to arrive at a style that is highly accurate, sharp and yet pervaded by an ongoing sense of disjunction, in an attempt to articulate the ongoing refusal of existing forms of power.[23] The focus on the act of walking is disrupted only when he notices that 'the water from the sewers overflowed everywhere' and that the 'smell was unbearable'.

This concentration on filth and excrement is part of the postcolonial aesthetics that Ibrahim employs in his critique of the excesses of the state. It reminds the reader of the degeneration of the urban metropolis and of the gradual disintegration of its infrastructure under Nasser's regime. As Joshua

Esty explains, 'shit has a political vocation: it draws attention to the failures of development, to the unkept promises not only of colonial modernizing regimes but of post independence economic policy'.[24] This is not the only time that putrid water overflows. The protagonist's bathroom floods covering the floor with water, an event he notes with characteristic detachment. The image of overflowing water connects public and private space; the latter is not impervious to the deterioration and decay of the outside world.

The alienation of the protagonist in the present and his detachment from his surroundings is undeniable when juxtaposed to the descriptions of the downtown streets of his past. Arriving at the area of his childhood home he decides to find the house he grew up in, even hoping that his mother still lives there. This is immediately followed by a nostalgic flashback, which takes us back to the protagonist's trips home with his father, undertaken on the once functioning tram:

> I used to love this quiet street because it was full of trees whose dense branches used to meet high across the middle of it, shutting out the light. I used to love the sound of the trolley-arm thrusting its way with difficulty between the branches overhead.[25]

Gone is the protagonist's detachment and instead here is a moment that recuperates his potential to feel. The memory is replete with emotion, the neighbourhood is described with a fullness and texture, and the experience is recreated in his mind through the sights and sounds of the streets. This vitality contrasts to the lackluster description of the street in the present: 'I turned to the right. The house I remembered was very high and had wide wooden balconies, from one of which my mother once threw herself and fell on the balcony below.'[26] The indifference with which he remembers his mother throwing herself off the balcony is the same indifference with which he receives the news of her death, at which point he realises his appointment with the parole office is approaching and he gets up to leave. The novel closes with the same routine actions that dominate the narrative: '"I must go now," I said . . . I crossed the side roads until I came to Ramses Square, then I turned off in the direction of the Metro tram stop.'[27]

State Surveillance and the Prison of Cairo

The closing event, the compulsory return home of the protagonist to meet his parole officer, is the primary structuring device of the novel. It is the action that organises the protagonist's days producing a sense of monotonous repetition (the officer visits the protagonist approximately ten times). In fact, at the very start of the novel, the officer declares 'we have to know your whereabouts' at all times.[28] Ibrahim's is an account of life in the prison that Cairo has become under the surveillance of the modern state apparatus of Nasser's police state.[29] This work presents a system of state coercion and control as described by Foucault, capturing how discipline, as a political technology of power, is exercised through surveillance and examination, maintaining control at the level of the mechanism of the body itself and of the body in space. If for Foucault the prison is the microcosm of society, for Ibrahim it is also the microcosm of the city, in which the citizen is continually observed, monitored and examined.[30] (This relationship reappears in Ashour's novel discussed later in this chapter). Here the rhetorical function of the city is transformed and expanded; instead of only fulfilling a metonymic role in which the city is a stand in for the entire nation, Ibrahim's Cairo is also a metaphorical prison.[31] This association is explicitly made when, after being released from prison but having no home, he is forced to return there to spend his first night of freedom.

The operation of time in the novel reinforces the sense of incarceration and surveillance that dominates the protagonist's relationship to the space of both home and city. The repetition of the protagonist's routine creates a monotony and tedium mirroring the experience of imprisonment. One day is indistinguishable from the next: he rides the metro, visits relatives or old acquaintances, unsuccessfully attempts to write, making sure he is back home in time for the officer's visit. This repetition calls into question the linear time with which the reader is familiar. Linearity, very much a convention of the realist tradition, is what the sixties generation sought to challenge, introducing innovative representations of time and space. In Ibrahim's case circularity and repetition replace linearity and progress, and we are presented with a protagonist stuck in time and place who repeats the same actions with no sense of movement or progress.

(Creative) Impotency

Surveillance is so crucial to Ibrahim's novel not only because of what it reveals about the repressive nature of the state apparatus, but also because it is tied up with the figure of the writer. *The Smell of It* is a literary expression of surveillance, a book about the inability to write a book, precisely because of state surveillance exercised upon the writer, limiting his/her ability to produce and circulate work. We see this on the level of plot with regards to the protagonist's ongoing struggle to write and in terms of the author's autobiographical experience. In both *al-Lajna* (*The Committee*, 1981) and *Bayrut Bayrut* (*Beirut Beirut*, 1984), Ibrahim takes up the issues of publication and censorship that dominated his experience with *The Smell of It*, using it as material for his creative works.[32]

Writing is presented in the novel as an alternative to acts of political resistance, or more precisely as a form of political resistance to state repression. The inability to engage in direct confrontation with state power drives the individual to wage war in the intellectual realm. He is the citizen born of the Nasserist regime, disappointed by the failures of the postcolonial state, monitored and imprisoned by the system he supported, alone in a city that was once his home. It is also a reflection of the importance of the writings of Jean-Paul Sartre and Albert Camus whose works were translated into Arabic in the 1950s and continued to exercise enormous influence on writers and intellectuals in the Arab world.[33] In Ibrahim's protagonist we can recognise the sense of estrangement, the process of 'detachment and separation' central to Camus' philosophy of alienation.[34] But there are also the echoes of Sartre's 'commitment', a sense that literature has a role to play in the political and social struggles of the contemporary moment. This is the cause of the protagonist's relentless battle to create, even as he continues to fail in this endeavour.

Despite numerous attempts to sit and write, the protagonist is paralysed. He chooses instead to masturbate, the empty pages in front of him a constant reminder of his failure: 'I put my hand down to my own thigh and began playing with myself. At last I gave a deep sigh . . . After a while I got up and gingerly stepped over the traces left by me on the floor under the table.'[35] The bodily traces left on the ground are another example of Ibrahim's use of the aesthetic of excremental fiction in his writing. Like the sewer water that flooded the streets of Cairo, this is a symbol of human excess. His semen, his bodily residue staining the floor is, like the blank paper, another testament to his inadequacy, an embodiment of failed potential.[36] It is also recognition of his own implication in 'ethical, aesthetic, or political failure'.[37] It is not only that the state has failed its people but that the intellectual, represented by Ibrahim's protagonist, is failing to challenge the repression of the state either by political action in the public sphere or by subverting power through literary production.[38]

The attention Ibrahim pays to the simplest, most banal details of the everyday, down to the basest physical bodily functions such as passing wind and masturbation, was the cause of much the criticism (and indeed part of the cause of its banning upon publication) levelled against the novel by the critics at the time.[39] In his column in the weekly newspaper *al-Masa'*, Yahya Haqqi launched a virulent attack of Ibrahim's work. Haqqi was most troubled by the representation of the masturbating protagonist, which he found 'truly disgusting' and prevented him from 'appreciat[ing] the story in the slightest, despite the outstanding skill evident in it'.[40] He concludes by insisting that 'this is a shameful repulsiveness which must be checked, and which the reader must be spared from having to swallow'.[41] Haqqi, who belonged to an earlier generation of writers, resisted the innovative move on the part of Ibrahim and his contemporaries to present all aspects of human existence, even the most sordid elements of private life. For Haqqi literature should depict life realistically and sincerely in the service of progress and socio-political advancement, exposing social inequalities, poverty, and the struggle for justice and freedom, very much in line with the social realism of his time. Descriptions like those in *The Smell of It* served no purpose in Haqqi's vision of literature as a revolutionary tool for social change.

Ibrahim offered an answer to Haqqi's critique in the introduction to the 1986 edition of his work saying:

> Doesn't the situation require a little baseness to express the baseness exemplified in physiological behavior like that of hitting a defenseless individual until death or placing an air pump in his anus and an electrical wire in his genitals? And all this because he expressed a different opinion or defended his freedom or his national identity?[42]

The 'baseness' of masturbation or passing wind is, according to Ibrahim, a necessary means of representing the baseness of a repressive system which continues to torture its citizens.

Sexual activity thus becomes the privileged site of (male) agency, solitary masturbation taking the place of political or intellectual action. The rape of the prison inmate which the protagonist witnesses upon his return to prison presents one example of the exercise of male power and dominance through sexual violence. Outside the prison walls the protagonist, the writer, is both sexually *and* creatively impotent. The transformation of the urban space of Cairo into a space of imprisonment, where the state monitors and controls its citizens, inhibits the writer from engaging in the very act of creation.[43] Sterility, as the absence of creative production, is paradoxically scripted in a creative work. And it is in using a postcolonial aesthetics, which departs from the space and time of the realist novel, that Ibrahim reimagines the capital as a fraught space, the site of an ongoing struggle between the regime and its citizens.

Gamal al-Ghitani's *The Zafarani Files*: An Ordinary Alley?

From the centre of downtown Cairo, we move to the alleys and backstreets of the old quarters of the city, familiar to any reader of Egyptian novels from the first half of the twentieth century. Life in the Egyptian *ḥāra* (alley) is captured most vividly, though not exclusively, in the novels of Mahfouz, who transformed this urban space into a familiar narrative trope, 'a microcosm of the city', replicating its social and economic divisions.[44] It is this tradition that Gamal al-Ghitani relies on in his 1976 novel *The Zafarani Files*, which draws on elements of the fantastic to tell the story of a Cairene alley gravely transformed by a mysterious impotency curse that strikes its male inhabitants.[45] The Egyptian *ḥāra* is no longer the heart of al-Ghitani's Cairo, but rather has become 'the margin to the center, dwelling place for the predominantly poor and underprivileged, whose lives and actions are monitored and controlled from without'.[46] Moreover, in *The Zafarani Files* the periphery becomes the centre, with the alley and all its social inequalities coming to represent the larger Egyptian nation. But is al-Ghitani, as a native of Jamaliyya and an inheritor of the Mahfouzian legacy, merely documenting the transformations of this neighbourhood? And if not, how then are we to understand his return to the *ḥāra*? And what of his reimagination of its literary function?

At first glance, al-Ghitani paints a picture of a typical Cairene street. We are told from the first page of the novel that the alley lies in the neighbourhood of al-Husayn (in the heart of what is known as Old or Islamic Cairo), near the mosque, not far from Masmat alley. Even if it is not a real *ḥāra* the reader can imagine its existence, assuming it to be a realistic depiction of a familiar urban space. (In much the same way as Mahfouz based his work on actual places.) But this is not the realism of Mahfouz. Instead of vivid descriptions of the intricacies of the alley, of the sights, smells and sounds which bring it to life, al-Ghitani provides a simplified map of the *ḥāra*, an aerial view that focuses on the location of every building. Each time a character is mentioned we are told *exactly* where his/her house lies. With our first introduction to Sheikh Atiya for example, we learn that he lives 'on the ground floor of house number 7 in Zafarani Alley'.[47] A little later we are given more details: 'Zafarani, it should be noted, is a dead end that leads nowhere. House number 7 stands at the far end, and it is here, in a narrow room tucked under the main staircase, that Sheikh Atiya resides.'[48] Looking for the home of Sayyid Effendi one would know that:

> his apartment is situated on the top floor of Umm Kawsar's house, which is fifth on the right as you enter Zafarani Alley but, as it stands opposite the low house belonging to Hagg Abdel Alim, which only has two stories, his apartment faces a wide, empty space.[49]

This seemingly unnecessary information adds little to the stories being recounted. Rather this attention to geographical space and the layout of the *ḥāra* is part of the form of the novel, which is presented as official government files collected about the events (*waqāʾiʿ*) taking place in Zafarani, after the discovery of the impotency curse. It is because of this state project of monitoring the alley, its inhabitants and their movement, that exact location is of utmost importance.

The Impotency Curse: The Alley as Fantastic Space

What at first appears as an alley like any other quickly transforms into a space where supernatural occurrences are the norm; this is the fantastical element that allows al-Ghitani to move beyond a realistic depiction of the *ḥāra*. It is also one of the ways to read his literary innovations. As the author notes in an interview with Issa J. Boullata, old Cairo 'is my take-off point from which I set out toward all humankind. I don't limit myself by merely portraying reality in a naïve way.'[50] With the impotency curse that Sheikh Atiya puts on the men of the alley, the people of Zafarani find themselves in the realm of the fantastic, having to accept the impossible as possible. Zafarani is no longer the quintessential Egyptian alley; this is the *ḥāra* gone awry. What al-Ghitani does here is in line with what Rosemary Jackson describes as the way fantastic narratives function:

> They assert that what they are telling is real – relying upon the conventions of realistic fiction to do so – and then they proceed to break that assumption of realism by introducing what – within those terms is manifestly unreal.[51]

Al-Ghitani uses the fantastic as a subversive strategy, to undermine the existing social order. The curse changes the world as the Zafaranis, and the readers, know it. Gender roles are both overturned and reversed, and socio-economic differences are eliminated. The transmutation of the men of Zafarani, resulting in a loss of virility, establishes a form of equality amongst the inhabitants. Beyond this, the Sheikh takes advantage of the inhabitants' fear to establish rules, which ultimately have a levelling effect. All the people of Zafarani are forced to wake, sleep and eat at exactly the same time, eradicating the socio-economic differences representative of social stratification.

The revolutionary possibilities offered by these changes extend beyond the limited space of the alley to the outside, thus 'transform[ing] this world'.[52] In the unique space that the alley has become, al-Ghitani is able to imagine an alternative to the current world order, a liberatory moment in which state power might be thwarted and social justice achieved. Because the curse is not limited to the people of Zafarani but, as the Sheikh informs the inhabitants, any man to enter the alley will be 'impaired' and any Zafarani woman to sleep with a man anywhere will 'impair' him, the alley is increasingly isolated from the rest of the city.[53] Gradually non-Zafaranis stop entering the alley and most of the inhabitants stop exiting it. The creation of a space of 'enclosure' where the extraordinary has become the norm is, according to Jackson, a fundamental way space is transformed in fantastic literature.[54] Here the alley as enclosure oscillates between a space of liberation and one of imprisonment; while it is temporarily out of the reach of state control, this freedom is at the same time something of a burden. The once bustling alley has fallen dead: it is so quiet in fact that it is 'as if the whole of Zafarani were taking part in a funeral procession somewhere'.[55] Rumana, an inhabitant of the alley, compares the silence to the time he spent in prison, to 'the cells in solitary confinement, the prison-within-the-prison'.[56] Here too we witness a rhetorical shift whereby the alley takes on a metaphorical purpose, coming to symbolise a prison.

Literary Expressions of Surveillance

Al-Ghitani's novel centres on questions of revolution and change and yet the intellectual does not figure in the narrative as directly as in Ibrahim's novel (or that of Aslan or Ashour). Nevertheless, many of the same issues are raised, this time in the form of the work itself. Al-Ghitani uses the tools of the state to represent a moment of resistance *against* the state. As with Ibrahim's novel, here too is a literary expression of surveillance. But while Ibrahim's protagonist could not produce his novel because of state surveillance, al-Ghitani's novel *is* the record of surveillance. The first section of the novel entitled 'File One' is followed by the following explanation: 'Containing Profiles of Certain Subjects Residing in Zafarani Alley; Information Drawn from Sources Who Are Closely Informed about All that Goes on in the Alley'.[57] And so the story unfolds, through the files, reports, memorandums and appendices from the various State Security departments that get involved in the Zafarani case. These documents are written in a style that remains detached, maintaining a distance between the narrator and the events being described. As the author explains: 'In *Zafarani* I expressed events with an objective spirit because it is a report and it's not possible to [be emotional] in a report.'[58] This objectivity and distance stand in contrast to the fantastical, almost mythical, nature of the events themselves. The tension between the real and the fictive, the official and unofficial narrative is fundamental to al-Ghitani's larger literary project. Mehrez notes that al-Ghitani 'displaces the borderlines which are usually set between the "fictional text" and the "historical text"; between the two worlds which have so conveniently been separated into the "imaginary" and the "real"'.[59] In this novel the conflation is less between the historical and the fictional text, but rather between the official format of the files and their content.

Within these documents occasional references are made to dates and times as if to remind the reader of the veracity of the information they contain. Early in the novel we learn of an event that took place on 8/4/1971 – this appearing to be a few years prior to the current events. Later in the novel reference is made to the defeat of 1967. Other than that, very few allusions are made to real time such that a sense of timelessness dominates the novel, undermining the time of the realist narrative and strengthening the idea that Zafarani Alley is not a part of the real world but has entered a mythical realm because of the fantastic impotency curse.

As the events in Zafarani unfold, the presence of the state is imposed upon the lives of its people. The secret police try and infiltrate the alley and a slew of state agencies and bureaus are established to combat the influence of the Sheikh. Here lies al-Ghitani's critique of the police state established under the rule of Nasser and its suffocating hold over the citizen population. To combat the perceived threat in the alley, the state creates organisations such as the 'Special Security Authority', the 'Department for the Suppression of Religious Fanaticism', the 'Department for the Suppression of Subversive Ideas,' and the more ridiculous 'Supreme Department of Eavesdropping' and 'Supreme Authority for Buildings Built with Red Bricks', clearly meant as parodies of the political climate under Nasser. Not surprisingly, however, these agencies are unable to discover the source of the Sheikh's power and instead propose an alternative plan. As word of the events in Zafarani leaks out to the rest of the world, the government fears tarnishing the image of the nation. Its response to the media frenzy that ensues is to flatly deny the claims made about the curse. When this strategy fails the government decides to solve the problem once and for all by erasing the alley from existence:

> This had to be carried out simultaneously with an emergency plan, for which immediate allocations had to be made and which consisted in notifying all the inhabitants of the alley that *they* must vacate their homes, upon which they would be moved into government housing in different, distant places in such a way that no two families would be close to each other. Then a new plan would be drawn up for Zafarani in such a way as to preserve the old style in new buildings.[60]

This plan fails, but here al-Ghitani draws attention to an important dimension of state power, the organisation of bodies in space. When unable to adequately police its citizens or control their existence in space, its response is to alter the physical and material reality of that space.

It is in taking on this literary project of surveillance that al-Ghitani undermines and critiques the repressive power of the state apparatus. The writer here uses the official tools of state documentation to present a portrait of Zafarani Alley, whose fantastic nature provides a liberatory moment and the opportunity for the people to reclaim their right to the alley.

Sexuality as Agency

The possibility for change that comes from the mobilisation of the inhabitants of the alley is once again built upon a privileging of male sexuality as the site of agency. The impotency that befalls the men of Zafarani calls into question their masculinity. Here we see the way in which gender is defined by sexuality; the alley becomes what Joseph Massad calls 'a postmanly world full of women and their equals'.[61] The men struggle to protect their wives from the pimps who enter the alley, their wives taunt them for their weakness and lack of masculinity, and they are no longer able to satisfy the women's sexual or reproductive desires.

The curse reveals the relationship between sexuality, reproduction and the technologies of power. As Foucault explains in *The History of Sexuality* the political significance of sex is its relationship to both the disciplines of the body and the regulation of the population. Refusing to comply with the state, the inhabitants of the alley insist on solving their situation alone. The end of the novel witnesses their movement against the Sheikh, violating all his rules and refusing to succumb to his power. Instead they stage what is described in the official sources as an 'insurrection'.[62] It is at this moment that the space of the alley is transformed into what Lefebvre calls a 'differential space', the space of subversion, opposition and dissent, a space that 'accentuates differences'.[63] This internal uprising is accompanied by the spread of the curse worldwide, with a number of bulletins and cables from cities around the world reporting the spread of the Zafarani epidemic.[64] This global phenomenon suggests an international revolution, an attempt to overturn the forces of repression and persecution and establish a new world order. The novel closes with the following declaration:

Farewell, old time, eras of darkness and distortions of truth; farewell to death by starvation, to miserable love, to frustrated hopes, to suppressed desires, to deferred promises, to unjust systems, to relative justice, to complicating that which is simple and making difficult that which is easy. It will not be long now. The era of the spell is here, to change the world.[65]

This potential for change seems possible only because of the extraordinary context created in the space of the alley. Al-Ghitani, like Ibrahim, provides a marked shift in the representation of the urban space of Cairo. This time however, he employs the well-known trope of the *ḥāra* but through an aesthetics of the fantastic. Al-Ghitani dispenses with the time and space of the realist novel to present possibilities of subversion and difference. The marginalised alley is thus recuperated within the changed political and economic context of postcolonial Cairo and produced as a potential space of opposition.

Ibrahim Aslan's *The Heron*: Placing Imbaba in Time and Space

The protagonist of Ibrahim Aslan's 1981 novel *The Heron* is the district of Imbaba, a site that encapsulates memories of a glorious past, the struggles of a tempestuous present, and the uncertainty of a fragmentary future. If Mahfouz is the chronicler of Jamaliyya, then Aslan is surely the chronicler of Imbaba, and it is this work more than any other that has placed the people and places of this district on the literary map.[66] As with al-Ghitani, the periphery is pushed to the centre. Reflecting the socio-economic and political changes of the post-revolutionary period, Aslan presents the hitherto ignored Imbaba as the site of resistance against the encroachment of the state. In a novel that prizes multiplicity over singularity, and circularity over linearity, the reader is forced to contend with the transformations of Cairo in the literary and national imagination. Though not originally from Imbaba, Aslan spent much of his life in this popular neighbourhood, moving only late in life to the wealthier suburb of Muqattam. Imbaba dominates his literary oeuvre, in novels and shorts stories populated by the same cast of characters.[67]

Located on the West Bank of the Nile, across from the upper-class neighbourhood of Zamalek, Imbaba once stood amidst a vast area of agricultural land. A small rural village that dated back to at least the medieval period was to undergo vast change, becoming by the beginning of the twentieth century, one of Cairo's fastest growing areas. Much of Imbaba's growth occurred in the early decades of the twentieth century; the completion of the Aswan Dam in 1902 as well as the building of the tram line in 1918, meant that land was available for development and a firm connection was at last established with the rest of the city. Beginning in the 1940s, formal housing was developed in the district, in areas such as Madinat al-Tahrir and Madinat al-ʿUmmal that were meant to serve as low-income housing. This marked the beginning of the transformation of the largely agricultural area to an urban one. The period that followed the 1952 revolution saw continued construction, this time in the form of Soviet-style housing projects constructed by Nasser's regime. Neither these housing blocks, nor the earlier colonial-style construction were able to cater to the ever-growing population. The state's attempt to incorporate the rural migrants into the growing urban proletariat proved increasingly difficult, leading to the development of informal communities or shantytowns (ʿashwāʾiyyāt). This situation was only exacerbated with the end of the Nasserist regime and the dismantlement of the welfare state by Sadat. Imbaba's position on the outskirts of Cairo, both geographically and economically, resulted in the absence of basic infrastructure such as water, electricity and sewage for much of its population.[68]

The Heron, Aslan's first novel, tracks the lives of Imbaba's inhabitants during a single day, 17 January 1977, the day of the famous Bread Riots in Egypt that erupted in opposition to Sadat's implementation of World Bank and IMF directives aimed at terminating basic food subsidies.[69] It is also a searing critique of the 'Open Door' (*infitāḥ*) economic policies initiated by Sadat's regime, against which the riots erupted, and which heralded the end of any hope of a socialist state in Egypt.[70] The compression of time in the novel to a single day is significant as a strategy employed by a number of sixties writers. In this case Aslan both limits the actions of the novel to a single day and uses numerous techniques of flashbacks and recollection to make sure that the past(s) is ever-present.[71] Here again we are led to question the linear progression associated with realist texts and are instead presented with constant repetition. The book opens and closes with references to the rain; the first paragraph of the novel begins: 'YESTERDAY IT RAINED. It poured.'[72] The novel ends in a very similar fashion; the penultimate section is entitled 'Some Rain' and is a description of the wet night of the siege of

Imbaba. What we are presented with then is a circular, rather than a linear, progression of narrative: the actions of the novel take place in one day only, which ends as it has begun, or begins as it has ended.[73]

It is a novel that refuses a simplistic understanding of the district; remembered as the site of the famous Battle of the Pyramids, where the Egyptian people stood against Napoleon's invading armies, it remains frozen in time in the national imagination.[74] When Imbaba is mentioned within a contemporary context it is often as a den of drug-dealers and prostitutes, or as a breeding ground for religious fundamentalism and an example of the dangers posed by the urban poor.[75] It is this picture of Imbaba that Aslan complicates, providing a portrait of the neighbourhood as a model of resistance for the rest of the nation. The representation of Imbaba's streets, its geographical location, and its relationship to surrounding areas comes alive before the reader's eyes through the wanderings of a host of characters; once again the focus is upon the dweller, the pedestrian, the practice of walking and living. What is interesting in comparison to Ibrahim's narrative, is the way Aslan focuses on a multiplicity of perspectives; we learn of a character's movement for example from a first-, second- and third-person perspective such that one journey is narrated from several different vantage points. This is one of Aslan's innovative techniques, encouraging the reader to understand space through the ways in which it is inhabited by its people.[76] The familiarity of street names is assumed, particularly with the streets that lie *inside* Imbaba, as if they were intimate and known characters.[77] So, for example, we trace the steps of Usta Qadri trying to avoid bumping into his neighbours as he makes his way home:

> For a number of weeks he continued to leave his house and walk along the Nile until al-Mounira. He would turn and return through the worker's projects to the railway station until Sidi Ismail al-Imbabi. He would then enter from the al-Garn school, passing by Ahmed ᶜAshur the grocer and from Murad street he would sneak through Qatr al-Nada until Fadlallah ᶜUthman in order to return home.[78]

In the English translation, Elliot Colla excises some of the detailed geographical description and replaces them with the following: 'For a number of weeks, he continued to leave his house and go along the Nile until al-Mounira, then return through the workers' projects toward the train station. From Murad Street, he'd sneak through Qatr al-Nada and Fadlallah Osman and return home.'[79] This excision points to an assumption that the reader needs a familiarity with the geography of the area to fully appreciate aspects of the novel. I would add that many of Aslan's Arabic readers may also be missing this familiarity and it is precisely such descriptions which are intended to introduce Imbaba and its surroundings to them.

This route is followed soon after with an alternative mapping, that is necessitated by Sheikh Hosni's ongoing inquiries into Usta Qadri's whereabouts:

> He used to leave from Fadlallah ʿUthman to al-Salam street from the back, until al-Mudir garden, passing by the nuns, then crossing Sudan street and passing through *Iskan Nasser al-Shaʿbi* [Nasser's housing for-the-people] until *Nadi Talʿat Harb* [Talʿat Harb Club]. He kept walking in the garden facing the Zamalek bridge looking at the side entrance to the Balloon Theatre until he reached *Tariq al-Nil* [Nile Road]. Turning left he would head to Kit Kat square.[80]

The above passages are just two of many examples that proliferate in Aslan's novel. The reader gradually becomes familiar with the geographical layout of the neighbourhood and its relationship to the rest of the city. Obvious immediately is the juxtaposition of the wealthier upper-class neighbourhood of Zamalek across the river from Imbaba. It serves as a constant reminder to the residents of Imbaba of what they are not: the most affluent of Egyptian society who inhabit spacious apartments in Cairo's most sought-after locations. While Amm Omran is destined to spend his days in 'a wooden room in the rear of the small rooftop with its cramped, covered toilet', his view is of the 'other' Cairo, 'the nearby river covered by a layer of light mist, the trees on the opposite bank, the bright lights in the windows, and the closed balconies of the massive Zamalek apartment buildings stretching off into the pitch-darkness of night'.[81] The characters of *The Heron* do not ever interact with this 'other' Cairo, but remain on its outskirts, allowed only to pass by these prosperous areas during late night strolls, or stare at the buildings from across the river. The bridges that the characters return to time and again, serve as much as dividers as they do as connectors, segregating Imbaba from the rest of the city.

Resisting the New World Order: The Café and the Square

Where the characters end up however is invariably Kit Kat Square, the site of the café that brings the community together; it is here that eventually all the people of the neighbourhood gather on this fateful night. The focus upon Kit Kat Square is emphasised in Egyptian film director Dawud Abdel Sayyid's adaptation of the novel entitled *al-Kit Kat*, which was released in 1991 and became an instant success. The two spaces, of square and café, are transformed in this novel into Lefebvre's 'differential spaces' in which possibilities of opposition and resistance are temporarily available. Kit Kat Square, named after the cabaret famous for entertaining the British soldiers during the colonial period, is ever-present throughout the novel. With its 'dancing and drumming and kings and ministers and singing' Kit Kat became the favorite haunt of King Farouq, until the revolution in 1952.[82] We learn of its significance as the site where the Mamluk soldiers faced the invading armies of Napoleon, an event that is memorialised in the architecture of the square 'its giant stone entrance, [with] the writing on the lofty arch: "The battle of the Pyramids took place here on the 21st of July 1798."'[83] It is once again the site of confrontation, this time between the Egyptian security forces and the people of Imbaba. As the people stand in front of the 'giant stone entrance' defending their neighbourhood against the riot police, the reader cannot help but draw parallels between the contemporary Egyptian government and the invading forces of Napoleon. Aslan allows us to see the multiple faces of Imbaba and its infamous Kit Kat Square: it is at once a site of resistance, a place famed for lascivious entertainment, and home to neighbourhood communities struggling to survive in an ever-changing world.

The fear of foreign domination, represented in the past by the Napoleonic armies, lives on in the present. Throughout the evening the characters discuss an important story reported in the day's newspaper, that of the foreigner who is claiming ownership of Imbaba. Listening to Qasim Effendi read from his daily copy of *al-Ahram*, the customers of the café hear of the legal battle that is unfolding over their neighbourhood. The reader learns of this second-hand, through the re-telling of this reading by Abdullah, the café's waiter: 'It says in Qasim Effendi's *Al-Ahram*' Abdullah explains 'that the owner of the café – and the cinema and the bookstore and Husayn's fish shop and Hagg Hanafi's milk store and the mosque, in fact, the owner of all of Kit Kat Square – turns out to be some foreigner. He's alive and well and is going to sue in court.'[84] This is a significant technique employed by the author throughout the novel. The same events are often told from various perspectives, and in this case the contents of the article are re-told to the group by Abdullah. In another part of the novel the group is given a different version of the same account by Qasim Effendi himself. Here, and throughout the novel, the reader is rarely given a definitive version of any one event and can as such make no claim to knowledge of any one truth. We are never sure what exactly happened or whose version of events to believe. This strategy is in line with the epigraph with which the novel opens, a quote by Paul Valéry which states, 'Oh Nathaniel. I urge you to be accurate not clear.'[85] In presenting multiple versions of these events Aslan is choosing a form of accuracy over clarity.

We are told a little later that this foreigner is an 'Italian named David Mousa who was visiting Egypt and had filed a complaint with the Chief of Police in Imbaba against the citizens of the Kit Kat neighbourhood on the grounds that they had illegally appropriated land which was his rightful property'.[86] This illegal appropriation is explained in the *al-Ahram* newspaper article as the presence of 'squatters all over the place' (the inhabitants of the *ʿashwāʾiyyāt* that proliferate in the area) and the 'tall buildings and commercial areas' that have appeared everywhere.[87] However, as the reader comes to discover (and what Abdullah himself already knows), the real threat to the café and the neighbourhood at large is not from a foreigner trying to retrieve the land he lost after leaving Egypt in 1956, but from the capitalist, exploitative ventures of Maallim Subhi and his ilk. These men, the *maallims* (bosses) of Imbaba, represent the benefactors of Sadat's economic policies, and the harbingers of the new world order, who possess the economic means to alter the spatial reality of the neighbourhood.

Once again, we see the contestation over power articulated as a contestation over space: Maallim Subhi, the poultry vendor, persistently harasses Maallim Atiya to sell him his lease to the café so that he can carry out his plans of knocking down the entire building and erecting a large apartment block in its place. This drive to develop, construct and reap profits from such endeavours is part of a larger critique levelled by the novel against the 'Open Door' policies initiated by Sadat, in which black-market trading and speculation were the hallmarks of the day. The battle over Awadallah's café, and the plans to construct an apartment building in its place, reveal the effects of the economic policies of the state upon the urban space of the city. What we witness here is the production of a new space, a shift from 'the representational space' of the café, the space of the social life and the lived reality of the everyday, to the 'representation of space' in the form of the planned apartment building, the space 'constructed by planners, professionals, technocrats, and urbanists', a space that is 'tied to the relations of production and to the "order" which those relations impose'.[88]

Awadallah's café is important in the novel as a homosocial space that here belies its reputation as a space of idleness, instead fomenting male bonds and providing revolutionary possibilities. Not only do the characters inevitably end up there throughout the evening but it features prominently in the endless flashbacks that present the community's past: the time of the action may differ, but the site remains the same. It is at the café that all the characters gather before the outbreak of the riots that shake their entire world, and it thus serves as the physical embodiment of this potentially transformative moment. But just as the riots that flare up on that fateful night are extinguished and their political possibilities smothered, the café too is destined for demolition.

The end of the café and the crumbling of the world it represents seem inevitable by the close of *The Heron*. If the neighbourhood's residents cannot stop the onslaught of Maallim Subhi, the people of Imbaba nevertheless put up a fight against the violence of the state and its encroachment upon their space. The novel, and the night it depicts, culminates in the violent protests of the 1977 Bread Riots. The police siege of Imbaba is bravely resisted by its inhabitants who refuse to be bombed or gassed into submission. As the demonstrators make their way down Sudan Street, the riot police block off the Zamalek bridge, trying to force them to surrender at Kit Kat Square. What ensues is a scene of street warfare in which the government troops are held at bay by the Imbabans who emerge victorious, even if only momentarily: 'The young men occupied the streets of their neighbourhood and were sitting in the doorways of the buildings, leaning against walls, exchanging whispered remarks and laughing.'[89] This scene is the climax of events that have been taking place throughout the day in different parts of the city. Much earlier, as Yusif al-Naggar, the novel's other protagonist, goes to meet Fatima downtown, he witnesses the demonstrations that have erupted in the streets of downtown Cairo and that represent the reclamation of the streets by the people in their attempt to confront and resist the violence and repression of the state. Aslan thus succeeds in connecting the different parts of the city through this one political moment, while also allowing Imbaba to momentarily emerge as the primary, or in fact last, site of resistance.

'He Wanted to Write Everything Down'

Not all the inhabitants of Imbaba share in this moment of popular uprising and potential resistance. In fact, Yusif remains largely disengaged from the unfolding events. If, as a number of critics have argued, Yusif is to be seen as the heron of the novel's title, then he seems destined to stand on the sidelines watching in despair the injustice that surrounds him.[90] The book's epigraph, which the author seems to be directing at his protagonist, points us to the grief that will follow: 'They say you sit near the waters of streams and creeks and that if these waters were to dry up, grief would overwhelm you, and you'd fall silent, mournful.'[91]

When he first sees the demonstrations downtown he is unable to take part in them, preferring instead to get drunk alone in a bar. He notices the gathering crowds as he is going to meet Fatma. Sitting on the bus heading downtown he remembers his earlier sexual failure with her. Here again, as in the novels of Ibrahim and al-Ghitani, political agency is associated with sexual potency.[92] His inability to take part in the demonstrations in the streets of Cairo is mirrored by his sexual inability. Both forms of paralysis find further resonance in his inability to write. He is the figure of the disillusioned intellectual, poised to act, but never able to do so.

The figure of the isolated individual is part of Aslan's critique of the intellectual and artistic climate of the time. Much of the state sponsorship of the arts that characterised the earlier decades disappeared with the establishment of Sadat's regime, which increasingly severed the ties between the social, cultural and political realms, leaving artists and intellectuals to fend for themselves. This also meant that the cultural and intellectual battle that remained ongoing between Nasser and his cultural critics was increasingly stifled. Yusif is shut out from the Writers' Union and during the student demonstrations members of the cultural institutions withdraw their support for the protests fearing the potential backlash.[93]

Throughout the novel we are subjected to Yusif's extended deliberations about his inability to write, or specifically his inability to write about the *right* things. As he sits in the bar he thinks of the novel he has spent years trying to write, saying to himself: 'Despite the years that have passed and your present drunkenness, you still remember everything, because you've already written it dozens of times, though you did nothing with the material afterwards.'[94] Interestingly, both Yusif's yet to be written novel and *The Heron* begin with rain, alerting us to the parallels with the novel that the reader holds in his/her hands. Is *The Heron* the novel Yusif would have wished to write? Are Yusif's own struggles with his role as writer and intellectual those of Aslan himself?[95] The fact that Aslan's novel took almost a decade to write is evidence of a trying labour of love and of the difficulties the author faced with writing.

If throughout the duration of the novel Yusif is unable to come to terms with his role as a writer, this is to some degree resolved *after* the siege of Imbaba. When the violence has subsided, he achieves a moment of clarity in which his purpose as a writer is finally revealed to him:

> He wanted to write everything down. To write a book about the river, the children, the angry crowds taking revenge on the storefront windows, and the trees along the Nile road and the advertisements for products and films. Write about the cafe and Omran and everybody: Write about the world of insomnia, the smoke, the trees at night, and the little birds. The afarit of Imbaba.[96]

Yet if Yusif's past is any indication, the reader is justified in doubting the completion of his project. Given that the novel ends with the demise of the café, the siege of Imbaba which the reader knows will not end in the residents' favour, and the sense that in some ways we are back where we started, Yusif's intellectual awakening might just be too late.

Radwa Ashour's Cairene Prison

Radwa Ashour's 2008 novel *Faraj* (*Blue Lorries*) is a particularly apt way to conclude the discussion of the Cairo novels in this chapter.[97] Written as the memoir of the protagonist Nada Abdel Qadir, the novel interrogates the connections between biography and history, situating real world events within the context of the fictional. *Blue Lorries*, a prison novel that spans three generations, casts the city of Cairo (and the country at large) as a space of incarceration and confinement. Here too Ashour, the urban novelist par excellence, contends with the difficulties of writing; throughout the novel Nada struggles with her desire to write a book, a novel about the experience of prison. In this self-reflexive text that blurs the boundaries between fact and fiction, the author and narrator/protagonist intersect and diverge. And yet, unlike her male contemporaries, Ashour does not posit (male) sexuality as the primary form of agency. Instead, the reader is left questioning the efficacy of both political and creative practice.

This is not the first time that the urban metropolis takes centre stage in Ashour's fiction. At least half of her novels take place in Cairo; her first novel *Hajar Dafiʾ* (A Warm Stone, 1985), *Khadija wa Sawsan* (Khadija and Sawsan, 1989), *Atyaf* (*Spectres*, 1999) and *Qitʿa min Urubba* (A Piece of Europe, 2003) being principal among them. The space of downtown Cairo for example is a central character in *Qitʿa min Urubba*, a work that seeks to interrogate the history of the city, focusing on the Cairo fire of 1952. Mara Naaman reads the novel as a 'textual reclaiming of the downtown for purposes of recovering the nationalist project as the natural inheritor of the project of modernity'.[98] As such, Ashour deliberately traces the history of the streets, buildings, squares and stores so central to the geography of downtown Cairo.

This is a decidedly different picture of the city than the one that appears in *Blue Lorries*. It is largely the experience of detention that dominates Nada's childhood and adult life – first through her father's imprisonment, then her own, and finally with her brothers' experience. Furthermore, it is the prison system writ large that connects the various spaces both within and beyond the boundaries of Egypt. To read *Blue Lorries* is to experience six decades of Egyptian history, from the 1950s until the early 2000s.[99] It is also to experience the penal system that dominates the contemporary world.

Ashour's novel opens in Cairo train station where the young Nada and her mother embark upon a journey to visit Nada's father, incarcerated in Asyut, in Southern Egypt. The Cairo train station, known as 'Mahattit Masr', alerts the reader to the centrality of the Cairene capital; '*Masr*', the word for

Egypt, is also used colloquially to refer to Cairo (as noted by Soueif at the start of this chapter). This opening scene simultaneously acknowledges the capital's dominance and points to its connections to the rest of the country. Imprisoned as a political prisoner under Nasser's regime, her father's absence dominates Nada's early childhood years. So too does the presence of Nasser, who figures as a paternal substitute and a figure of constant comparison with her father.[100] Haunted by those years, Nada tries to imagine the details of his prison experience, devouring pages of prison literature searching for answers, as she says 'filling the gaps in my imagination'.[101] And thus she masters the details of all of Egypt's prisons; Abu Zaʿbal and al-Qanatir in Cairo, al-Wahat in Egypt's Western Desert, al-ʿIzab in Fayoum and Tora, between Cairo and Helwan.[102] Memorising the layout of the prisons and the locations of the various cells, Nada recreates the narrative of her father's absence, a narrative which he never shares.

The generational stories in *Blue Lorries* are connected largely though the experience of prison; in many ways repression and persecution connect the regimes of Nasser, Sadat and Mubarak. Thus, Nada finds herself in prison a few decades after her father. Part of the student movement that erupted in the 1970s, Nada takes part in the activism and mobilisation that erupts across Cairo, participating in the demonstrations and sit-ins that unfold on her campus at Cairo University, in opposition to the policies of Sadat.[103] She is at first able to evade imprisonment when her father insists she travel to Paris to be with her mother, but after her return to Cairo a few months later, the police arrest her. In the chapter '*Nahtagik Saʿa aw Saʿtayn*' (We need you for an hour or two) referring to the colloquial phrase uttered by police when taking someone in for questioning, we find Nada contemplating the dark, desolate streets of the city:

> I hadn't been afraid when they were coming into the house and searching it, nor did the appearance of the two armed security officers standing by the door of the flat frighten me, nor the three armed men I found unexpectedly at the bottom of the stairs near the entrance of the building. But when I was sitting between the two officers who had taken me in, watching the dark, deserted streets, I was engulfed all at once by a feeling that I was suffocating.[104]

This is one of the few instances when the reader is offered a glimpse into Nada's anxieties in the face of imprisonment. Just as her father reveals little of his experience, so too does our protagonist.[105] And yet the constant threat of imprisonment in a city that is transformed into a space of incarceration and fear looms large over the characters' lives.

The third generation of Nada's family also experience time in a Cairene prison. Her two brothers, Nader and Nadeem, to whom she figures as a surrogate mother, are students in the early 2000s, and participate in university demonstrations against the US invasion of Iraq in 2003. The stifling political climate and the state's crackdown against dissent is captured in the protests that erupt in the streets of Cairo. Worried for her brothers' safety, and filled with a sense of foreboding, Nada scours the downtown streets around Tahrir Square, the same area that Ibrahim's protagonist traversed. The iconic streets, immediately recognisable to her readers, are heavily guarded by armed police, with their dogs and armoured trucks:

> I walked to Kasr al-Aini Street and headed from there to Tahrir Square. The square was peaceful, cars streaming through it as usual, although greater numbers of security vehicles had been stationed there of late. I turned right on Tahrir Street, making for Bab al-Louk Square, then went left toward Talat Harb Square. As soon as I got to Sabri Abu Alam Street I took note of the dense ring of soldiers blocking access to the square . . . The demonstrators proceeded toward Tahrir from the direction of Mahmoud Bassiouney Street or Kasr al-Nil Street . . . Before I reached the next intersection – the junction of Al-Bustan and Talat Harb Streets – I saw a row of security vehicles on the opposite side of the street from the Nasserist party headquarters, and I noticed the ground was wet, that there was in fact a great deal of water, along with a residue of stones – large ones, small ones, crumbled ones. Then I saw the dogs: big dogs, and with each dog a special guard holding it leashed by an iron chain. I carried on in the direction of the square and found the way to it blocked by a circle of helmets and truncheons. I retraced my steps to Al-Bustan Street . . . Suddenly I said to myself that something dreadful must have happened to Nadeem. I began to run.[106]

The chapter that describes these events is tellingly entitled '*al-Sayyārāt al-Zarqāʾ*' (Blue lorries) in reference to the large trucks that are used to transfer prisoners in Egypt. The chapter ends with Nadeem's release from prison, and the death of Nada's friend and comrade Siham. Thus, the ominous feelings that drove Nada to pursue the 'blue lorries' at the start of the chapter are realised by its end. There seems to be few ways to avoid the 'grave that is growing, snatching, and brutalizing', the grave that is the city and nation at large, devouring its own citizens.[107] The choice for Nader and Nadeem, like Nada before them, is imprisonment or departure from Egypt. (Briefly arrested for his activities, Nadeem is soon released and travels to Dubai to join his brother.) Political activism and street demonstrations provide little possibility for change.

Blue Lorries does not remain contained within the boundaries of Cairo, but rather the prison network connects the capital to various locations around the country and across the Arab world. Thus, Nada travels south as a child to the prison in Asyut, but also through her reading to countless prisons across the country; in Cairo, al-Wahat, al-Fayoum and Tora. As an adult she visits the famous al-Khayyam prison in Southern Lebanon after the departure of the Israeli troops. And it is in the Tazmamart prison in Morocco that the novel ends; Nada recounts in great detail the prison narrative of Ahmed Marzouki, imprisoned there for eighteen years. *Faraj*, the name of both the final chapter and the novel itself (in the Arabic original) refers to a pigeon cared for by Marzouki and the other inmates. Freed after almost two decades Marzouki explains his indebtedness to Faraj on the day of his release: '"Farewell," I murmured, "and thank you"'.[108]

The Panoptican: Foucault as Interlocuter

Blue Lorries is a novel about the actual experiences of prison, the suffering wrought upon generations of prisoners across Egypt and the Arab world. It is also about the forms of discipline and surveillance enacted by the state and thus Foucault becomes in many ways Nada's interlocutor. While Foucault's work sheds light on the novels discussed thus far, Ashour brings him explicitly into her text. Analysis of Foucault's work appears in the narrative, often as an alternative to descriptions of Nada's time in prison – the chapter that follows her arrest is strikingly entitled 'The Panoptican'. Thus, the reader is invited to consider prison both as an actual, tangible, physical space in which real bodily and psychological harm is wrought on the individual and also as the myriad of ways in which the state monitors, scrutinises and controls its citizens.

Abandoning her discussion of Foucault's theoretical exposition, Nada hungrily devours the pages of the state department's files concerning the arrest of members of the student movement in the 1970s. As such we are made privy to the tools of the state, the network of spies and investigators employed by the state security apparatus to surveil the citizen population; this is not unlike the enterprise undertaken by al-Ghitani in *The Zafarani Files*. Here, it is also an opportunity to hear a multitude of voices within Nada's narrative; she recounts interviews conducted with her classmates, with the voice of Siham Sabri taking centre stage. Not only is the central protagonist Nada a woman, but also the collective history she records is heavily focused upon the voices of women – a glaring absence in the three novels discussed thus far. The files, part of the repressive apparatus of the state, come, ironically, to represent a collective history, recording the voices of Nada's generation:

> Be that as is it may, the fact remains that the files are much like a mirror, in which I stare at my own face, which is not mine alone, but is rather the face that belongs to us all together, as a collective of young men and women who took part in a dream, a movement, a pulse; in terror and confusion and disappointment – a face some strip bare and then call history.[109]

Foucault's work becomes the means to come to terms with the devastation of her generation. Faced with decades of disappointment, failure, and the suppression of the possibilities of political transformation and change, Nada's friends pass away prematurely one by one. Left to deal with this loss, Nada realises at the end of the novel that the prison walls are permeable, and that the state's control over its citizens extends beyond the space of incarceration:

> It decides for him when to wake up and when to sleep, when to work, when to eat, when to rest, when to talk and when to keep quiet. It defines the movements of his body, and appropriates his physical and spiritual resources. Such is prison, albeit with variations. Here or there – it makes no difference.[110]

While these words belong to Nada, could they not have been uttered by the narrator of *The Zafarani Files*? The prison is the same even if it differs, 'here or there – it makes no difference' precisely because it ceases to be only a physical space, but rather is also inside the individual. As Ahmed Hilmi states, for Ashour 'prison is a tight space within each of us, which we built ourselves, over which we placed a low ceiling, and no windows. Then we sat in the space of our own free will and began to scream.'[111] It is this realisation that drives Nada's contemplation that she write a book, a novel 'that would invert the usual order of things, whereby it is those living outside the prison who are the prisoners, not the other way round'.[112]

How to Write a Prison Novel?

Ashour's novel is a narrative concerned with the possibilities and limitations of writing. If *Blue Lorries* is presented as Nada's autobiography, a memoir of sorts, that records the events of her life and simultaneously those of her generation, it is also a work that is fraught with anxieties about the very act of writing. This tension pervades a great number of Ashour's works, self-reflexive meta-narratives about the complexities of the creative process; 'the preoccupation with writing is present in every one of Radwa Ashour's texts'.[113] In *Spectres* Ashour and her alter ego Shagar struggle with the impossibilities of writing, with how to tell their own stories, with how to record massacres such as Deir Yassin, and with the entanglement of literature and history. Likewise, *Qitᶜa min Urubba* is the outcome of the narrator's project to write an account of downtown Cairo. The nameless narrator/protagonist referred to as '*al-nāẓir*' (literally: the looker) once again contends with the meaning of authorship, unsure if he is producing history or literature. Such deliberations are also embedded in Ashour's autobiographical works that explicitly engage with her journey as a writer.[114]

This anxiety permeates *Blue Lorries*, not least in the convergence of fact and fiction, significant as one of the primary ways Ashour calls into question the form of the realist text. *Blue Lorries* is clearly a novel, though one in which the first-person narrative resembles an autobiography; each chapter is given a title that reflects an idea, phrase or event that stands out in Nada's recollections. Furthermore, by the end of the novel the reader is left questioning whether the whole work is in fact a flashback, Nada's reckoning of her life brought about by her journey to visit her aunt in Southern Egypt. The novel ends as it began, on a train from Egypt to al-Saᶜid that precipitates in Nada's memory the flashback of her train ride as a young girl to visit her father in prison. This circularity is not unlike that which the reader encounters in Aslan's text, and once again the linearity of the narrative is undercut. As such *Blue Lorries* becomes a story within a story, the frame of which is only revealed by the work's end. And yet it is a narrative that employs actual events from the historical record, and more importantly is populated by real people. In Arwa Salih and Siham Sabri we find characters based upon two of the leading figures from the student movement in Egypt in the 1970s.[115] That Ashour includes real people, namely two women that were her contemporaries during this period, raises further questions about the intersection between author and narrator. Here, as in a multitude of her works, Ashour blends genres and forms; *Blue Lorries*, like *Spectres* 'is an evocative tapestry of history, autobiography, fiction, and philosophy'.[116]

This tapestry is a hallmark of Ashour's innovative works. The case of *Blue Lorries* stands out, I would argue, as an attempt to contend with the question: How does one write a prison novel? Throughout the novel Nada struggles with this question; it looms over the entire work though she never explicitly utters it aloud. And yet she is haunted by this desire for much of her adult life, a desire which she continues to defer. Ignited by the need to understand her father's own experience Nada is first drawn to reading prison literature, deciding that she will write a book about all prison experiences, in Egypt, Israel, Lebanon and South Africa. Later, the idea comes to her for a novel about the prisoner outside of prison but she dismisses this claiming 'I am not a novelist, so where did I come up with this mad idea of writing a novel, anyway?'[117] In fact she does neither, although she returns to the idea repeatedly, and almost obsessively, throughout the novel.

Just as the protagonists in the works of Ibrahim and Aslan struggle with what it means to be a writer, in an urban environment that has become increasingly oppressive, so too does Nada. It is only through writing that narrator and author deal with prison as an actual place and as the condition of existence in the modern world. Brahim El Guabli, in an article that focuses upon the famous Tazmamart prison with which Ashour ends her novel, explores prison literature as a form of resistance within the context of the 'Years of Lead' in Morocco.[118] El Guabli argues that such texts are one of the only ways for prisoners to insist on the truth of their experiences, particularly in a context where the authorities may destroy the official record: 'all that is left for the former prisoners is the process of writing and their claims of veracity'.[119]

Ashour echoes this sentiment in her lecture 'Arab Prison Literature', citing examples of narratives from Egypt, Morocco and Palestine. Like El Guabli, Ashour this time in her literary critical work recognises the productive necessity of documenting the horrors of prison and torture. She ends her lecture by acknowledging that prison narratives in the Arab world represent a small victory in the midst of great atrocities:

> No Picasso did a drawing of any Palestinian or Lebanese detainee; no Guernica has been produced to commemorate the atrocities of Khiam, Tazmamarte or al-Wahat. However, the body of writings by political prisoners in the Arab world, is, in a sense, a large canvas whose every detail has been paid for in sweat and blood, a Guernica of a sort produced not by an individual genius but by a collective who went through hell and came out, not with retaliatory feelings but with a sense of triumph, and the confidence, to quote Habashi, that humans can grow a flower even in the midst of hell.[120]

In *Blue Lorries* we confront the multiplicity of sources that contribute to the production of this prison novel: memoir; childhood reflections; prison literature; state records; philosophical texts; poetry; song; political slogans. All these texts intertwine in the production of a complex and multi-faceted account of the prison that is Cairo, Egypt, and even beyond. As Ashour explains, writing is a 'reappropriation of a threatened geography and a threatening history . . . [when] I write, the space becomes my own, and I am no longer an object acted upon but a subject acting in history.'[121] In struggling to own space, to fulfil the role of the writer as 'national recorder', Ashour and her narrator Nada encounter a plethora of voices and accounts. Nada does not produce her definitive book about prisons, although the reader suspects that *Blue Lorries* is intended to be that text. Ultimately however, it is not Nada's voice with which the novel closes but that of Marzouki whose account of his departure from Tazmamart suggests a glimmer of hope, the *faraj* of the title.

Conclusion

To re-visit the novels of the writers of the sixties generation with an attention to spatial representations exposes not only the transformation of Cairo in the decades following the revolution, but also the socio-economic and political changes that beset the capital (and the nation at large) throughout the second half of the twentieth century. To read the novels in this way is to examine the different strategies undertaken by the novelists in their attempts to come to terms with the changing space of their city. More than this though, these literary representations can be read as part of what Lefebvre terms the social production of space, producing images and understandings that contribute to our imagination of the social space of Cairo and the spatial practices of its inhabitants. As we have seen, Ibrahim juxtaposes the newer neighbourhood of Heliopolis with the downtown Cairo of his youth. Al-Ghitani creates a fantastical space based upon the Jamaliyya district of which he is a product. Aslan brings to the foreground the neighbourhood of Imbaba where the author lived for much of his life, and Ashour connects Cairo to the world beyond through the pervasive system of incarceration. In doing so they compel their readers to reconsider the space and significance of the city of Cairo in the literary and national imagination, within the context of postcolonial Egypt. The metropolis is no longer the idealised space of the nation, the site of a fiercely hopeful struggle for independence, but has become an increasingly repressive urban environment where its citizens struggle to halt state encroachment and violence.

This anxiety about state surveillance and violence permeates all four works, which should be read as allegories of the writer's vocation, presenting the ways the respective authors struggle to render legible both the urban setting that surrounds them and their own position within it. For the three male writers it is the sexual terrain that becomes the site of confrontation. For Ashour the battle continues to be waged in the political and textual realms. These novels, as reflections on the role of the writer as a public intellectual in Egyptian society, speak of a relationship between intellectual experience and the urban, and the continued dominance of Cairo as the perceived hub. It is in the writing of urban narratives that the authors confront their own predicament as writers, particularly as they contend with the transformation of their Cairene metropolis. In turning to Alexandria in the next chapter, we confront the challenges facing writers of fiction as they struggle to capture the multiple and varied identities of the Mediterranean city.

Notes

1. Soueif, *Cairo*, p. 6.
2. A number of significant works in Arabic and English have explored this tradition of urban narratives. See, for example, Hishmat, *al-Qahira fi al-Adab al-Misri al-Hadith wa-l-Muʿasir*; Hammuda, *al-Riwaya wa-l-Madina*; Hafez, 'Jamaliyyat al-Riwaya al-Jadida'; Naaman, *Urban Space in Contemporary Egyptian Literature*; and Mehrez, 'From the Hara to the ʿImara'.
3. Mahfouz, *Midaq Alley*, p. 1.
4. Mehrez, 'From the Hara to the ʿImara', p. 145.
5. This is not to suggest that Mahfouz's own depiction of the city of Cairo did not undergo any transformation during this decade. Critics have noted Mahfouz's own shift away from realist representations in novels such as *Awlad Haritna* (*Children of Gebelawi*, 1959), *al-Liss wa-l-Kilab* (*The Thief and the Dogs*, 1962) and *Tharthara Fawq al-Nil* (*Adrift on the Nile*, 1965). Rather what I am suggesting is that the writers of this generation were consciously moving away from the realist mode epitomised by the novels cited in the opening of this chapter.
6. I rely on the English translations of the novels unless otherwise noted. A point about the titles: *Waqaʾiʿ Harat al-Zaʿfarani* is translated by Farouk Abdel Wahab as *The Zafarani Files*, although a more accurate translation is 'The Events of Zafarani Alley'. Radwa Ashour's *Faraj* which can be translated as 'Freedom from Grief', 'Release from Suffering', 'Joy' or 'Relief' appears as *Blue Lorries* in Barbara Romaine's translation.
7. Ghannam, *Remaking the Modern*, p. 22.
8. Mehrez, 'From the Hara to the ʿImara', p. 149. See also Mehrez, *Egyptian Writers Between History and Fiction*.
9. Said, *Representations of the Intellectual*, p. 11.
10. Mehrez uses the term 'literary architects of the city', arguing that their role is to 'reconstruct and remap the city'. 'From the Hara to the ʿImara', p. 145. In this chapter, Mehrez charts the transformation of the alley as the dominant literary metaphor to that of the apartment building.
11. *Tilka-l-Raʾiha*, first published in 1966, was immediately confiscated by the censor. It appeared in print again in 1968, in the Lebanese magazine *Shiʿr*,

though in an edited version. This was followed by its reissuing in 1969 by a small publishing house in Cairo, again in a heavily censored version of the original and without the author's permission. The complete novel appeared in 1971 in an English translation of the text. The Arabic original was published in its entirety in 1986. This first complete edition in Arabic includes an introduction by Ibrahim in which he recounts the history of the novel's censorship and publication. See Ibrahim, *Tilka-l-Raʾiha*, pp. 5–19; and Stagh, *The Limits of Freedom of Speech*, p. 184.
12. Ibrahim returns to the prison experience in his 1997 novel *Sharaf* (Honor) and in *Yawmiyyat al-Wahat* (Oasis Diary) in 2005.
13. For more, see Gordon, *Nasser's Blessed Movement*; Jacquemond, *Conscience of the Nation*; Idris, *al-Muthaqqaf al-ʿArabi wa-l-Sulta*; and ʿIsa, *Muthaqqafun wa ʿAskar*.
14. For more, see Stagh, *The Limits of Freedom of Speech*; Jacquemond, *Conscience of the Nation*; and Mehrez, *Egyptian Writers Between History and Fiction*.
15. For a reading of Ibrahim's extensive oeuvre, see Starkey, *Sonallah Ibrahim*.
16. Ibrahim, *The Smell of It*, p. 1. Citations in this chapter are from Denys Johnson-Davies' English translation of the text. It should be noted that a translation entitled *That Smell and Notes from Prison* has appeared more recently by Robyn Creswell. Creswell also includes an annotated selection of the author's prison diaries *Notes from Prison*, handwritten notes smuggled out of jail that were the precursor to the novel. For the passages I cite, Johnson-Davies' translation more accurately captures the essence of the text, particularly in the staccato punctuation used in Ibrahim's urban itinerary.
17. For more on the history of Heliopolis, see Raymond, *Cairo*, pp. 329–33.
18. De Certeau, *The Practice of Everyday Life*, p. 119.
19. Ibid. p. 119.
20. Ibrahim, *The Smell of It*, pp. 49–51.
21. De Certeau, *The Practice of Everyday Life*, p. 121.
22. Ibid. p. 121.
23. Al-Kharrat, *al-Hassasiyya al-Jadida*, pp. 19–20. See also Jacquemond, *Conscience of the Nation*, pp. 93–4.
24. Esty, 'Excremental Postcolonialism', p. 32.
25. Ibrahim, *The Smell of It*, pp. 50–1.
26. Ibid. pp. 53–4.
27. Ibid. p. 56.
28. Ibid. p. 1.

29. Ideas about surveillance appear in Ibrahim's novel *al-Talassus* (*Stealth*, 2007), though this time it is the child narrator who spies on the adults.
30. Foucault, *Discipline and Punish*.
31. For more on the shift from metonymy to metaphor, especially as it pertains to the writing of Abd al-Hakim Qasim, see al-Musawi, *Islam on the Street*, pp. 110–25.
32. For an examination of the way the three works construct an ongoing narrative about their own publication and reception, see Mehrez, 'Sonallah Ibrahim and the (Hi)story of the Book', pp. 39–58.
33. For more on the influence of existentialist thought on Arab writers, see al-Musawi, *al-Nukhba al-Fikriyya wa-l-Inshiqaq*.
34. Sagi, *Albert Camus and the Philosophy of the Absurd*, p. 23.
35. Ibrahim, *The Smell of It*, p. 32. This is one of the passages that was removed in early versions of publication.
36. The protagonist also passes wind in the company of others. The 'smell of kaka' detected by the child harks back to the stench of the novel's title. Ibrahim, *The Smell of It*, p. 16.
37. Esty, 'Excremental Postcolonialism', p. 34.
38. The use of excremental aesthetics recalls the fiction of James Joyce. The connection to the latter is made explicit in the novel's epigraph where Ibrahim quotes the protagonist of Joyce's *Portrait of the Artist as a Young Man* to set the stage for what the reader is about to encounter: 'This race and this country and this life produced me . . . and I shall express myself as I am.'
39. For the censored passages, see Stagh, *The Limits of Freedom of Speech*, pp. 193–5.
40. Haqqi quoted in Ibrahim, 'The Experience of a Generation', p. 20.
41. Haqqi, ibid. p. 20.
42. Ibrahim, "ʿAla Sabil al-Taqdim', in *Tilka-l-Raʾiha*, p. 13.
43. For more on this in Ibrahim's most recent novel, see Colla, 'Revolution on Ice'.
44. Mehrez, 'Re-Writing the City'.
45. The relationship between Mahfouz and al-Ghitani, especially as far as the city of Cairo is concerned, is well documented. In *Mahfouz Yatadhakkar* (Mahfouz Remembers, 1987) for example, al-Ghitani writes the city as seen and remembered by the great author, but in doing so also writes his own city. See Mehrez, 'Re-Writing the City'.
46. Mehrez, 'Re-Writing the City', p. 146.
47. Al-Ghitani, *The Zafarani Files*, p. 1.
48. Ibid. p. 3.

49. Ibid. pp. 4–5.
50. Boullata, 'New Directions in the Arabic Novel', p. 8.
51. Jackson, *Fantasy*, p. 34.
52. Ibid. p. 18.
53. Al-Ghitani, *The Zafarani Files*, pp. 80–1.
54. Jackson, *Fantasy*, p. 46.
55. Al-Ghitani, *The Zafarani Files*, p. 87.
56. Ibid. p. 86.
57. Ibid. p. 1.
58. Al-Ghitani, 'Jadaliyyat al-Tanass', p. 79.
59. Mehrez, 'Re-Writing the City', p. 149.
60. Ibid. p. 257.
61. Massad, *Desiring Arabs*, p. 326.
62. Al-Ghitani, *The Zafarani Files*, p. 323.
63. Lefebvre, *The Production of Space*, p. 52. I take this reading of differential space as oppositional space from al-Musawi's *Islam on the Street*, pp. xxii, 74.
64. Al-Ghitani combines the real and the imaginary in presenting the locations hit by the curse. Paris and India appear alongside places like Galantia and Isteffendial. Al-Ghitani, *The Zafarani Files*, p. 330.
65. Al-Ghitani, *The Zafarani Files*, pp. 330–1.
66. The novel's original title was *Imbaba: Madina Maqfula* (Imbaba: A Closed City). See Badawi, *al-Riwaya al-Haditha fi Misr*, p. 156.
67. An example of this is the sequel ʿ*Asafir al-Nil* (*Nile Sparrows*, 1991).
68. See Raymond, *Cairo*; Abu-Lughod, *Cairo*; Bullard, 'Informal Development in Cairo, the View from Above'; and O'Malley, 'Scenes from Cairo's Camel Market'.
69. Waterbury, *The Egypt of Nasser and Sadat*, pp. 229–31.
70. The 'Open Door' policies (*infitāḥ*) refer to the increasingly liberal economic policies Sadat instituted. Along with the dismantlement of many of the socialist policies of the Nasserist regime (such as the subsidisation of staple goods) came rampant inflation; the abandonment of basic welfare programmes; greater intervention on the part of the World Bank and IMF; a turn towards foreign investment; a focus upon private investment; and a steady increase in the importing of consumer goods.
71. See Hafez, 'The Egyptian Novel in the Sixties', p. 186.
72. Aslan, *The Heron*, p. 3. Hammad argues that the drought symbolises the dearth of literary and cultural production in the decade of the seventies. While there

is merit to his analysis it relies on an overly romanticised notion of Aslan as the sole literary producer, the heron saddened by the disappearance of the river. See Hammad, *Malik al-Hazin*.

73. Hammad argues that Aslan's preoccupation with time is distinguished according to different types of light. This, he notes, is more a characteristic of the short story than the novel. This is significant not only because Aslan does not in fact consider himself a novelist, but also because he first intended to write a collection of short stories but was pushed to make it into a novel after winning the prize awarded only for the writing of novels. Hammad, *Malik al-Hazin*, p. 73.
74. For references to this historical incident, see Stewart, *Great Cairo*, p. 175; Rodenbeck, *Cairo*, pp. 118–23; and Abu-Lughod, *Cairo*, p. 97.
75. For more on the siege of Imbaba that took place in the 1990s and the crackdown on the Islamists, see Singerman, 'The Siege of Imbaba'. For more on the urban poor as a political threat, see Denis, 'Urban Planning and Growth in Cairo'; and Denis and Bayat, 'Who is Afraid of the Ashwaiyyat?
76. Badawi, *al-Riwaya al-Haditha fi Misr*, p. 132.
77. Al-Hajmari, *Takhayyul al-Hikaya*, p. 131.
78. Aslan, *Malik al-Hazin*, p. 33. This is my translation. Fadlallah Uthman and its people becomes the focus of one of Aslan's short story collections entitled *Hikayat min Fadlallah Uthman* (Stories from Fadlallah Uthman, 2003).
79. Aslan, *The Heron*, p. 36.
80. Aslan, *Malik al-Hazin*, p. 36. This is my translation. In the English text, Colla replaces this description with the following: 'When he heard that Sheikh Hosni had been coming around, asking about him, he began to change the course of his walks, wandering all over creation before he finally returned to Kit Kat Square.' Aslan, *The Heron*, p. 36.
81. Aslan, *The Heron*, p. 127.
82. Ibid. p. 116.
83. Ibid. p. 113. For references to the Battle of the Pyramids, see Rodenbeck, *Cairo*; and Raymond, *Cairo*.
84. Aslan, *The Heron*, p. 10.
85. Aslan, *Malik al-Hazin*, p. 5. The translation of the epigraph is my own; it is omitted from the English translation.
86. Aslan, *The Heron*, p. 68.
87. Ibid. p. 68.
88. Lefebvre, *The Production of Space*, p. 33.
89. Ibid. p. 156.

90. See, for example, al-Hajmari, *Takhayyul al-Hikaya*. Colla points to *Kalila wa Dimna* as the original source of this story, in which the heron teaches a pigeon how to escape the tricks of the fox, only to eventually succumb to them himself. Colla, 'Translator's Introduction', p. v. This utilisation of Arabic *turāth*, the literary and cultural tradition, is also to be found in the titles of some of the stories that seem to mimic the story cycles of *Kalila wa Dimna* and the *1001 Nights*. For an extensive explanation of the *Kalila wa Dimna* tale and its significance, see Hammad, *Malik al-Hazin*, pp. 62–5.
91. Aslan, *The Heron*, p. 2.
92. Yusif never uses the key to his friend Magid's apartment. Instead of being the key to consummating his relationship with Fatima, Yusif uses it to empty canisters during the police raid on Imbaba. Yusif's actions are in contrast to those of Faruq, Shawqi, his son Abduh, and Gaber the grocer who, during the raid, pick up the canisters and throw them back at the soldiers. Aslan, *The Heron*, p. 152.
93. For more, see Stagh, *The Limits of Freedom of Speech*; Jacquemond, *Conscience of the Nation*; and ʿIsa, *Muthaqqafun wa ʿAskar*.
94. Aslan, *The Heron*, p. 73. Yusif's struggle to write is in stark contrast to Amm Omran's oral narratives from which we learn a great deal about past and present Imbaba.
95. See Hammad, *Malik al-Hazin*; al-Kharrat, *al-Hassasiyya al-Jadida*; and al-Hajmari, *Takhayyul al-Hikaya*.
96. Aslan, *The Heron*, pp. 154–5.
97. As noted earlier, the Arabic title *Faraj* can be translated as freedom from grief, release from suffering, joy, or relief. It is, as will be discussed, also the name of a pigeon which appears in Ahmed Marzouki's prison narrative which Nada reads and discusses. The title was rendered as *Blue Lorries* in the English translation in reference to the armoured vans that are used to transport prisoners in Egypt, unfortunately losing the aforementioned connection. I cite from the English translation of the text and will therefore refer to the novel as *Blue Lorries* in the body of this chapter.
98. Naaman, *Urban Space in Contemporary Egyptian Literature*, p. 41. Naaman offers an excellent reading of this novel in Chapter 2.
99. The historical is fundamental to Ashour's literary enterprise. *Thulathiyyat Gharnata* (The Granada Trilogy, 1994–5), *Siraj: Hikaya ʿArabiyya* (*Siraj: An Arab Tale*, 1992) and *Qitʿa min Uruba* (A Piece of Europe, 2003) are all works of historical fiction.

100. Ashour, *Blue Lorries*, p. 11. The second chapter of the novel is explicitly entitled 'Which of the Two Men is Better?' For a reading of the figure of Nasser in the novel, particularly related to the letter that Nada's aunt writes to the President, see Khalifah, *Nasser in the Egyptian Imaginary*, pp. 54–7, 125–9.
101. Ashour, *Blue Lorries*, p. 25.
102. Al-Wahat prison is where Sonallah Ibrahim spent much of his sentence. He published his prison diary under the title *Yamiyyat al-Wahat* (Oasis Diary) in 2005.
103. The university campus as a site of political struggle appears also in Ashour's earlier novel *Spectres*. See Morsi, 'al-Jamiʿa fi Riwayatay "al-Bab-al-Maftuh" wa "Atyaf"'.
104. Ashour, *Blue Lorries*, pp. 80-1.
105. This stands in sharp contrast to other prison narratives, particularly those written by women. See, for example, Nawal El Saadawi's *Mudhakirat fi Sijn al-Nisaʾ* (*Memoirs from the Women's Prison*, 1984) and Salwa Bakr's novel *al-ʿArba al-Dhahabiyya la Tasʿad ila-l-Samaʾ* (*The Golden Chariot*, 1991).
106. Ashour, *Blue Lorries*, pp. 212–13.
107. Ashour, *Faraj*, p. 166. My translation. Romaine translates this as 'I saw the grave yawning wide-open and grim'. *Blue Lorries*, p. 79.
108. Ashour, *Blue Lorries*, p. 239.
109. Ibid. p. 92.
110. Ibid. pp. 228–9.
111. Hilmi, 'Riwayat *Faraj*: Ahaduhum Tara Fawqa ma Tabaqqa Minna'.
112. Ashour, *Blue Lorries*, p. 33.
113. Mazid, 'Radwa Ashour fi *Athqal min Radwa*', p. 45.
114. Among Ashour's autobiographical works are *al-Rihla: Ayyam Taliba Misriyya fi Amrika* (The Journey: Days of an Egyptian Student in America, 1983), *Athqal min Radwa: Maqatiʿ min Sira Dhatiyya* (Heavier than Radwa: Excerpts from an Autobiography, 2013) and *al-Sarkha: Maqatiʿ min Sira Dhatiyya* (The Scream: Excerpts from an Autobiography, 2015).
115. Arwa Salih (1951–97) and Siham Sabri (1951–2003) were both students at Cairo University and significant members of the student movement that erupted in the 1970s against Sadat's policies. Salih, a writer and translator, was also part of the Egyptian Communist Party. Her non-fiction book, *al-Mubtasarun: Dafatir Wahda min Jil al-Haraka al-Tulabiyya*, was published in 1997, the same year Salih took her own life. An English translation of the work has been produced by Samah Selim entitled *The Stillborn: Notebooks*

of a Woman from the Student-Movement Generation. Sabri is famous for her encounter with Dr Ahmed Kamal Abu al-Magd, the Secretary-General of the Socialist Youth Organization and the Minister of Youth, in which she demanded that the President himself come to answer the students' questions given that Abu al-Magd considered himself only a go-between. This, and other episodes for which Salih was famous, appear in *Blue Lorries*. For more, see Imbabi, *Siham Sabri Zahrat al-Haraka al-Tulabiyya*.

116. Radwan, '*Spectres* by Radwa Ashour and Barbara Romaine', p. 98. For a more extensive discussion of Ashour's literary oeuvre as a tapestry, see Sami, 'Balaghat al-Bayan fi Nasjiyyat Radwa Ashour'.
117. Ashour, *Blue Lorries*, p. 33.
118. 'The Years of Lead' refer to the period 1956–99 when, in the aftermath of Moroccan independence, King Hassan II ruled with an iron fist. This reign of terror included the forced disappearance of political dissidents and army officers, the silencing of political opposition, and the gross violation of human rights. For more, see El Guabli, '"The Hidden Transcript" of Resistance in Moroccan Tazmamart Prison Writings'.
119. El Guabli, '"The Hidden Transcript"', p. 180. El Guabli draws heavily upon the writings of Ahmed Marzouki's *Tazmamart Cell 10* and Aziz BineBine's *Tazmamort: Eighteen Years in the Jail of Hassan II*. It is Marzouki's memoir that Nada reads in the closing pages of Ashour's novel.
120. Ashour, 'Arab Prison Literature'.
121. Ashour, 'Eyewitness, Scribe and Story Teller', pp. 88–9.

2

Of Other Cities

My Alexandria. Passion (and loss) in the marble city
Edwar al-Kharrat, *Iskandariyyati*[1]

What does Alexandria have to do with a war in Europe?
Ibrahim Abdel Meguid, *No One Sleeps in Alexandria*[2]

This chapter expands the literary map beyond the boundaries of Cairo and moves us to the coastal city of Alexandria, one that had been largely absent from the literary landscape throughout much of the twentieth century, but that is front and centre in the fiction of the sixties generation. Two natives of the city, Edwar al-Kharrat and Ibrahim Abdel Meguid, have produced Alexandria Trilogies (*Thulāthiyyāt al-Iskandariyya*), expansive works spanning numerous decades that contend with the city's colonial and postcolonial realities, delving into its Egyptian, Arab, Coptic, European and Islamic identities. Both writers present Alexandria as a city with a complicated past and present, calling into question Cairo's position of dominance. In focusing upon the outbreak of the Second World War and its aftermath, the writers compel the reader to grapple with Alexandria's greatly celebrated cosmopolitan diversity within the context of colonial occupation and military siege.[3] With independence, the attack on ethno-religious diversity is coupled with the attack on political diversity, and the forging of the city's identity within the postcolonial context of Egypt is fraught with contradictions.

In re-writing the modern history of Alexandria, al-Kharrat and Abdel Meguid offer more than representations of a cosmopolitan haven or a surrogate for the capital. Instead, what we are given are rich, heterogeneous representations of the city and its inhabitants. The novels focus upon the urban landscape of Alexandria, the roads, routes, streets and neighbourhoods that make up the city. The working-class areas, populated by labourers and rural migrants, are given as much, if not more, attention than the neighbourhoods once inhabited by the Greek, Italian and Jewish communities.[4] The changing architecture is registered as much in nightclubs and brothels as in ancient relics and ruins. What emerges then is a narrative of Alexandria as varied and pluralistic, both in terms of the ethno-religious communities of the past, and the socio-economic and political groups of the present.

There is a marked shift in the representation of Alexandria that sets the writers apart from their predecessors, both Western and Egyptian. This is not the Alexandria of Lawrence Durrell, E. M. Forster and Constantine P. Cavafy. Nor is it the Alexandria of Naguib Mahfouz. While European writers by and large imagined the city as the paragon of cosmopolitan coexistence, an idealised foil for the complicated capital, Egyptian writers presented it as a destination for those fleeing Cairo. Both writers are keenly aware of this, purposely positioning their works as departures from these narratives.

While one should approach the critical assertions of the author about their own work with caution, al-Kharrat is not wrong in pointing to his writing as marking a significant shift in the literary representation of Alexandria – I extend this shift to Abdel Meguid as well. Al-Kharrat argues that Lawrence Durrell, the greatly celebrated British writer and author of the famous *Alexandria Quartet*, knew only one particular aspect of Alexandria, that of the upper-class, foreign communities.[5] It is not only Western writers with whom al-Kharrat takes issue. Naguib Mahfouz, he argues, considered the city in general as mere background for his novels and not, as al-Kharrat demands, as having 'potential for action' (*quwwa fāʿila*).[6] While I would argue that this generalisation regarding Mahfouz is overstated, particularly in regard to his Cairene novels, it is certainly true that Alexandria is not front and centre in his literary oeuvre. Even his greatly celebrated 1967 novel *Miramar*, which takes place in a pension in Alexandria in post-revolutionary Egypt, presents the coastal city as an escape from the Cairene capital.[7] Written as a critique of the political climate of the 1950s and 1960s, and as a foreshadowing of the catastrophic defeat of 1967, Miramar (the novel and the pension) brings together a group of exiles largely from Cairo. The novel's engagement with the Alexandrian natives focuses on the foreign communities increasingly driven out of the country. We follow Marianna, the Greek owner of the

Miramar pension, as she is forced to reckon with her place in the postcolonial Egyptian nation during a period of instability and uncertainty.

In writing chronicles of Alexandria both al-Kharrat and Abdel Meguid engage with the multiplicity of communities that made the city their home throughout the twentieth century. The question thus becomes: how to write a history of the city given this diversity and multiplicity? Al-Kharrat creates texts that defy categorisation, blending autobiography and fiction, simultaneously narrating the story of an individual and an entire city. He does so in works that echo and repeat each other, and that resist a linear chronology of events. I thus discuss al-Kharrat's three works in conjunction in this chapter, and not in separate sections. Abdel Meguid merges the monumental and the everyday, drawing upon a plethora of songs, sayings, newspapers, letters and movies, in the creation of a more expansive and multifaceted history. He does so in novels that are more readily accessible as individual works of fiction and that proceed in a more chronological manner, and as such I have chosen to discuss each work in turn. In both cases the authors unsettle the time and place of the realist novel bringing together the worlds of dreams and reality. Hala Halim argues that 'Alexandrianism' is 'the Western construct of the space of Alexandria as an ur-archive, an archive of archives' that draws upon the canonical texts of Forster, Cavafy and Durrell, among many others.[8] The works of Abdel Meguid and al-Kharrat can be read as alternative archives of Alexandria, which do not do away with the aforementioned writers, but that seek to expand the possible contributors. The position of Alexandria vis-à-vis the nation and the world is as important as the fragments of the everyday. What they create then are trilogies of the city that try to capture decades of the city's history while simultaneously reimagining the formal possibilities of the urban literary chronicle of Alexandria.

Al-Kharrat's Trilogy: Which Alexandria?

A native of the city, al-Kharrat reclaims a place for Alexandria in the literary landscape of Egypt, most significantly in his trilogy composed of *Turabuha Zaʿfaran: Nusus Iskandaraniyya* (*City of Saffron*, 1986), *Ya Banat Iskandariyya: Riwaya* (*Girls of Alexandria*, 1990) and *Iskandariyyati: Madinati al-Qudsiyya al-Hushiyya: Kulaj Riwaʾi* (*My Alexandria: My Sacred Strange City: A Narrative Collage*, 1994).[9] Born in 1926, to a Coptic Christian family, al-Kharrat spent much of his childhood and early adulthood in Alexandria. His larger literary project is inextricably linked to the city of his birth. It features prominently in works such *Rama wa-l-Tinin* (*Rama and the Dragon*, 1979), *al-Zaman al-Akhar* (The Other Time, 1985), *Yaqin al-ʿAtash* (The Certainty of Thirst, 1996) and *Hariq al-Akhyila* (Fire of Fantasies, 1994).

The Alexandria Trilogy follows Mikhail and spans the period between the 1930s and the 1980s.[10] These are, however, no ordinary coming of age novels. All three works suspend the adherence to chronological progression, moving through time and space freely, according to processes of association, to recreate the workings of memory and connect it to the urban landscape. According to Calvino,

> [a] city is a combination of many things: memory, desires, signs of a language; it is a place of exchange, as any text-book of economic history will tell you – only, these exchanges are not just trade in goods, they also involve words, desires, and memories.[11]

All three works capture Mikhael's memories, presenting and repeating incidents from his life; his childhood home; his relationships with many members of his boisterous family; the celebrations of Coptic holidays; and his many romantic pursuits. We follow him as he attends university, participates in demonstrations against the British, is imprisoned, and eventually reneges on his political commitments. In reading the entirety of the trilogy, the reader has the feeling that he/she has heard many of the stories before, stories which tell of the city as much as the protagonist.

Mikhael's childhood is spent mostly in Gheit el-Enab (Ghayt al-ʿInab), a working-class neighbourhood inhabited by migrant workers from Upper Egypt and the Delta, as well as by Coptic families like that of Mikhael's.[12] Gheit el-Enab is located in the area of Karmuz, which according to Muhammad Subhi Abdel Hakim's extensive study of the city, was one of the most densely populated areas of Alexandria, noteworthy for its working-class population, most of which worked in the factories that proliferated in the area.[13] Through his childhood wanderings and later adult experiences, we follow Mikhael down Alexandria's streets, as he crosses its squares, explores its varied neighbourhoods and sits at its seaside cafés. The three works thus recreate the city in its material reality: in fact, each installment of the trilogy opens with a reference to geography. The first line of the first work, *City of Saffron*, is 'I went back to *shari*ᶜ Raghib Pasha [Raghib Pasha street]', locating us in Karmuz.¹⁴ The first line of *Girls of Alexandria* reads as follows: 'It is as if I am entering the house in *haret* el-Gullanar [Gullanar alley]', once again situating the reader at street level.¹⁵ *My Alexandria*, however, describes the city in more lyrical, impassioned terms: 'My Alexandria. Passion (and loss) in the marble city – white and blue – that the heart continuously weaves, and that always floats over her luminous, scintillating face'.¹⁶ Al-Kharrat's city is both real and imagined, tangible and ephemeral, captured in the materiality of the streets and alleys and in the metaphorical rendering of its beauty as a feminine face.

Here, as in the works examined in Chapter 1, walking is fundamental to the urban experience. It is recreated in descriptions that are pointed and precise, recreating a form of mapping, predominantly through walking but also on the buses and trams Mikhael rides. Mikhael as pedestrian (and passenger) is, as de Certeau would claim, producing the city of Alexandria both in the act of walking and in the act of remembrance.¹⁷ Recalling a memory of his mother giving him directions to the Masalla Market, Mikhael recounts the directions with precision:

> My mother said to me: 'You take the tram from in front of the house. It passes by Raghib Pasha [street] until Khedive Tawfiq Street, then al-Nabi Daniel, and it turns into Sultan Husayn until you reach the street from which we can see the sea, Masalla Street, and you get off at the stop before al-Raml.'¹⁸

The tram here is important as a symbol of mobility, movement and interaction. In reorienting Alexandria cosmopolitanism 'geographically, socially, and culturally', William Hanley cites the tram as an example of 'everyday cosmopolitanism' or 'vulgar cosmopolitanism' where people from the different religious, ethnic and national groups mixed.¹⁹ Mikhael traverses different socio-economic spaces via the tram, leaving his working-class neighbourhood of Gheit el-Enab, passing through the commercial centre of the city and the mercantile centre of al-Attarin, to the final destination of al-Raml, a station overlooking the sea.

The ethnic, national and religious diversity is captured in the materiality of the city, the physical remnants of the past, the monuments and statues. In a lyrical passage from *Girls of Alexandria*, Mikhael recounts an ode to his city: 'Alexandria my great city, God preserved harbor, golden haven, vision of Alexander and work of Socrates, the mighty engineer, pearl of Cleopatra the eternal beauty, shining marbled city which at night need no illumination so white she is.'[20] What follows is a hymn to the various monuments, areas and sights of the city, called by their Arabic *and* Greek names. Throughout the trilogy the Alexandria of past and present is at once Arab, Muslim, Greek, Roman and Coptic. We are also witness to Mikhael's encounters with Muslim neighbours, with friends and political comrades of Greek, Italian and Jewish lineage; the various foreign communities that made Alexandria their home throughout the early twentieth century.[21] The diversity of the city is thus captured both in the city's landmarks and in its inhabitants.

Al-Kharrat's presentation of Coptic Alexandria is one of the most important dimensions of the trilogy. That Mikhael, a Coptic boy, is the main protagonist and not a peripheral character is itself noteworthy. Furthermore, the vivid descriptions of Mikhael's childhood, his home, extended family, and the religious celebrations in his neighbourhood means that al-Kharrat provides a full and vibrant picture of the community's experiences. One such recollection is of celebrating the Epiphany with his mother and cousin: 'we put lighted candles inside hollowed and re-folded globes of orange-peel so that they glowed with a flickering light and the pimples on the peel appeared to be made of some brittle and translucent gemstone'.[22] Such moments of warmth and tranquility are not limited to Mikhael's home but extend beyond its walls to include the family's neighbours and friends, many of whom are Muslim. Much of this communion is played out through the exchange of food, particularly during the various religious holidays that the different groups celebrate: 'We exchanged plates of *ka'k* and biscuits and *ghurrayiba* and crisp milk crackers, at the feasts of Easter and Adha and Christmas and Fitr: plates covered with ironed tea-towels, checked or white', Mikhael recounts.[23] These descriptions serve to paint a vivid picture of Mikhael's childhood experiences and the community of which he was a part, one in which Copts and Muslims are cherished neighbours. This also works to expand the representation of the Christian community beyond that of a persecuted minority, a problematic rendering with which al-Kharrat repeatedly takes issue.[24]

This inter-religious community is captured poignantly in a scene in which the neighbours all gather in a bomb shelter during a German air raid on the city – this scene will find remarkable resonance in a similar description by Abdel Meguid in the first installment of his own trilogy. Nuris Fakhri, one of Mikhael's many loves, tells of the intermingling of prayers and languages, the Greek and the Italian, heard alongside the Muslim and Coptic prayers:

> She also told me that Madame Teresa the Italian lady and her children, the boys and two girls, had burst into muffled sobs when they heard the rattle of the anti-aircraft guns, and that when the bombing became intense 'Our Father's' mingled with the Chapter of the Chair from the Quran, prayers in Greek and Italian with cries of 'O Kindly One, O Kindly God whose Graces are unseen, deliver us from Terror'.[25]

Though a symbol of the diversity of the community, the utterances are punctuated by the sounds of falling bombs. A similar effect is registered in a description that catalogues the areas of the city during the same aerial bombing campaign:

> from el-Anfushi to el-Mandara and el-Montaza, from el-Rand and el-Ban and el-Nakhil in Gheit el-Enab to el-Labban and Raʾs el-Tin and Anastasi; from Glymonopoulo and Zizinia to Stanley and el-Nuzha and el-Wardyan; from Hagar el-Nawatiya to Kom el-Nadura, from Sidi Gabir and Sidi Bishr and Bacos to Samuha and el-Maks; from the Cairo railway station and el-Rassafa to Mustafa Pasha, and back again to ʿEzbet el-Sayadin. All the treasures of Alexandria lay prostrate and naked, veiled only by the network of beams which stabbed the sky.[26]

This is not unlike the passage in Ibrahim's novel discussed in Chapter 1 that lists the streets of downtown Cairo. Here too the areas and landmarks almost overwhelm a reader unfamiliar with the geography of Alexandria. They do, however, once again alert us to the long and varied history of the city, that inscribes Alexandria as Ancient Greek, Roman, European, Islamic, Arab and Coptic. The diversity is also socio-economic; the working-class neighbourhoods of Gheit el-Enab and el-Labban, the more affluent el-Montaza and Zizinia, the industrial areas of el-Maks and Bacos, the beaches of Sidi Gabir, Sidi Bishr and Stanley are all subject to the aerial bombing, 'prostrate and naked' to the destruction from above. And thus there is no possibility of idealising the world that Mikhael inhabits. The scenes of war remind the reader of the reality of life in colonial Egypt, and thus there is no disentangling the cosmopolitan from the colonial in al-Kharrat's texts. The bombing that the people of Alexandria must endure by the Germans is a direct consequence of the colonial presence of the British in Egypt. Given that the majority of the plot of the trilogy takes place in the 1930s and 1940s, the reality of the Second World War and the presence of the Allied troops in Alexandria is one of the dominant features of Mikhael's memories and hence of the three texts.

Al-Kharrat further complicates the category of the cosmopolitan, reminding the reader that it does not entirely erase the differences of religion, ethnicity and nationality. In describing one of the neighbours, the narrator states that the boy (in reference to Mikhael who is here mentioned in the third person) 'did not, then, fully understand the import of the word *grigiya* – Greek woman. For him, back then, differences between people were part of the natural course of things.'[27] Difference is registered through language, and we are told that there 'was something in her voice, the faintest traces of a Greek accent. She was almost like a native Egyptian in her speech, but she had a particular delicacy – the slightest softening of the hard consonants.'[28] Thus the claim that difference is 'part of the natural course of things' is immediately undercut. Even as a child, Mikhael understands that his neighbour is 'almost like a native Egyptian in her speech' but not quite. This is not unlike the difference he feels because of his religion. Throughout his childhood Mikhael articulates an anxiety about his Coptic name: 'there on the echoing verandah I told her, and my unmistakably Coptic name sounded odd even to my ears – odd and somehow unjustifiable, as it has all my life. Has it been so, in another way, with my whole existence?'[29]

As an adult, Mikhael continues to interrogate these ideas of authenticity and belonging. His reflections are precipitated by the political climate of the 1950s and 60s, which witnesses the maturation of Mikhael, and his involvement in and then denouncement of political activity. Mikhael grapples with the predicaments of the post-revolutionary postcolonial regime in Egypt. The 1952 revolution and the rise of Nasser are described as momentous events in history, ending colonial rule in Egypt but also causing the exodus of 'foreign' communities from the country.[30] Remembering Zaki Ibrahim Sadduq, a Jew and a fellow revolutionary forced to leave Egypt for Genoa in 1949, Mikhael describes him as '*ibn al-balad al-yahūdī al-iskandarānī al-quḥ*' (the native Jewish Alexandrian, through and through).³¹ The Arabic phrase '*ibn al-balad*' here identifies Zaki as truly an Egyptian, as one who really understands and belongs to place, primarily the city of Alexandria. As a true Alexandrian, he is also a true Egyptian. But within the context of revolutionary Egypt he is cast as foreigner and outsider because of his Jewish identity. Zaki's religion, as a sign of difference, recalls the young Mikhael's anxiety about his own religious identity. Zaki's departure, as part of a larger exodus from Alexandria and Egypt, is largely registered by Mikhael in the form of a question, a melancholy rhetorical statement concerning a friend or acquaintance forced to emigrate to Europe or the United States: 'Where are you now Gabir? Are you still living in Alexandria?'³² Mikhael's question, laden with longing, represents his struggle with the postcolonial project that brings about an end to much of the diversity he remembers, a diversity represented in the urban environment and in its inhabitants. And this is a diversity that al-Kharrat continues to complicate throughout his trilogy. The opposition here is not between an idealised cosmopolitanism and an exclusionary nationalism. Instead, al-Kharrat reminds us of the relationship between the colonial and the cosmopolitan while also rejecting a limited understanding of national identity. Instead he suggests a more expansive identity that includes ethnic, religious and socio-economic differences that are captured in the urban landscape of Alexandria and its people.

Girls of Alexandria: Gendered City

If the trilogy is a celebration of the Mediterranean city that acknowledges it as multiple and varied, then so too are the women of Alexandria. Throughout all three works Mikhael tells of the different women he meets, pursues and pines over. This host of female characters reflects the religious and ethnic diversity of the city; Suᶜad al-Samahi of Bahari, Sumaya the Englishwoman's daughter, the Coptic Nagiya, Layla the Bedouin, Janine the Yugoslavian and Stepho the Greek girl are just some of the many women we encounter.³³ His loves feature prominently in the 'hymn of *nūn*' that appears in *City of Saffron*, alongside the heroines of Ancient Greece, Egypt and Rome.³⁴ He sings to Venus and Persephone, as well as to Mona and Niᶜma, in a verse in which all the women are one, eternal and ultimately bound to Alexandria. The medley of names that appears in the hymn speaks to the heterogeneity of the city in the past and present. The women at once multiple and single cease to be real, but instead intertwine with the city and the sea. This image is the very opening of *Girls of Alexandria*, in an epigraph that casts the women as born of memory and fantasy:

> Girls of Alexandria, multiple, single, peerless; who are you? I have never met you face to face but I know you like a lover: and no one knows more than a lover. Paradise-girls of memory and fantasy, appearing ever in bodies and souls gone and forgotten now. Reveries aeons old, they throng my boyhood, youth, my later years: even now they undulate through my dreams with a life more carnal than that of any woman.
> Girls of Alexandria, sea of Alexandria: constant unending seduction which cannot perish.
> However many she is, she is one: however fleeting, she is eternal.
> How can I resist her?[35]

The final lines of the passage solidify the association between city and woman, thus recreating the 'well-worn trope of feminization of cities and nations', a trope not limited to but certainly embedded within orientalist, colonial discourses.[36] These 'paradise-girls' that consume Mikhael from childhood are by and large described according to physical attributes; we repeatedly encounter the 'shadowy place, plump and mysteriously compelling, between their bared thighs',[37] and the 'fresh young golden body [that] could hardly contain the womanhood which bloomed and flowered, the first fruits of her fullness'.[38] This focus upon the female form can be attributed to the trilogy being a coming of age tale that foregrounds Mikhael's sexual awaking, an awakening in which his constant desire for consummation remains unrealised. Thus, like the novelists of Cairo, al-Kharrat connects agency to male sexuality, suggesting implicit ties between the erotic and the political, the two conditions that undergird much of the three novels.[39] Just as we read of Mikhael's many loves, so too do we encounter his embrace and then abandonment of political activity and struggle. In the chapter of *Girls of Alexandria* significantly entitled 'Bullets and the Passions of the Clinging Vine' (*al-Raṣaṣ wa-l-Lablab*), the young Mikhael expounds upon his deep desires, both for justice and love:

I yearned with all my rebellious, trembling heart for some form of justice and truth. And in the days when I was the licit spoil of a love which determined to choke me in its vice, when I was the prey of a despair I imagined to be cosmic metaphysical, absolute, and when the November afternoon skies blazed with a refreshing damp-winded fire which nevertheless appeased me not at all and conveyed to me no meaning at all – then I would drag my heavy limbs down to Stanley Bay to lose myself in dark meditation on the lure of death, on its futility, on all the impossibilities of life.[40]

As in the epigraph cited earlier, al-Kharrat's texts combine the realms of the body and the soul, the worlds of dreams and reality. 'You girl of Alexandria, single however many you are; too many for me. You force me to silence. And in the end is there anything else but silence, however long my Alexandrian songs are sung, silence to the end of time?'[41] Mikhael's obsessive descriptions of both city and woman are perhaps intended to hold the silence at bay, the eternal silence of death that looms over the texts.

Both Magda al-Noweihi and Marlé Hammond concur that the women in al-Kharrat's text are at once single and multiple, unique and archetypal; 'for what is important is the beloved as an ideal, as a fulfillment of needs and desires'.[42] While this may be the case, I would argue that this representation nevertheless results in a host of female characters who only reflect Mikhael's desires, both physical and spiritual. It is hard to ignore the fact that Mikhael's primary mode of interaction with the female other is that of the erotic, even if, as Hammond argues, this reinforces the 'central importance of desire as the driving force behind all forms of union with the other'.[43] It is then difficult to locate instances in the trilogy in which the girls and women enact examples of their own agency. Rather they seem to reflect and represent Mikhael's own yearnings and urges, even as these culminate in the very sincere though perhaps impossible hunger for unity with the other.

The distancing that occurs between Mikhael's desires and those of the female characters of the trilogy is also a result of the narrative technique employed by al-Kharrat. While al-Kharrat moves between the first and third person in telling Mikhael's story, the female characters only ever narrate in the third person. Thus, while Mikhael's position is destabilised by the constant movement between the 'I' and the 'he', the women of the novel are never granted the narrative 'I'. I then caution against a reading, such as the one proposed by Hammond, that suggests that this narrative technique necessarily results in 'mutual empowerment' for both Mikhael and the women of the novels, but rather it is important to remember that the female speech and representation remains filtered through the male protagonist.[44] And thus, while on the one hand al-Kharrat strives to capture the rich and varied history of the city, the mix of ethnic, religious and national groups that made Alexandria their home, he does so by drawing on existing gendered tropes of the spatial and the feminine. The city of Alexandria is cast as a 'maiden . . . of unruptured virginity' and the women of the city, who are too numerous to count, are represented first and foremost through the eyes of the male protagonist.[45]

'More, Perhaps, a Becoming'

The attempt at classifying and describing al-Kharrat's Alexandria Trilogy is no simple matter; the impossibility of narrating a conclusive history of the city thus coincides with the difficulties of capturing one's own story. Mikhael shares many similarities with al-Kharrat: both character and author are born to Coptic families, spend their childhoods and early adult lives in Alexandria, and are imprisoned for political activities and participation in anti-colonial demonstrations against the British. Despite the similarities between author and protagonist, and the fact that the narrative continues to shift between first and third person, the texts resist being classified as an autobiography in the conventional sense. In fact, the first work, *City of Saffron*, opens with the following declaration by al-Kharrat:

> These writings are not an autobiography, nor anything like; the flights of fancy, the artifice herein, bear them far beyond such bounds. They are illusions – incidents and visions – figures; the kernels of events which are but dreams; the clouds of memories which should have taken place, but never did. More, perhaps, a 'Becoming' than a 'Life'; not *my* life.[46]

What are we to make of this introduction? Is this al-Kharrat demanding that his text not be read as an autobiography, at the very moment that he insinuates himself into the text? Or is this declaration intended to cast doubts on Mikhael's story even before it has begun? Interestingly, the English translation, unlike the Arabic original, does not specify the introductory statement as being penned by al-Kharrat, leaving a heightened ambiguity regarding its authorship.

Such suspicions continue to arise throughout the trilogy. Mikhael frequently interjects as a commentator on the truth of the memory he has just recounted:

> Is this a touching scene, is it predictable or required in this narrative? Is it touching at all? Or did it happen at all? I said: Given that I am telling it then it must actually have happened.[47]

Mikhael is aware of the tricks of memory even as he obsessively recounts his autobiography:

> Does my memory deceive me or does my imagination create things that are more realistic than any reality? Or is this what really happened? What does my writing here have to do with what really happened? Do I write what happened? And what I write, happen? And what could have possibly happened?[48]

That the reader is required to occupy a position between fact and fiction, dream and reality, autobiography and invention, is declared in the very first page of the trilogy and continues to undercut the narrative. At all moments we are made to question the relationship between the narrative and the events of Mikhael's (and al-Kharrat's) life, and to contend with the creative process inherent in remembrance.

It is not only that the convergence of author and protagonist complicates the issue of categorisation. There is also the question of what to call the works themselves.[49] *City of Saffron* has the subtitle '*Nusūs Iskandarāniyya*' (Alexandrian Texts), which signals to the reader that this is a collection of texts identified as something other than a novel, the illusions and kernels that are described in the passage quoted earlier. It also suggests the constant interplay of fact, fiction and memoir in the trilogy. Both *City of Saffron* and *Girls of Alexandria* are similar in form; each one being divided into nine chapters; each chapter being given a title. Interestingly however, despite its similarities to its predecessor, *Girls of Alexandria* is specifically referred to as a '*riwāya*' (novel). *My Alexandria*, however, is described by al-Kharrat as a '*kulāj riwāʾī*' (narrative collage). This third and final work also stands apart from its antecedents in another respect. *My Alexandria* begins with two sections; the first, an introduction entitled 'My Alexandria: The Saffron City' and the second entitled 'Al-Kharrat's Alexandria: According to English Critics' in which we are introduced to al-Kharrat the critic. It is here that al-Kharrat explains that this work is a 'collage', a 'combination of things' that can be compared to the visual arts.[50] The label of critic must then be added to the description of al-Kharrat in thinking about the creation and construction of his Alexandrian trilogy.

Whether labelled text, novel or collage, the three works are remarkably similar in style; all three suspend the adherence to a chronological progression, moving through time and space freely by processes of association, in an attempt to recreate the workings of memory. According to al-Noweihi, *City of Saffron* 'follows the process of remembrance that is tinged with imagination in an exploration of how a child experiences his world, and how his experience converges with that of the adult he has become'.[51] We read about his childhood, the girls (and then women) he desires, and his involvement in anti-colonial demonstrations. Mikhael repeats the same recollections, changes details, expands upon events, with the ultimate effect of leaving the reader in what al-Kharrat termed earlier, the 'clouds of memories'. If Mikhael is ultimately unsure what is true, what he remembers and what he imagines, then so too is the reader. In assembling the multifarious and contradictory kernels that together tell of the city's complicated history, the author creates a series of texts that defy categorisation. The works of the trilogy are at once texts, autobiographies, visions, memories and collages. It is in this way that al-Kharrat showcases his innovative contribution to the urban narrative of Alexandria.

No One Sleeps in Alexandria: Colonial Cosmopolitanism

Ibrahim Abdel Meguid's Alexandria Trilogy is an expansive work spanning almost four decades, from the 1940s until the 1980s. In his three novels, *La Ahad Yanam fi al-Iskandariyya* (*No One Sleeps in Alexandria*, 1996), *Tuyur al-ʿAnbar* (*Birds of Amber*, 2008) and *al-Iskandariyya fi Ghayma* (*Clouds over Alexandria*, 2012), Abdel Meguid contends with the city's colonial and postcolonial realities, delving into its Egyptian, Arab, European and Islamic identities.[52] As a native of Alexandria, Abdel Meguid's larger literary project is inextricably linked to his city; other than the trilogy, *Bayt al-Yasmin* (*House of Jasmine*, 1984) and *Adagio* (2016) are also set in the city of his birth.[53]

In the first installment, *No One Sleeps in Alexandria*, Abdel Meguid masterfully recreates the Alexandria of the 1940s, a city in turmoil as the world erupts into chaos with the advent of the Second World War. The novel opens on 25 August 1939 with Hitler signing the order to invade Poland. A few days later, as troops invade the country, the protagonist Magd al-Din and his wife Zahra leave their village for good, driven out by an order from the mayor and a threat of a vendetta supposedly settled long ago.[54] As rural migrants, they make their new home in Alexandria where, having escaped the threat of violence from the villagers, they live amidst the violence of war, a violence that is immediately suggested in the novel's title, an allusion to Federico García Lorca's apocalyptic poem *City that Does not Sleep*.[55]

If, as scholars have argued, the Roman phrase '*Alexandrea ad Aegyptum*' has animated much of the discourse concerning cosmopolitan Alexandria, then Abdel Meguid is conscious here, and throughout the trilogy, of Alexandria's connection to the rest of Egypt.[56] As Khaled Fahmy argues 'Alexandria was always written about as if it was *appendaged* to Egypt ("Alexandrea ad Aegyptum") rather than being an integral part of it.'[57] The insistence in the novel that Alexandria is part of and not apart from Egypt is neither an assertion of nationalism, nor a claim about who the authentic Alexandrians are. Rather, Abdel Meguid's characters undermine the binary of native and foreigner at almost every turn, capturing the realities of migration. In fact, migrants had been central to Alexandria's growing population throughout the nineteenth century; Will Hanley describes the city as 'a nineteenth century boomtown with almost no truly native inhabitants'.[58]

Alexandria of the 1940s is not here the cosmopolitan haven long celebrated for its diversity – or rather, that is not all it is. The novel does engage with the multiple communities that called the city home: the Greeks, Italians, Maltese and Jews who populated Alexandria until the middle of the twentieth century. Yet Abdel Meguid focuses on the context of war, and the colonial context in particular, that results in Alexandria being thrust into the foreground of conflict. This also signals a temporal shift of sorts, highlighting an earlier moment of displacement and exodus. While historical accounts by and large privilege the 1952 revolution and Nasser's rise to power as the significant turning point in Alexandria's contemporary history, Abdel Meguid, not unlike al-Kharrat, recalls an earlier moment in the previous decade that put all the city's inhabitants at risk. Deborah Starr argues that

> the demise of cosmopolitanism in Egypt in the middle of the twentieth century needs to be understood in the context of the rise of a range of parochial nationalisms and divided loyalties in wartime – the Second World War, the Arab-Israeli war of 1948–1949, and the Suez Conflict – not just as a result of anti-colonialism.[59]

Abdel Meguid reminds the reader of earlier tumultuous events that prompted Alexandria's residents, Egyptian and foreign, to flee the city to escape the dangers of war.

To read Abdel Meguid's novels is to encounter a meticulous and intentional mapping of the spaces of the city of Alexandria and the changing urban landscape of the twentieth century. Throughout the novels the characters traverse the cityscape, often by foot, crossing roads and squares in countless excursions. As the author himself notes, walking is a central component of all his literary works.[60] As in the novels of al-Kharrat, the focus upon working-class neighbourhoods is notable; Abdel Meguid was born and raised in Karmuz, which features prominently in all three works. In *No One Sleeps in Alexandria*, Magd al-Din settles in Gheit el-Enab (the same neighbourhood upon which al-Kharrat focuses his attention). While Magd al-Din encounters a host of the city's inhabitants, the novel pivots around his friendship with Dimyan. The two men eventually find employment with the railroad company and their travels to work are a constant refrain throughout the narrative:

> They were to leave Ghayt al-Aynab [Gheit el-Enab] and walk along the bank of Mahmudiya Canal to a point midway between Karmuz Bridge and Kafr Ashri bridge. There they would find a big housing compound for railroad workers, next to which they would find a smaller housing compound for traffic workers who also worked for the railroad.[61]

The Mahmudiya (Mahmudiyya) Canal mentioned in the description of the walk to work is also a symbol of the city's connection to the rest of Egypt. Completed in 1820, under the auspices of Muhammad Ali, the canal provided the city with fresh water, as well as ensuring its connection to the Nile Valley and contributing to the growth and prosperity of Alexandria.[62] Trains transporting the troops figure prominently in the present world of the novel, not least because Magd al-Din and Dimyan are employed by the rail company. The troops themselves, allied soldiers from Britain, Australia and India, populate the streets of Alexandria, another form of cosmopolitanism rarely included in the nostalgic recollections about the foreign communities of the city.

If the cosmopolitan diversity of the city is complicated by the colonial context of war, Abdel Meguid foregrounds another diversity in the form of inter-religious cooperation. Most importantly, the central friendship of the novel is between the Coptic Dimyan and the Muslim Magd al-Din. As Starr notes, Abdel Meguid's first installment of the trilogy was published in the midst of the rising tide of Islamist militant violence in Egypt in the 1990s and was received as part of a larger 'reaction against intolerance and intercommunal violence'.[63] Upon Magd al-Din's arrival in Alexandria, he resides in the building of the Christian Khawaga Dimitri, a space of cooperation across ethnic and religious lines.[64] As we are told early in the novel, the conflicts in the neighbourhood are not strictly religious; Zahra, for example, 'was surprised to hear about the tensions between the Christians and the Muslims and how they had subsided now, and that the real tensions were now between northern and southern Egyptians'.[65]

It is Zahra who regularly crosses such lines, in her friendship with Sitt Maryam, Khawaga Dimitri's wife. As a result of their friendship, Zahra comes to know and explore the city:

> 'We'll get off at Attarin,' Sitt Maryam told her. 'This streetcar goes around in a circle, from here to Attarin, then Abd al-Munim Street, then Istanbul Street, and Safiya Zaghloul, and the Chamber of Commerce, then Manshiya and Bahari from Tatwig street, and comes all the way back with the same ticket – something of a joy ride.'[66]

Again, as noted earlier in the work of al-Kharrat, the tram is an important symbol of mobility, a means for characters to navigate the socio-economic spaces of the city. Leaving the poorer neighbourhood of Gheit el-Enab, the tram route weaves through the more affluent Safiya Zaghloul and the

Chamber of Commerce, then Manshiya and Bahari. Through Zahra's walks we, as readers, are introduced to the spaces of the city. That we follow the movement of a female character as much, if not more, than the movement of the two male protagonists is important to note.

The unity captured in Khawaga Dimitiri's building is heightened during moments of impending danger; one of the most poignant scenes in the novel takes place during a fierce air strike, when the inhabitants of the neighbourhood band together. In an episode that strongly recalls those in al-Kharrat's trilogy, a six-hour air raid wreaks havoc on the city, with 'fire burning in the sky'.[67] Amidst the destruction the inhabitants of the building take shelter together, and the prayers of Muslims and Christians mix in a powerful image of religious harmony in the face of frightening circumstances:

> Magd al-Din, still swaying, began reciting the Quran again after his prayer. Dimitri continued his own prayers. The words intermingled in such a way that one could only make out that they were the prayers of sincere souls devoting every bit of their being to God, the Savior.[68]

This is followed by a dialogue in the form of the recitations, which alternate between the phrases from Muslim and Christian prayers, in a harmonious interlude amid discord.

A similar interlude is to be found at the end of the novel, in a scene that is certainly the emotional climax of the narrative. Returning from al-Alamein, where Magd al-Din and Dimyan are stationed for much of the war, their train is bombed. The attack results in Dimyan's death, a ghastly tragedy which Magd al-Din casts as a magical episode that recalls the slaying of the dragon by Saint George; 'he saw him rising through the fire with a golden body and a golden face, holding in his golden hand a long golden lance, riding a gold horse and transfixing the heads of the fire-spewing dragons'.[69] Dimyan, as golden knight, then ascends to the heavens. This is just one of many fantastical episodes that occur throughout the three novels and is one of the innovative ways that Abdel Meguid moves away from the realism of previous decades. While this is not the magical realism of novels such as Abdel Meguid's *al-Masafat* (Distances, 1984) and *Burj al-ᶜAthraʾ* (Virgo, 2003), episodes such as this call into question the reality depicted.

As Magd al-Din cries out for his friend, his Qurʾanic prayers intermingle with Dimyan's name. He recites the chapter from the Qurʾan, 'the only chapter he could still remember', a chapter (*Sūrat al-Raḥmān*) which describes how man was created from clay, and the jinn from fire.[70] Magd al-Din stops at numerous words that rhyme with his friend's name.[71] So following the words '*yasjudānī*', '*al-mīzānī*', '*tukadhdhibānī*', Magd al-Din cries out 'Dimyan. Dimyan'.[72] While at other moments in the narrative Muslim and Christian symbiosis plays out in the simultaneous recitation of religious texts, here Dimyan's (Christian) name, harmoniously mixes with Magd al-Din's Qurʾanic recitation. Throughout the novel Dimyan and Magd al-Din's friendship signals the connection between Muslim and Christian traditions within the Egyptian context. That Magd al-Din is initially a stranger to the city of Alexandria, who is befriended and saved by Dimyan, elicits from the reader a reconsideration of the context of colonial cosmopolitanism and the possibilities of Alexandrian diversity.

Birds of Amber: The Promises of Postcolonial Nationalism

From the Second World War, Abdel Meguid moves deftly to the 1950s, beginning the second novel of the trilogy, *Birds of Amber*, with yet another war. Bypassing the events of 1952 and the end of the British presence in Egypt, the author instead takes the 1956 Suez crisis and the nationalisation of the canal as his starting point. Leaving behind almost the entire cast of characters of *No One Sleeps in Alexandria* we find ourselves in the same place, the workers' projects near the Mahmudiya Canal, in the context of postcolonial Alexandria. It is this geographical juncture, not the characters themselves, that connects the first and second parts of the trilogy. Mahmud, the novel's aspiring filmmaker, gives us an aerial view that takes us across the city to the project:

> Alexandria's beautiful breeze quickly lifts him up in the air with a camera passing over Umar Ibn al-Khattab Street, going through Masgid al-Sultan Street to Piazza to Bab Sidr to Pompey's Pillar, to Karmuz Bridge and Kafr Ashri, and then he lands carrying the camera. Here's the Railway Authority workers' housing. In front of the houses is Mahmudiya and the ferry that carries people back and forth to the tram stop and to Kom al-Shuqafa.[73]

It is on the banks of the canal that the novel opens; 'No boats, large or small, on the Mahmudiya Canal. Not a single tram moving on the opposite bank.'[74]

This eerie silence, a result of the impending attack by Israel, foreshadows the turbulent times to come. Central to the opening description are the warehouses of Salvago the Greek, 'quite a celebrity in Alexandria', and a symbolic reminder of future upheavals, and the departure of the foreign communities of Alexandria in the wake of the 1956 Tripartite Aggression and the nationalisations that took place in the following years.[75]

The city thus becomes the site where questions over the national identity of post-independence Egypt are played out; with the departure of a majority of Alexandria's foreign communities and the transformation of the spatial realities of the city that ensue, the characters of the novel struggle to define the contours of their urban environment. What is so striking about Abdel Meguid's narrative, however, is the ways in which the multiple identities of Alexandria are conjured in the text. The legacies of the colonial cosmopolitanism of the previous novel encounter the limits of postcolonial national identity. Those who struggle and suffer with the transformation of Alexandria are not just the members of the foreign communities, compelled to leave Egypt as a result of Nasser's policies of nationalisation and the fall out over the Suez crisis: *Birds of Amber* also presents the difficulties of marginalised communities, particularly those of the workers' projects, and the persecution of political groups in a world where definitions of national identity are continually contracting. Throughout the novel, news of arrests, disappearances and imprisonments of communists and leftists reaches the characters through their newspapers and radios, a constant reminder of the myriad forms of oppression in the postcolonial period.[76]

The exodus of the foreign communities of Alexandria is largely presented through the experiences of the workers of the project. We are told initially that 'the war ended and Alexandria became preoccupied with the mass exodus of the English and French and Jewish communities'.[77] The narrator then continues that 'the departure of the French made no difference to anyone in the Project; nor for that matter, did the departure of the English'.[78] This is, however, with the exception of Sulayman, the young writer in love with British Jane Bancroft, who is left heartbroken after her departure. Distinctions are also made between the nationals of the colonial powers of Britain and France, and the Jewish communities, who as the narrator tells us were Egyptians who had been living in Egypt for centuries; 'the city' we read, 'turned its back on the Jews'.⁷⁹ The same attitude is largely taken in relationship to the *shawām* (Levantine), Greek, Italian, Cypriot and other European minorities, increasingly compelled to leave the city.⁸⁰ For Arabi, a young inhabitant of the Project working in the atelier of the Greek Katina, the transformation of the city means the loss of both his employment and his much older lover.

If loss is registered in the exodus of communities, and particularly in the departure of many of the novel's characters, it is also apparent in the physical landscape of the city. Here I draw attention to one scene in which Arabi leaves Katina and wanders the streets of the city, only to mistakenly wind up in the Jewish quarter, now deserted:

> He almost slipped on the slippery street as he made his way quickly and aimlessly. He slowed down, his nose assailed by other smells, muffled smells of neglected walls and neglected homes. Garbage was strewn on both sides of the street. Faint lights barely escaped from three-story houses, old houses leaning together in the street paved with slabs of basalt, whose cracks were filled with water, that no one had swept (hence the slipperiness). He was walking on a narrow side-walk that couldn't be wider than half a meter. But the whole alley was almost totally dark and almost all the doors were closed with locks covered with grease, which meant that they would be locked for a long time, at least a year, as they did with the cabins on the beach. Cats and dogs were sleeping in corners. The walls were dingy. This all happened in a few short months. How did the Jews ever live here? They must have taken care of their quarter when they lived here. So, he had entered the Jewish quarter without realizing it, unintentionally.⁸¹

This lengthy description is noteworthy for its attention to detail and for the pungent, oozing filth that emanates from the quarter, a description not unlike that of Sonallah Ibrahim's *The Smell of It*, discussed in the previous chapter. Furthermore, the insistence that Arabi finds himself amidst the dilapidated buildings and the garbage filled streets 'without realizing it, unintentionally' is striking for the ways in which Alexandria's squalor refuses to remain hidden but imposes itself on the narrative. The deserted quarter and the exiled communities are the consequences of post-independence, and the end of colonial rule in Egypt that is symbolised in Nasser's victory in the Suez war in the novel's beginning. The abandoned Jewish quarter and its exiled inhabitants are the price to be paid for Nasser's nationalist policies. This episode also reminds the reader that the communities of the city do not live in isolation, with Arabi noting how 'there were a few Muslims and Christians who lived in the quarter, perhaps they hadn't deserted it'.[82]

It is Arabi who moves most frequently across and between different socio-economic and ethnically marked spaces. Like the Jewish quarter, Katina's atelier is another remnant of a cosmopolitanism that is slowly disappearing. Here, Arabi is part of a socio-economic world quite different from that of his native project. At some moments this appears as a space that encapsulates the nostalgic cosmopolitanism celebrated for its harmonious diversity: 'Armenian, Maltese, Greek, Turkish, Swiss, Austrian, Russian, and Hebrew, among others. The atelier was like the tower of Babel around which different sounds of strange languages flew around.'[83] On the one hand Arabi is granted access here to a female space, an intimate world of women, which in this case also encapsulates the cosmopolitan diversity for which Alexandria was greatly celebrated. On the other hand, however, this is no egalitarian utopia. Arabi is clearly socio-economically inferior to the women who frequent the shop and is never rid of his position as employee of the atelier. Furthermore, though he professes great love for Katina, both she and the other women primarily seduce him for sex. This disparity in power prevents the reader from embracing the atelier as a female space of ethno-religious diversity. Instead one is constantly aware of the politics and economics at play in both the colonial and postcolonial contexts.[84]

This contradiction is at the heart of the excursion Katina, Arabi and friends take to Stanley beach on the day of '*shamm al-nasīm*', a holiday that follows Coptic Easter and is significantly traced back to Ancient Egypt, and thus celebrated across religious lines.[85] The beach, once populated almost exclusively by foreigners, is now bustling with Egyptians. The women note this with some fear and hostility, remarking that 'this beach is no longer our beach' and 'there are more and more Egyptians ... They look at us defiantly.'[86] If Arabi feels sympathy for the plight of Katina and her friends, he is unable to ignore Asmahan's response to his question as to the impact of this increased Egyptian presence: 'Now the beach is natural' she replies, 'there are Europeans and Egyptians just like any zoo: there are gazelles and monkeys'.[87] The exclusivity that the women crave, and that is increasingly diminishing, is highlighted as the group leaves the beach. Riding in a taxi through the city, Arabi witnesses the festivities being held all along the corniche:

> The music would not stop on all the beaches along the coastal road. The distance from Manshiya to Attarin was the most arduous as wave upon wave of pedestrians returning to southern working-class neighbourhoods choked the road. Their voices filled the air with laughter, jokes, and a cacophony of percussion instruments – tablas, tambourines, and finger cymbals that boys and young men attached to their fingers as belly dancers did.[88]

The passage continues to describe the plethora of people celebrating in the streets; men, women, children, wearing all kinds of clothes, a 'sea of humanity'.[89] The corniche, the beach promenade, is here truly a 'public space' open to all of Alexandria's residents, as opposed to the beach itself, which retains its exclusivity.[90] While Katina watches the scene in despondent despair, Arabi catches himself before he parrots Asmahan and declares Alexandria full of gazelles and monkeys. Instead he bitterly rejects the city, saying: 'why should he care about Alexandria, which hadn't paid much heed to him yet?'[91] Thus while the reader recognises the 'wondrous mix and ceaseless chaos' as worthy of celebration, Arabi's words insist upon the foregrounding of marginal communities within the city, ignored despite the promises of the postcolonial regime.

It is this marginalisation that is associated with the workers and inhabitants of the Project. While they may occupy a peripheral position vis-à-vis the city at large, many of the inhabitants consider their neighbourhood as anything but marginal; as Khayr al-Din tells the younger Karawan: 'It seems to me that we live at the center of the earth . . . Strangely enough, as soon as we return to the Project we never think of the world beyond.'[92] And in some ways the 'world beyond' pays little heed to the people of the projects. Early in the novel, during the momentous events of 1956, we are told of a Friday when the workers from the Project eagerly await the radio broadcast of Nasser's speech from al-Azhar mosque in Cairo. With all of the city turning out to the demonstrations, the people of the projects are ignored; 'They were truly prepared to sacrifice themselves for the country, but they were quite far away, on the margins of Alexandria, and no one would hear them on that day that they'd never forget.'[93]

The speech in question recalls Nasser's earlier speech in July 1956, delivered in Manshiya Square in Alexandria, in which he announced the nationalisation of the Suez Canal, leading to the attacks by Israel (with help from Britain and France) that are already underway at the start of the novel. Manshiya Square (formerly Muhammad Ali Square) with its lavish colonial architecture, elite commercial establishments and bordering French Gardens reappears a number of times throughout the novel, its transformation representing the broader transformation of Alexandrian society.[94] As Sulayman notes: 'Manshiya Square is Alexandria.'[95] Both Sulayman and Arabi take note of the changes to the square, the closed stores and the sense of desolation that come in the aftermath of the departure of the foreign communities from Egypt. And yet, as Starr argues, the square is representative of 'wealth and state power', both foreign and national.[96] Focusing on the scene in which the seamstress Abla Nargis and the young women of the projects cross the square, Starr notes that their interest in the removal and replacement of statues, from one regime to the next, speaks to the understanding of the square as signalling 'state structures, power and order' in both colonial and postcolonial contexts.[97] In both cases, it is a power that does little for the marginal inhabitants of the Project.

Abdel Meguid's work then writes against the marginalisation of the workers' communities of Alexandria and insists on their centrality to the narrative. Furthermore, if the question of 'What is Alexandria/Alexandrian?' is the underlying refrain of this trilogy, then the inhabitants of the Project are the ones that encourage an expansive definition of this question. One of the most compelling ways in which this is achieved is through the narrative of the spice seller Pepper, who tells numerous stories about his familial history.[98] Tracing his roots back seven centuries, Pepper tells his listeners of his grandfather, a renowned merchant, whose caravansary was 'filled with ambergris, safflower and all kinds of spice'.[99] Pepper's stories also educate the neighbourhood's men about the old trade routes and position Alexandria at the centre of an important commercial thoroughfare, while simultaneously suggesting the city's connection to the East as well as to Europe. It is from Pepper's tales that the novel itself acquires its name; in a fantastical tale we learn of his grandfather's quest for amber, 'the perfume of the princes'.[100] Hearing of the bird in the Maldives who emits amber, his grandfather moves to the island and awaits the magical creature. His quest, however, fails when massive winds blow his home away, forcing him to become a whale hunter in Oman instead (amber being a substance produced in the digestive system of sperm whales). And yet, at the end of the novel, Pepper himself decides to pursue the spice route. Having found old documents from the site of his family house, he describes his plan to his friend Sulayman:

> 'These documents have clear references to the Coast of Malabar, the western coast, the land of pepper, and the port of Calicut . . . For quite a long time now I have been longing to travel to India, the spiritual country. Imagine how much stronger the longing now that there is a treasure that I might obtain!'[101]

Like his tale of magical birds, Pepper's success is suspect. His importance lies in orienting, or reorienting, his city to other territories and possibilities. And this reorientation is achieved through the narration of fantastical tales that challenge the dominant narrative about Alexandria and its past.

If Pepper's expeditions suggest a connection between Alexandria and the Indian subcontinent, then Arabi's actions at the end of the novel reassert the Arab and Islamic identity of the city. In the aftermath of Katina's departure, Arabi decides that in these times he needs 'an Egyptian job, with Egyptians, in the midst of Egyptians'.[102] Eventually employed by the city's planning department, Arabi (whose name significantly means Arab) is tasked with renaming the streets of Alexandria, replacing the Greek and Italian names with 'the names of your people and your country'.[103] It is not until the very last street name that Arabi resists the exercise: 'Antar ibn Shaddad Street replacing Heracles Street. Heracles? He knows him. He's seen the movie at the Cinema Alhambra . . . He doesn't want to change this sign.'[104] Arabi's clever solution is then to Arabise the street, to fuse the Greek and the Arab, 'he also bought a small brush and added "h" to the "s" at the end and thus the name of the street became "Heraclesh Street" and he said to himself that now the street had become an Arab street!'[105] Once again, like in Pepper's excursion, the resistance to narrow articulations of national identity takes place on the geographical terrain, thus challenging and expanding what it means to be Alexandrian and by extension Egyptian. Abdel Meguid's critique of the postcolonial regime of Nasser is thus a critique of the limits of postcolonial national identity and the death of the ethno-religious diversity captured in *Birds of Amber*.

Clouds over Alexandria: The Intersection of the Religious and the National

The third and final installment of Abdel Meguid's Alexandrian trilogy takes place almost two decades later, at the start of 1975. While *Birds of Amber* is a work that writes against the exclusionary nationalism of Nasser's post-revolutionary regime, *Clouds over Alexandria* tackles the capitalist expansion and religious ideology that were the hallmarks of the Sadat era. Here too, the novelist pays careful attention to the physical transformation of the city, describing the explosion of construction that was to significantly alter the urban landscape, as well as the impact of the Islamic ideology upon the cultural and commercial landmarks of the city. What is at the centre of this narrative is not, however, the workers' projects but the university – this is reminiscent of Ashour's novel discussed in the previous chapter. In this work Abdel Meguid foregrounds Alexandria as a site of political mobilisation, and it is the group of university students and political activists who are at the heart of this novel. Here too, the focus is upon reclaiming the multiple and multifarious identities of the city and resisting the discourse that seeks to elevate Alexandria's Islamic identity above all else.

The Alexandria of *Clouds over Alexandria* is a city in the midst of rapid construction, fuelled by the 'Open Door' policies and the economic climate of the Sadat period. Much of this transformation is characterised by disorder and the absence of the rule of law; residents lay claim to abandoned land, and building occurs with little heed paid to zoning and permits.[106] We are told, for example, that in the southern part of the city in 'Sidi Bishr, al-Asafra, al-Mandara' people were selling or demolishing their summer homes to make way for houses or apartment blocks built 'with no order'.[107] These changes are also largely in response to the changing demographics of the city; the real estate sold and abandoned by the foreign communities whose exodus is documented in the earlier novel is not enough for the needs of the city's growing population, fuelled also by the 'invasion' of migrants from the Delta and the South.[108] Here, as in *No One Sleeps in Alexandria*, internal migration is key to the character of the city and serves to remind the reader of the connection between Alexandria and the rest of Egypt. While characters move through and experience an increasingly diverse array of spaces, much of the novel is anchored in the student apartment inhabited by Nader and Hasan. Located in the area of al-Ibrahimiyya, on al-Tanis Street, the students reside in what has come to be a red-light district, 'a school for teaching love and sex'.[109] Once again, masculinity and sexuality are intricately associated with political activity.

The capitalist expansion that encouraged the building of high-rises is accompanied by the rising influence of the Gulf States and the beginning of the influx of petro-dollars. This, in conjunction with the effects of the Islamic ideology embraced by Sadat, was to impact the social and commercial fabric of the city. (Of note, is the absence of the rise of Islamist ideology in the novels of al-Kharrat.) Throughout the novel, restaurants, night clubs and drinking establishments are closed and abandoned. Although some of these establishments were once owned by members of the Greek, Italian and Jewish communities compelled to leave in the 1950s, few still are. One such example is Bar al-Gaban (The Coward's Bar), whose owner, Matiakas the Greek, has not left Alexandria, but continues to call the city his home and runs his business in increasingly trying times. Our introduction to the bar is through ᶜIsa Salmawi, the communist and perpetual student, who seeks refuge from his loneliness amidst the patrons, all of whom are 'still as poor as they were'.[110] Enjoying the warmth and laughter ᶜIsa wonders why he does not come more often to spend time amongst 'the real spirit of the people'.[111] Deciding that he will 'watch, be happy, and be amazed' ᶜIsa sits back and enjoys 'a true Egyptian time'.[112] While there is no denying the problematic idealisation and essentialism that sustain this scene, ᶜIsa's experience of the bar and the deliberations it prompts are crucial to the commentary of the larger trilogy. First and foremost, that Matiakas the Greek is the orchestrator of the 'true Egyptian time' compels the reader to remember the other Egyptians forced to leave their city in the previous novel, and maintains Abdel Meguid's critique of the exclusionary policies, practices and discourses at the heart of the post-revolutionary national project. Furthermore, the bar is a space for recreation and entertainment for the lower and middle classes, one that is increasingly under threat in the current climate. ᶜIsa notes, as he leaves the bar heading to another establishment, that he wishes to look in on 'what remains of the middle class, soon to be crushed by the parasitic class of new money, in the age of *infitāḥ* [Open Door] inaugurated by the devout leader'.[113] His comments continue the mockery of Sadat's false religiosity instigated by the patrons of Bar al-Gaban, while also highlighting the violence of policies that helped the rich at the expense of the rest of the population.

Bar al-Gaban and Matiakas represent the diversity of Alexandria that has all but disappeared, but that continues to exist in the architectural landmarks of the city.[114] Throughout the novel, ʿIsa is consumed with reading, learning and observing as much as he can about Alexandria's rich and complicated past. His urban tours culminate at the cemeteries of al-Shatbi, the space, he insists, that 'preserves the history of Alexandria'.[115] In many ways it is as if the ethno-religious diversity that the entire trilogy tries to capture is distilled in the tombs of the city. As he tells his companion Bushr,

> There will come a day when I go with you to the old cemeteries of al-Shatbi, and to the Roman cemeteries of Raʾs al-Sawdaʾ. We will look even at the Muslim cemeteries in Qum al-Shaqafa that lie beside a rich historical area, as if declaring to the world that the history of Alexandria can't be separated by religion or ethnicity.[116]

The cemeteries, what Foucault called 'heterotopias', are the sublimation of the 'other city', the remnants of Alexandria's past that can no longer be incorporated nor can they be entirely cast out (not unlike the Jewish Quarter described in the previous novel).[117]

The impact of the transformation of the city is not just felt by the foreign communities. A central space in the novel is that of Nawal Boat, a restaurant and nightclub owned by the amateur singer Nawal. Interestingly, she is one of the few characters from *Birds of Amber* to appear in the final part of the trilogy. Trained as a nurse, Nawal's true aspiration is to become a singer in the cultural milieu of 1950s Alexandria. But her association with members of the Communist Party and her short-term imprisonment spell the end of her dreams. We encounter her in *Clouds over Alexandria* as a wealthy widow and proprietor of the nightclub where she often sings. It is also the establishment that the male communist students (Nader, Hassan and Bushr) frequent most often. Their friendship with Nawal, and their shared political vision, suggests that the significance of Nawal Boat extends beyond the recreational, and that like Bar al-Gaban it represents resistance against the transformation of the city. While Nawal Boat successfully staves off the advances of wealthy Gulf tycoons, who buy up its competitors and transform them into more 'reputable' establishments, it does not survive the end of the narrative. In the famous Bread Riots, the demonstrations that rage in response to Sadat's termination of state subsidies in January 1977, the Boat is burned and destroyed.

It is with the events of January 1977 that the trilogy culminates. If Aslan grants us a narrative of the Bread Riots from the vantage point of the working-class neighbourhood of Imbaba, then Abdel Meguid does so from the perspective of the students in Alexandria. Throughout the novel, Alexandria as a space of political mobilisation and possibility is enacted through the city's streets, squares and the university. It is the latter that dominates much of the narrative, with a great deal of the events unfolding within its environs. It is not only because the principal characters of the novel are students but also because Abdel Meguid is intent on capturing the forms of student organisation that dominate this period. The two couples – Nader and Yara, and Hassan and Kariman – join the underground Communist Party and engage in both public and covert forms of political mobilisation. It is in the university that they hang posters, distribute flyers and listen to ʿIsa's lectures. It is here too that they clash with security forces and their fellow students, many of whom have joined the 'Islamist groups'.[118] The university is connected to the rest of the city on the day of the riots with demonstrations spilling out beyond its gates, uniting students and workers. We are told how the demonstrators:

> take with them the workers from the Bata shoe company. And when they get close to the area of Mina al-Basal they take with them all the workers from the cotton mills, and the shipping companies. Behind them, far away, were the workers of the petrol, chemical, and cement companies who had also come from al-Maks. On the way the students from al-Wardiyan secondary school and Taher Bey Middle School joined them, and together they all headed to al-Manshiya square, crossing al-Sabaʾ Banat street.[119]

Once again, al-Manshiya Square takes centre stage and it is here that the confrontation comes to a head, becoming a 'center for freedom'.[120]

And yet the moment of possibility and change is short-lived; the demonstrations are shut down by the state security forces and dozens of demonstrators are arrested, among them Nader, Yara, Hassan and Kariman. Forced to marry against her will, Yara is isolated both from Nader and her friends. Hassan abandons Alexandria and Kariman for good. Tired of her abusive step-father, Kariman attempts suicide. The novel closes in the city's hospital, with a dejected Nader vowing to stay with Kariman as she recovers. By the end of the trilogy the clouds over Alexandria have not lifted.

How to Write a History of Alexandria?

Abdel Meguid's trilogy raises critical questions about genre; while not historical novels per se, it is a work which struggles with its own ability to capture the vast and manifold realities of twentieth-century Alexandria. This is most evident in the first installment, *No One Sleeps in Alexandria*, which took Abdel Meguid six years to write and is a heavily researched work, built upon what he refers to as '*tawthīq*', the process of gathering evidence; the author even spent time in the Western Desert visiting minefields in preparing for the task of writing.[121] While the trilogy follows a linear chronological progression of time, there exists a significant gap of about a decade in between each novel. Furthermore, with few exceptions, each novel deals with an entirely different set of characters. While each work can be read independently, the success of Abdel Meguid's project of writing the modern history of Alexandria depends on engagement with all three novels.

This ambitious project leads Abdel Meguid to draw on a capacious set of sources; all three novels are brimming with the history, literature, art and music that both creates and recreates Alexandria. In *No One Sleeps in Alexandria* Abdel Meguid begins each chapter with an anonymous epigraph; citations include ancient Egyptian proverbs, Jalal al-Din al-Rumi, Lawrence Durrell, Egyptian folk songs and Coptic prayers. If, as stated earlier, this novel insists on a diversity that is more complex than the idealised cosmopolitanism of the 1940s, then the reader is reminded of this with every new chapter. It is worth noting that the original Arabic text (unlike the English translation) does not identify the source of each epigraph until the end of the novel. Listing his sources, Abdel Meguid explains his decision to exclude the names from the text, so as not to break the 'continuity of the narrative'.[122] This also achieves an equivalence of sources such that folk songs are as valuable in the telling of the history of Alexandria as the work of famous poets.

Much of Abdel Meguid's material is embedded in the narrative itself, with similarities and echoes across the three works. In both the second and third installment of the trilogy countless song lyrics and lines of poetry are quoted. In *Birds of Amber*, the girls who gather at the home of Abla Nargis listen to the radio and sing along to the songs of the musical sensations of the time: Muhammad Fawzi, Abdel Halim Hafez, Shadia, Umm Kulthum, to name just a few. In *Clouds over Alexandria*, both the international pop music of the 1970s and the Arabic songs of the period are heard in the bars and nightclubs. Songs also animate the demonstrations and are sung in the prisons; the words of Sheikh Imam and Sayyid Darwish reverberate throughout the novel.[123] In an interview with the Iraqi writer Jabbar Yassin, Abdel Meguid notes that music is a central component to many of his works, constituting something of a language within the novel.[124] In *No One Sleeps in Alexandria*, it is not poetry but Muslim and Coptic prayers that are interwoven throughout the narrative. And so it is that the three works both contain and create an extensive archive of Alexandria that tries to come to terms with the heterogeneity of the urban experience.

Fundamental to Abdel Meguid's narrative is the incorporation of the monumental and the mundane, and thus throughout the trilogy the reader is aware of the interplay between the local and the global. The opening of *No One Sleeps in Alexandria* is telling in this respect. We begin with the description of Hitler, pacing in his office, deliberating about a decision that will irrevocably alter the world. At the same time, Magd al-Din is spending his last night in his village, before fleeing it for good – a decision that will irrevocably alter his world. And this movement between the consequential and the seemingly trivial continues throughout the trilogy. One of the principal ways in which this is achieved is through the newspaper reports that Abdel Meguid weaves throughout the chapters, what the author calls the 'records of life' as opposed to the 'historical records'.[125] With no indication of this switch, other than in the change of tone and content, the third person narrator of the trilogy turns away from the characters and towards recounting the 'news'. The news segments in the novels include everything from international events and national news, to local incidents. These are reported alongside, and with the same emphasis, as the latest film releases, gossip about actors and singers, and the census of birth and deaths in Alexandria. The news segments serve as a frame and a commentary upon Abdel Meguid's characters, whose everyday adventures are not catalogued in newspapers or history books.[126]

The news reports are dominated by the world of film. In fact, the entire trilogy is obsessed with cataloguing the movie theatres of Alexandria and the movie releases of the period. The theatres are a part of the architectural and cultural landscape of the city that Abdel Meguid wishes to preserve, part of a world which is transforming.[127] Many if not all of them have long since vanished. Characters in the novels are constantly going to movies, discussing the latest releases, walking past posters of the stars. Mahmud in *Birds of Amber* is an aspiring filmmaker, often citing Youssef Chahine as his greatest influence and guide. Chahine, the Alexandrian film maker par excellence, is arguably involved in a similar project to Abdel Meguid (and al-Kharrat), though in a different medium.[128] Cinema becomes another form of cosmopolitan experience, an exploration of diversity and difference, even as the diversity of Alexandria is increasingly threatened. It is also an experience that is available to a plethora of the trilogy's characters and not just the elite; the grand opulent theatres of the city appear alongside the second- or third-rate establishments frequented by the city's poorer inhabitants.

Abdel Meguid's trilogy also directly engages with the production and purpose of narrative and literature. Sulayman, the young student and aspiring writer from the workers' project, deliberates throughout *Birds of Amber* about how best to write a history of his city. Promoted by the departure of his love, the British woman Jean Bancroft, Sulayman turns to writing to deal with the rapidly changing world that surrounds him. Abandoning his initial idea to tell the story of Alexandria through the life of a famous singer, he decides instead to focus on the lives of the inhabitants of the Project; 'He has kept a record of many things that were happening, so why shouldn't that be his real material'.[129] Sulayman's project thus mirrors Abdel Meguid's (and echoes the words uttered by our protagonists in the Cairo novels), ensuring that the reader is constantly reminded of the construction of the narrative at hand. At several moments Sulayman intervenes in his own narrative, explaining his choices to his reader and drawing attention once again to his role as creator. He also reports on the latest local and international news, taking over the role of the news segments that proliferate in the novels. The most remarkable of Sulayman's writings is the story he pens towards the end of *Birds of Amber*, what he calls 'A Surrealistic Story' in which the Indian actor Sabu leads elephants through the city of Alexandria.¹³⁰ Sulayman, like Abdel Meguid himself, brings together the ordinary and the extraordinary, the mundane and the fantastical, in his narrative rendering of Alexandria.

Sulayman is not the only writer to take centre stage in the trilogy; Nader in *Clouds Over Alexandria* is an aspiring poet, who like Sulayman considers writing a novel about the city, though we are not informed whether he goes through with his plan. In discussing this with his girlfriend Yara, Nader claims that 'If I wrote stories like Hassan [their friend and comrade] I would write a novel about the Second World War and would have a hero named Rushdi'.¹³¹ This is of course a self-referential nod to Abdel Meguid's own novel, the opening work of the trilogy which features a character with the same name. Nader revisits this idea after his release from prison when, unable to describe his experience to ʿIsa, he remarks that maybe one day he will write about it instead. When Nader's political activities take him to Cairo, he encounters the cultural milieu of the capital. There he meets Faruq Abdel Qadir, the editor of the journal *al-Taliʿa*; the famous writers Amal Dunqul, Naguib Surur and Sulayman Fayyad; and visits Café Riche and the Madbuli bookstore. These episodes remind the reader of the position of dominance long held by Cairo as the cultural capital of Egypt. To succeed within the literary and cultural sphere, writers like Abdel Meguid, al-Kharrat, and others have in fact made the capital their home. After his release from prison and his discovery of Yara's marriage, Nader contemplates making this move himself; 'Everything around him has become a wasteland . . . Alexandria is a wasteland. A wasteland wherever he goes . . . He must leave Alexandria now . . . Cairo is the destiny of writers, artists, and political activists.'¹³² And yet it is not Nader who decides to leave Alexandria but Hassan, whose departure contributes (albeit unintentionally) to Kariman's demise. Nader decides to remain in the wasteland that his city has become, and it is with his lines of poetry that the entire trilogy comes to an end:

If you write our story
You write with it the story of the city

You will not write the story of the city
while you are in it
And if you find me
You will never write our story
Never ever.[133]

Abdel Meguid's trilogy thus closes with a reflection on the impossibility of capturing the story of self and city.

Conclusion

To read the trilogies of al-Kharrat and Abdel Meguid is to encounter the city of Alexandria with its complicated and entangled histories; not interested in merely celebrating a cosmopolitan nostalgia so long associated with the city, the writers instead engage with the multifarious and often conflicting identities of the city. For both writers Alexandria is at once colonial, cosmopolitan, Arab, Muslim, Coptic, European and Egyptian. In contending with this panoply of pasts and presents, both trilogies expand the existing archive of the city. Al-Kharrat's novels are not to be seen as discrete pieces in a larger trilogy but must be read collectively. That the events, descriptions, recollections and musings are repeated, reformulated and recomposed across the three works requires such a reading. As such al-Kharrat recreates the workings of individual memory for the purposes of collective recollection. Abdel Meguid's trilogy is perhaps more easily read as separate novels that fit a linear chronology. And yet in expanding the narrative material of the trilogy, and thus engaging with the local and the global, the exceptional and the everyday, Abdel Meguid also reimagines the contours of the Alexandrian novel. In both cases the writers move us beyond both the representation of the city as a cosmopolitan haven so long celebrated by Western writers, and a city subordinate to the capital, as found in Egyptian literature. Rather, both writers unsettle the time and space of the realist narrative in reimagining the urban narrative of Alexandria.

Notes

1. Al-Kharrat, *Iskandariyyati*, p. 1.
2. Abdel Meguid, *No One Sleeps in Alexandria*, p. 19.

3. Several notable works explore the relationship between the colonial and the cosmopolitan within the context of Alexandria. See, for example, Starr, *Remembering Cosmopolitan Egypt*; Halim, *Alexandrian Cosmopolitanism*; and Salameh, *Nom de Lieu*.
4. This can be read against the vast literary and historical material that focuses first and foremost on the foreign communities, for example, the work of Lawrence Durrell, E. M. Forster and Constantine P. Cavafy. See also Haag, *Alexandria* and Tzalas, *Farewell to Alexandria*.
5. Al-Kharrat, *Iskandariyyati*, p. 6. Halim, in her exploration of what she describes as the archive of Alexandrian cosmopolitanism, reads against the grain to show that while al-Kharrat's declaration may indeed be true, there are instances of resistance in the cosmopolitanism of Durrell, Cavafy, and others. Halim, *Alexandrian Cosmopolitanism*, p. 53.
6. Al-Kharrat, *Iskandariyyati*, p. 6.
7. *Miramar* showcases much of the stylistic transformation evident in Mahfouz's work from the early 1960s onwards: the departure from realism, the breakdown of the linearity of narrative time, and use of stream of consciousness. Earlier examples of this include *al-Liss wa-l-Kilab* (1961) and *Tharthara Fawq al-Nil* (1966).
8. Halim, *Alexandrian Cosmopolitanism*, p. 19. In the work of both writers Halim sees what she terms 'contrapuntal cosmopolitanism' in the Saidian sense.
9. I cite from the English translations of *City of Saffron* and *Girls of Alexandria*. The translations from *Iskandariyyati: Madinati al-Qudsiyya al-Hushiyya; Kulaj Riwaʾi* (My Alexandria: My Sacred Strange City: A Narrative Collage) are my own. The titles of the first two installments *Turabuha Zaʿfaran* (literally: Its Dust is Saffron) and *Ya Banat Iskandariyya* (literally: Oh, Girls of Alexandria) are taken from popular songs about Alexandria. See Halim [Youssef], 'The Alexandrian Archive', p. 302.
10. Mikhael also appears in *Rama wa-l-Tinin, al-Zaman al-Akhar* and *Yaqin al-ʿAtash*, which form their own trilogy.
11. Calvino, 'Italo Calvino On *Invisible Cities*', p. 41.
12. Halim [Youssef], 'The Alexandrian Archive', p. 301. I cite place names, like Gheit el-Enab as they appear in the English translation to avoid confusion.
13. Abdel Hakim, *Madinat al-Iskandariyya*, pp. 372–3.
14. Al-Kharrat, *City of Saffron*, p. 1.
15. Al-Kharrat, *Girls of Alexandria*, p. 1. It is interesting to note that the translator Frances Liardet chooses to leave the words *shāriʿ* and *hāret* in Arabic and

explain them in the glossary. Perhaps this is to suggest the Arabic names of streets, neighbourhoods and alleys as remembered by Mikhael. It also refers to geographical knowledge particular to natives of the city.

16. Al-Kharrat, *Iskandariyyati*, p. 21.
17. De Certeau, *The Practice of Everyday Life*, p. xxi.
18. Al-Kharrat, *Iskandariyyati*, p. 145. In describing the heart of downtown Alexandria and its mercantile centre, Abdel Hakim describes a map strikingly similar to the route that Mikhael undertakes in the novel. Abdel Hakim, *Madinat al-Iskandariyya*, p. 355. This is like the tram route described by Abdel Meguid later in this chapter.
19. Hanley, 'Foreignness and Localness in Alexandria', p. 24.
20. Al-Kharrat, *Girls of Alexandria*, p. 73.
21. Significant immigration to Alexandria had begun under the Ottomans in approximately the 1850s and included people from North Africa, the Levant, Europe and the Mediterranean. Robert Mabro distinguishes between a 'foreign national' such as those of European descent and 'non-Egyptian locals' who were of Ottoman descent. Mabro further analyses the different members of the groups based on patterns, eligibility, and desire for integration into Alexandrian and Egyptian society. See Mabro, 'Alexandria 1860–1960', p. 247. For more on the history of foreign communities in the city, see also Haag, *Alexandria* and Tzalas, *Farewell to Alexandria*.
22. Al-Kharrat, *Girls of Alexandria*, p. 33.
23. Al-Kharrat, *City of Saffron*, p. 87. For an extensive discussion of this scene and the significance of the exchange of food in the novel, see Halim [Youssef], 'The Alexandrian Archive', pp. 306–11.
24. Al-Kharrat argues against representing the Coptic environment as separate from the Egyptian one and thus rendering it a 'ghetto'. By extension there is no 'Coptic literature' for al-Kharrat, nor does he see himself as a 'Coptic Writer'. In rejecting this designation, he poses the question: 'Why don't we ask Naguib Mahfouz: Why do you write "Islamic Literature?"' Al-Kharrat, 'La Yujad Adab Qibti Muᶜasar', p. 101. In another essay, in the same collection, al-Kharrat critiques Lawrence Durrell's rendering of the Copts in his work as traitors and collaborators with the Zionists. Al-Kharrat, 'Lawrence Durrell Sammim ᶜAlam al-Iskandariyya bi-Baraᶜa', pp. 255–60.
25. Al-Kharrat, *Girls of Alexandria*, p. 158. This description reoccurs in *Iskandariyyati*, p. 126.
26. Al-Kharrat, *City of Saffron*, p. 142.

27. Ibid. p. 153.
28. Ibid. p. 155.
29. Al-Kharrat, *Girls of Alexandria*, p. 30.
30. Between 1937 and 1960 the percentage of the Alexandria population who were 'foreign nationals' dropped from 12.9% to 2.9%. Mabro, 'Alexandria 1860–1960', p. 248. While the departure of some groups, such as the Greek, Maltese and Italians, dates to the 1930s there is certainly an increased exodus following the revolution and as a result of Nasser's policies of nationalisation which meant that many Levantine, Greek and Armenian families saw their businesses and properties sequestered. For the Jewish population of Alexandria, the Arab-Israeli wars of 1948, 1956 and 1967 increasingly led to heightened tensions, incidents of violence and the community's departure. See Mabro, 'Alexandria 1860–1960', pp. 247–62.
31. Al-Kharrat, *Iskandariyyati*, p. 179.
32. Ibid. p. 78.
33. These examples are taken from a long descriptive cataloguing of the many loves of Mikhael and his friends. This section, which unfolds over many pages, appears in *Girls of Alexandria* (pp. 97–103) and then again in *Iskandariyyati* (pp. 188–91). It is not unusual for events and descriptions from the first two novels to reappear in the third installment, *Iskandariyyati*. For more on the intertextuality of his work, see Ostle, 'From Intertext to Mixed Media: The Case of Edwar al-Kharrat', and Starkey, 'Intertexuality and the Arabic Literary Tradition in Edwar al-Kharrat's *Stones of Bobello*'.
34. In the Arabic original the hymn is a celebration of language that, as translator Frances Liardet notes in his introduction, is full of 'sound and color' and in which every word alliterates with the letter *nūn* (n), the letter that signals the feminine ending. Another hymn, the hymn of *mīm* (m) appears in the following chapter. Liardet, 'Introduction', p. x. For the Arabic original, see Al-Kharrat, *Turabuha Zaʿfaran*, pp. 168–71, 192–3.
35. This appears in the opening of the novel *Girls of Alexandria*, before the first chapter, as an epigraph.
36. Halim, 'Forster in Alexandria', p. 237.
37. Al-Kharrat, *Girls of Alexandria*, p. 25.
38. Al-Kharrat, *City of Saffron*, p. 46.
39. Interestingly, there are also scenes of masturbation that recall my discussion of Sonallah Ibrahim's protagonist in Chapter 1. Marlé Hammond suggests that the scene between Mikhael and Nuris Fakhri in *Girls of Alexandria* is a

scene of masturbation in which the former is imagining and fantasising about the latter. Here too then is an example of individual sexual activity, though in this instance it can be read as an attempt to imagine and unite with the other. Hammond, 'Subsuming the Feminine Other', pp. 44–5.
40. Al-Kharrat, *Girls of Alexandria*, p. 71.
41. Ibid. p. 103.
42. Al-Noweihi, 'Memory and Imagination in Edwar al-Kharrat's *Turābuhā Zaʿfarān*', p. 52. See also Hammond, 'Subsuming the Feminine Other'.
43. Hammond, 'Subsuming the Feminine Other', p. 42.
44. Ibid. p. 39.
45. Al-Kharrat, *Girls of Alexandria*, p. 107.
46. Al-Kharrat, *City of Saffron*, p. xiv.
47. Al-Kharrat, *Iskandariyyati*, p. 158.
48. Ibid. p. 128.
49. The desire to unsettle the decisive boundaries between genres is part of al-Kharrat's larger literary project and is at the heart of his critical study *al-Kitaba ʿAbr al-Nawʿiyya* (1994) in which he focuses on 'al-qiṣṣa-al-qaṣīda' (the poem-story).
50. Ostle documents al-Kharrat's artistic collaborations with artists Ahmad Mursi and ʿAdil Rizqallah. He also notes how al-Kharrat takes his 'desire for confusion of the arts' even further, citing the art exhibition that al-Kharrat put on in December 2004 at the Hanager Art Center in Cairo. Ostle, 'From Intertext to Mixed Media', pp. 148, 146.
51. Al-Noweihi, 'Memory and Imagination in Edwar al-Kharrat's *Turābuhā Zaʿfarān*', p. 34.
52. I cite from the English translations *No One Sleeps in Alexandria* and *Birds of Amber*. The translations of *al-Iskandariyya fi Ghayma* are my own. I take the translation of the title as *Clouds over Alexandria* as used by the International Prize for Arabic Fiction, for which the novel was nominated in 2014.
53. Adagio won the first Katara Prize for the Arabic Novel in 2015. Abdel Meguid was criticised by some in the Egyptian cultural field for accepting a prize administered by Qatar. The Katara Prize is not, as the author was sure to point out, 'presented by the Qatari Ministry of Culture'. Abdel Meguid, quoted in Tewfiq, 'A Prize with a View'.
54. This may be intended to recall the rural peasant migrant Zuhra from Mahfouz's Alexandria novel *Miramar*, who also leaves her village for the city, this time to better her situation. While Zuhra is central to Mahfouz's novel she is not given

her own voice and heard only through the voices of the male characters. This is not the case with Abdel Meguid's Zahra, whose perspective on Alexandria and its inhabitants is central to the narrative.

55. Abdel Meguid quotes from Lorca's poem directly at the start of chapter sixteen. Lorca's poetry was influential upon the work of Arab poets and writers particularly in the 1950s and 1960s, not least because he considered himself an Andalusian poet, whose own work drew on the poets of Muslim Spain. Though he never aligned himself with any political group, he displayed a social and political awareness and a revolutionary spirit that contributed to his assassination by Francisco Franco's forces in 1936. His political commitment was also celebrated by Arab writers and poets. For more on Lorca's influence upon Arab modernist poets, and a reading of a number of poems specifically devoted to Lorca, see El-Enany, 'Poets and Rebels', pp. 252–64; and al-Musawi, *Arabic Poetry*, pp. 144–6.
56. See, for example, Halim, *Alexandrian Cosmopolitanism* and Rowlandson and Harker, 'Roman Alexandria from the Perspective of the Papyri'.
57. Fahmy, 'Towards a Social History of Modern Alexandria', p. 282. Fahmy proposes an alternative historiography (not unlike Abdel Meguid's literary one) by examining the Mahmudiyya Canal, the dockyard and the Quarantine Board, in order to focus upon the interaction between foreigners and Egyptians in nineteenth-century Alexandria.
58. Hanley, 'Foreignness and Localness in Alexandria', p. 1.
59. Starr, *Remembering Cosmopolitan Egypt*, p. 23.
60. Abdel Meguid, in Jamal al-ʿArdawi (dir.), 'Ibrahim Abdel Meguid . . . al-Iskandariyya . . . Ayna?'
61. Abdel Meguid, *No One Sleeps in Alexandria*, p. 114. Abdel Meguid's father worked for the railroad for much of his life. He is also, according to the author, the partial impetus for writing a novel about Alexandria during the Second World War. Abdel Meguid recalls that his father regularly told stories of the war throughout his childhood. See Abdel Meguid, 'Ibrahim Abdel Meguid . . . al-Iskandariyya . . . Ayna?'
62. Fahmy, 'Towards a Social History of Modern Alexandria', pp. 283–4. Fahmy notes that thousands of labourers from Lower Egypt were forced to work on the construction of the canal, with reports of casualties as high as 100,000.
63. Starr, *Remembering Cosmopolitan Egypt*, p. 59. Another example of this is the love story between the Muslim Rushdi and the Christian Camilla. Forced apart by their families, Camilla eventually joins a convent and is blessed with

the power of healing, while Rushdi decides to travel to France after the end of the war.
64. The term khawaga (*khawāga*) was used to refer to foreign residents of Egypt, particularly those from Europe and the Levant.
65. Abdel Meguid, *No One Sleeps in Alexandria*, p. 33.
66. Ibid. p. 39.
67. Ibid. p. 133.
68. Ibid. p. 132.
69. Ibid. p. 343.
70. Qur'an, Sura 55:14–15.
71. Abdel Meguid, *No One Sleeps in Alexandria*, pp. 343–4.
72. Abdel Meguid, *La Ahad Yanam fi al-Iskandariyya*, pp. 449–50. This is unfortunately lost in the English translation.
73. Abdel Meguid, *Birds of Amber*, pp. 37–8.
74. Ibid. p. 3.
75. Ibid. p. 3.
76. The characters in *Birds of Amber* are not primarily engaged in political activity. The main exception is Nawal, the nurse and aspiring singer, who is introduced to a group of writers and artists with communist leanings. After singing at their private New Year's Eve celebration, Nawal discovers that the group has been arrested. Her arrest follows soon after and her time in prison leads to the ruin of her voice and the end of her dreams of singing for the Egyptian Radio. Her politicisation is taken up in the following novel – Nawal being one of the only characters to reappear in the trilogy. Karawan also participates in political demonstrations in the novel.
77. Abdel Meguid, *Birds of Amber*, p. 105.
78. Ibid. p. 105.
79. Ibid. p. 106.
80. Much is made in the novel, for example, of the Greeks support of Nasser during the Suez Crisis of 1956. See also Fahmy, 'For Cavafy, With Love and Squalor', p. 278.
81. Abdel Meguid, *Birds of Amber*, p. 112.
82. Ibid. p. 112.
83. Ibid. p. 330.
84. The atelier is contrasted to the home of the seamstress Abla Nargis, where the girls from the Project convene on a nightly basis to sew, listen to the radio and socialise. The group includes Muslims, Christians and Jews, and is not unlike

Khawaga Dimitri's building in the first novel of the trilogy. The apartment as female space cannot, however, shelter the girls from the turbulent transformations of the time. By the end of the novel the group has been dispersed as a result of unhappy marriages, departure from the city, and even imprisonment.

85. Moore, 'Between Cosmopolitanism and Nationalism', p. 889.
86. Abdel Meguid, *Birds of Amber*, p. 261
87. Ibid. p. 261.
88. Ibid. p. 262.
89. Ibid. pp. 262–3.
90. Moore, 'Between Cosmopolitanism and Nationalism', p. 887.
91. Abdel Meguid, *Birds of Amber*, p. 263.
92. Ibid. p. 178.
93. Ibid. p. 51.
94. Manshiyya also appears in al-Kharrat's trilogy. See, for example, *City of Saffron*, p. 107. For more on the history and transformation of Manshiyya, see Halim, *Alexandrian Cosmopolitanism*, pp. 124–5; and Moore, 'Between Cosmopolitanism and Nationalism'.
95. Abdel Meguid, *Birds of Amber*, p. 91.
96. Starr, 'Recuperating Cosmopolitan Alexandria', p. 225.
97. Ibid. p. 225.
98. Farouk Abdel Wahab translates the Arabic *Filfil* more literally as 'Ground Pepper'.
99. Abdel Meguid, *Birds of Amber*, p. 90. Starr objects to Abdel Wahab's translation of the Arabic ʿ*anbar* into the English 'amber', noting that it also means ambergris. She also notes that Abdel Meguid distinguishes between *kahramān* (amber) and ʿ*anbar* (ambergris). It is also true that it is ambergris (and not amber) that is produced from the secretion of the intestines of whales. Starr, *Remembering Cosmopolitan Egypt*, p. 165 (note 26).
100. Abdel Meguid, *Birds of Amber*, p. 212.
101. Ibid. p. 403.
102. Ibid. p. 373.
103. Ibid. p. 376.
104. Ibid. p. 376.
105. Ibid. p. 377.
106. This is not unlike what Ibrahim Aslan depicts in *The Heron*.
107. Abdel Meguid, *al-Iskandariyya fi Ghayma*, p. 79. Translations are my own.
108. Ibid. p. 9.

109. Ibid. p. 49.
110. Ibid. p. 133.
111. Ibid. p. 136.
112. Ibid. p. 136.
113. Ibid. p. 139. Sadat was known as '*al-Raʾīs al-Muʾmin*' (The Devout President) and actively propagated his religiosity as a central component to his leadership.
114. It also exists in the private space of the home. An extended description of Yara's bedroom, early in the novel, catalogues the origins of each piece of furniture, listing the various streets and neighbourhoods from which each piece was purchased. Abdel Meguid, *al-Iskandariyya fī Ghayma*, pp. 11–12.
115. Abdel Meguid, *al-Iskandariyya fī Ghayma*, p. 224.
116. Ibid. p. 232.
117. Foucault, 'Of Other Spaces', p. 25.
118. Abdel Meguid, *al-Iskandariyya fī Ghayma*, p. 26.
119. Ibid. p. 336.
120. Ibid. p. 347.
121. Abdel Meguid, in Jamal al-ʿArdawi (dir), 'Ibrahim Abdel Meguid . . . La Ahad Yanam fi al-Riwaya'.
122. Abdel Meguid, *La Ahad Yanam fī al-Iskandariyya*, p. 365.
123. Sheikh Imam (1918–95) was a famous Egyptian singer and composer, known for his collaboration with the colloquial poet Ahmad Fouad Negm. Together they wrote, composed and sang songs of the struggles of the poor and working class. They were particularly popular in the 1960s and 1970s amongst leftists and revolutionaries. Sayyid Darwish (1892–1923), a native of Alexandria from the Qum al-Dikka neighbourhood, was a singer and composer known for great innovations in classical Arabic music. He too was committed to the political struggle and the anti-colonial movements of the early twentieth century. He composed '*Bilādī Bilādī*' (My Country, My Country) which became Egypt's National Anthem. See Staff Writers, 'The Legacy of the Late Sheikh Imam, Creator of Modern Arabic Political Song'; Salloum, 'Sayyed Darwish, The Father of Modern Arab Music'; and Goldschmidt Jnr, 'Darwish, Sayyid', p. 47.
124. Abdel Meguid, in Jamal al-ʿArdawi (dir.), 'Ibrahim Abdel Meguid . . . al-Iskandariyya . . . Ayna?'
125. Ibid.
126. The impetus to construct an alternative history through the incorporation of newspaper sources is not unlike the project under taken by Sonallah Ibrahim in *Dhat* (*Zaat*, 1992).

127. Abdel Meguid, in Jamal al-ʿArdawi (dir.), 'Ibrahim Abdel Meguid . . . al-Iskandariyya . . . Ayna?'
128. Chahine's *Iskandariyya Lih* (*Alexandria Why*, 1979), *Hadduta Misriyya* (*An Egyptian Tale*, 1982), *Iskandariyya Kaman wa Kaman* (*Alexandria Again and Forever*, 1989) and *Iskandariyya . . . New York* (*Alexandria, New York*, 2004) span the period from the 1940s until the early 2000s. Here too, Chahine manipulates chronological time, includes archival footage in the feature films, and blurs the lines between autobiography and fiction. For more on the trilogy, see Halim, 'Alexandria Re-inscribed', and 'On Being an Alexandrian'; Starr, 'Why New York?: Youssef Chahine'; Anishchenkova, 'Visions of Self'; and Massad, 'Art and Politics in the Cinema of Youssef Chahine'.
129. Abdel Meguid, *Birds of Amber*, p. 215.
130. Starr, *Recuperating Cosmopolitan Alexandria*, p. 226. Starr reads this story as 'a recovery of the repressed postcolonial subject (Sabu acting out) and repressed sexuality (the acting out of sexual fantasies)'. Starr, *Recuperating Cosmopolitan Alexandria*, p. 227.
131. Abdel Meguid, *al-Iskandariyya fi Ghayma*, p. 72.
132. Ibid. pp. 402–3.
133. Ibid. pp. 454–5.

3

Re-imagining the Rural: The Mystical and the Mythical

I am the son of the village and I will remain that way.
Yahya Taher Abdullah[1]

From here the center of my life became rediscovering my village.
Abd al-Hakim Qasim[2]

If a great number of the writers of the sixties generation chose urban environments as the setting of their novels, this does not mean that the Egyptian countryside disappeared from the narrative landscape. Quite the contrary in fact: the writers of this generation reimagined the rural in new and captivating ways. Abd al-Hakim Qasim, Yusuf al-Qaid and Yahya Taher Abdullah all produce novels that are situated in the Egyptian countryside, focusing on a rural world that is harsh and severe, the site of suffering and difficulty for the peasant population. Abd al-Hakim Qasim's *Ayyam al-Insan al-Sabᶜa* (*The Seven Days of Man*, 1969), Yusuf al-Qaid's *Akhbar ᶜIzbat al-Minisi* (News from the Minisi Farm, 1971) and Yahya Taher Abdullah's *al-Tawq wa-l-Iswira* (*The Collar and the Bracelet*, 1975) take place in villages that are isolated from the rest of the country, peripheral spaces, forgotten by the centres of power, ignored by the urban metropolises of Cairo and Alexandria.

The three writers foreground the villages from which they themselves hailed.[3] Qasim locates his narrative in a small village close to Tanta, in the Egyptian Delta. Al-Qaid, also from the Delta, sets his novel in the village of al-Dahriyya, in the governate of al-Bihira, the place of his birth and childhood. Abdullah, noteworthy as one of the few writers to write about the villages of the South, chooses al-Karnak, the site of the ancient city of Thebes, in Upper Egypt (al-Saᶜid). All three writers represent examples of rural intellectuals whose narrative worlds stand outside the spatial and temporal parameters of the nation, operating within their own cycles of repetition, in works that undermine the time and space of the realist novel. They do this at a time when novelists largely did not focus on rural space. Muhammad Siddiq attributes this to the centrality of Cairo in the 1960s, stating that 'any conjecture about this phenomenon must take into account the high political drama unfolding in the capital Cairo, at the center of which for better or worse was always the towering image of Nasser'.[4] In representing marginal spaces ignored by the centres of power and outside the sphere of revolutionary possibility, all three writers bring the oral tradition to bear upon their textual practice. Qasim recreates the time and space of mystical Sufi ritual; al-Qaid undermines the official discourse of the state with the memories and musings of the villagers; and Abdullah creates a novel in the form of folkloric tales from the oral tradition. The shift in space, from the urban to the rural, brings with it a shift in narrative devices and in the attitude towards the role of the writer.

These writers bring the Egyptian village to the fore at a time when the rural question – and particularly agrarian land reforms, 'an example of state-sponsored projects originating at the center' – dominated the political and economic climate.[5] This is not to suggest that agrarian reform was not part of the political discourse in the years preceding the revolution; reformists had advocated programmes for change throughout the first half of the twentieth century in response to growing disturbances in the countryside.[6] But agricultural reform and the redistribution of land became a fundamental tenant of the post-revolutionary Nasserist regime, and were framed under the rubric of 'the social revolution'. The first agrarian reform law initiated by Nasser in 1952 targeted large landowners, limiting the land ownership of both individuals and families. Individual ownership could not exceed two hundred feddans, while an additional one hundred feddans was approved for a family with two or more children.[7] Expropriated land was parcelled out amongst small farmers, not divided amongst the landless peasants. The agrarian reforms were implemented gradually until, in 1969, the limit was set at fifty feddans per individual, or one hundred per family.[8] While these policies were initially intended to 'maintain equity through redistribution', the Nasserist regime failed to raise the necessary revenues and chose not to further burden the dominant class, instead 'maintain[ing] social peace by sacrificing equity'.[9] The reforms instituted during this period thus 'failed to satisfy the expectations of the peasant masses' and what was witnessed instead was 'a rise in the influence of rich and middle-class peasants'.[10] By the time of Nasser's death in 1970,

> the 'feudal' landowners had been swept away through successive land reforms, but there were still millions of landless peasants and about half the agricultural surface was still farmed by tenants. A new kind of capitalism, state capitalism as some call it, had taken over the power structure of the country and instituted monopolies in the name of the people in several domains. The distribution of income remained sharply skewed, absolute poverty probably continued to involve most of Egypt's population, and disease and illiteracy were only marginally eroded.[11]

This trend was extended under Sadat who instituted policies of desequestration to the detriment of small peasants.[12] Throughout the decade of the 1970s, food deficits grew, and land fragmentation, dwarf-holdings, rural poverty and landlessness all increased.[13] The agrarian reforms remained limited in scope and the focus on the rural question failed to improve the lives of the peasant population.

The three novels are thus significant for their spatial shifts and can be read in contrast to the social realist works of the previous generation, for example, Abdel Rahman al-Sharqawi's classic novel *al-Ard* (The Land, 1954).[14] This work, arguably *the* village novel of this earlier period, is replete with descriptions of the fields, the land and the toil of the rural workers. While the author presents an unromantic view of rural life, aware of the hardships the peasants must endure, he concentrates on the possibility of revolutionary struggle; the peasants are able to mobilise against the power of the government that imposes itself upon their lives. The 'land' of the title, representative of the larger Egyptian countryside, serves a metaphoric purpose, as a symbol of the Egyptian nation. It is also the focus of the entire novel as the villagers band together to fight both the landowners and the state for control over their land and access to crucial water sources.[15] *Al-Ard*, published only two years after the 1952 revolution, expresses a moment of optimism and opportunity. Set in the 1930s, the novel presents the rural as the space of political transformation and change, the heart of the fight for social reform and justice during the colonial period (and beyond) in Egypt.

It is this within this context that Qasim, al-Qaid and Abdullah produce their rural novels, works which provide truncated descriptions of the village. The move away from the social realist depictions of the countryside, and the alternative spatial representations that emerge, articulate a disillusionment with the policies of the state, and the recognition of the ongoing marginalisation of the rural populations of Egypt. The three writers recast the village as a mythical and magical space that stands apart from the nation and the transformative possibilities of political mobilisation and change. In reading the novels in this way, I suggest that while the authors are indeed articulating their own sense of alienation or existential crisis, a hallmark of their generation – as has been argued by scholars such as Muhsin al-Musawi, Samah Selim, Samia Mehrez and Muhammad Dhannun al-Sa'igh – they are also drawing attention to the division, separation and marginalisation of their rural communities, despite the hopes of the post-revolutionary period.[16] The failed policies of agricultural reform and land redistribution, and the absence of meaningful political and economic transformation within the context of social revolution are ultimately laid bare.

The Struggle for Survival: Rural Life in *The Seven Days of Man*

Abd al-Hakim Qasim's first novel *The Seven Days of Man* is a complex and moving work built around the practices of Sufi ritual. Set in a small village near the city of Tanta in the Egyptian Delta, the novel describes the week leading up to the annual pilgrimage to the shrine of Sayyid Badawi (spelt Bedawi in the translation), one of the foremost Sufi saints in Egypt. Told from the perspective of the young Abdel-Aziz – the son of Hagg Karim, the leader of the Sufi brotherhood in the village – the narrative follows two threads simultaneously, the ritual practices that take place throughout the week and the maturation of the young Abdel-Aziz. Each chapter is both a stage in the Sufi rites and a different moment in Abdel-Aziz's own life, moving the reader through a week and a lifetime simultaneously.[17] This is significant as an early work that focuses on the practices of a Sufi brotherhood, marginalised by the ideology of the revolution. A number of Qasim's works are set in the same village and continue to trace the growth and development of Abdel-Aziz, whom Mehrez describes as the author's 'Dedalus-like protagonist'.[18] The choice of this setting reflects Qasim's own biographical background, having grown up in the small village of Mandara in the district of Gharbiyya and having moved to Tanta to complete his schooling. His novellas *al-Mahdi* (*al-Mahdi*, 1984) and *Turaf min Khabar al-Akhira* (*Good News from the Afterlife*, 1984) also take place in similar rural locales, which are the setting for much of his work.[19]

Here, the Egyptian countryside, as represented by the fields, is the space of labour and struggle. The villagers' lives are wretched, dominated by their work on the land in their continued endeavour to survive. It is, in the words of Badawi, 'the underworld of the lowest worlds of the Egyptian countryside'.[20] Descriptions foreground the glaring sun beating down upon the backs of the farmers. In the opening chapter of the novel, '*al-Ḥaḍra*' (The Evening Gathering), one of the brotherhood's meetings is depicted. This nightly ritual stands in opposition to the difficulties of the day, the misery of the morning 'when the sun blazed at its hottest and its harshest, unrelenting rays reached every corner'.[21] The daily struggle, the toil that the peasants must endure, is captured in Hagg Karim, whose very countenance reflects the division between day and night. While he appears happy and content in the evening, we are told

> during the day he was fearsome. He gripped the lead rope of his two animals with a rough fist and lashed back with his whip. The blade of his plow split the belly of the earth as the two beasts pulled and twisted beneath the yoke, dripping white foam from their mouths onto the cracked surface of the land.[22]

'The belly of the earth', 'the cracked surface of the land' is not here an image of fertility and abundance, the metaphor of a productive nation. Instead it is rough and barren, the site of the suffering of the village men, forever labouring under the burning sun. Later, as he walks through the fields, Abdel-Aziz notices 'the brown earth [that stretches] to the horizon, bare except for a few thin, indiscriminate wheatstalks' and is reminded of the 'few joys' in the villagers' lives.[23] In fighting these experiences of suffering and adversity, the 'whirlwind of toil and misery', the villagers recall memories of their annual journey to the shrine of Sayyid Badawi to help them endure their otherwise wretched existence.[24] The festival (*mawlid*) provides stories and laughter that nourish them year round, helping them survive 'the long days of hardship and suffering under the scorching heat of the sun'.²⁵ It is against this backdrop of destitution and poverty that the world of Sufi ritual is cast as an alternative.

Spaces of Possibility and Transformation

The first chapter of the novel takes place in the *dawwār* of Hagg Karim, the area attached to his home, where the members of the Sufi brotherhood come together for their meetings, to reinforce the bonds of friendship and community between the brothers through the reading of sacred texts, but also through the indulgence of bodily desire, understood to be part of the culture and practices of the mystic path. Returning from the mosque, the symbol of official religion, the villagers, 'feeble, broken ghosts', pass by Hagg Karim's house, only to be 'swallowed up by the darkness of the lane'.²⁶ While Hagg Karim's house is bathed in the light and warmth of spiritual community and fidelity, the surrounding spaces are those of darkness and isolation. The ritual and sociability of the brotherhood, 'the delights of the evening gathering' are a means for the villagers to resist their marginalisation and to create inclusivity in a world of exclusion.²⁷

The world of the village is transformed through the rituals that take place in the *dawwār*, through the recitations of poetry, the telling of stories and the readings of sacred texts. The Arab and Islamic textual and oral traditions are brought to bear upon the individual experiences of the men. The group listens to readings of the famous *Burda* poem of al-Busiri, recitations from the Qurʾan, and the oral epics of the Bani Hilal tribe, but they also tell each other tales of their own fortunes and losses, 'the hardships and the joys' each had experienced.²⁸ It is here that Qasim weaves the oral practices of the village into the textual fabric of his narrative, bringing together personal narrative and the texts of the larger tradition. Through their conversations and recitations the men transcend the world of the village, moving beyond its borders, as if recreating the longed-for journey to the Saint's shrine; 'In these moments there would emerge behind the limited world of everyday life another world, a marvelous and boundless world, one that awakened men's longings and filled their hearts with fervor.'²⁹

This other world brings together the past, present and future. The continuous present of Sufi ritual, proceeding in constant cycles, governs the entire narrative. Moving through the different stages in the *mawlid* of Sayyid

Badawi, the novel dispenses with historical linearity in favour of circularity and repetition, drawing upon the rituals that shape and govern village life. This manipulation of time is itself significant when read in light of the writers of Qasim's generation, who as al-Kharrat explains, 'destroy the progression of time in a linear path', moving away from the realist tradition and its narrative conventions.[30] The creation of a 'marvelous and boundless world' extends beyond the house of Hagg Karim through the performance of the Sufi *dhikr*, which transforms the physical space of the village, connecting it to the larger universe, to the 'deserts and sands, seas and rivers, trees, clouds, and tiny specks'.[31] This 'strange journey' performed through the recitation of the name of God, changes the village into what Selim describes as 'the timeless circle of the mythic, utopian community, mythic because imaginatively constructed, as dream, as refuge' and thus cast as an alternative to the degradation of village life.[32]

Just as the *dawwār* of Hagg Karim is the space of brotherhood and community, a sanctuary amidst the harsh world of the village, so too is the shrine of Sayyid Badawi. Located outside of the village, in the town of Tanta, the shrine represents the peasants' hopes and dreams. Arriving at the shrine, we are told how the men are unable to look away, their 'eyes clung in awe to Badawi's shrine . . . They were like flecks of iron drawn toward the pole of a magnet.'[33] In what turns out to be the men's final visit, Qasim provides us with a rich and detailed description of the physical surroundings:

> They were going into the immense halls of the mosque. These men who had lived for thousands of years in mud huts were filled with yearning for the splendor and beauty of these immense halls.
>
> With this longing and devotion, with these rough hands, domes, columns, and great halls had been erected, and temples had been hewn out of solid rock. Coolness and shade had been created in the heat of the desert . . . The two leaves of the door had been swung wide open. Inside loomed the great structure of thick brass latticework that surrounded the tomb. The polished metal scintillated in the light of the huge chandeliers with their hundreds of dazzling eyes. The men stood humbly in the opening of the door for a moment. Then they entered and moved counterclockwise around the tomb, holding on to the brass grill and rubbing their faces against it . . .

> Ahmed Bedawi was searching for his own world in the things he saw around him, that world he had created for himself out of the books with the yellow pages. Every time he found something from it he was carried away with joy. He kissed the rock and looked toward Abdel-Aziz.[34]

What is so telling about this passage is the connection that is made between the material and the spiritual. The halls of the mosque, in all their beauty and splendour, stand in opposition to the homes of the villagers, the 'mud huts' they have inhabited for thousands of years. The inviting 'coolness and shade' of the mosque is nothing like the scorching heat that beats down on the men in the fields. The end of the description brings together the experience of ecstasy and devotion experienced in the village *dhikr*, in Hagg Karim's *dawwār* and in the shrine of Sayyid Badawi. The 'books with the yellow pages' remind us of the readings that took place in Hagg Karim's home. The brothers transform and transcend the physical world by drawing upon the sources of their textual and oral tradition, in rituals that recreate the space of the sacred shrine and ultimately connect the worldly and the divine.

This scene is so central to the novel not only because it marks the culmination of the entire journey undertaken by Hagg Karim and the men, but also because it signals the beginning of the end of their lives. The 'farewell' (*al-wadāʿ*) of the chapter's title connects the end of the yearly pilgrimage to the Saint's tomb to the ever-looming death of the group. The men are aged and ailing; the once strong and powerful Hagg Karim is old and frail. The others suffer from blindness and decrepitude. The next and final chapter tells of the slow demise of Hagg Karim and his eventual death foreshadowed here 'in the eyes of a man about to die'.[35]

Connecting the Urban and the Rural

The shrine is central to the novel, not only as the site that draws the villagers, the manifestation of their hopes and desires, but also as the connection between rural and urban space. During the annual *mawlid* of the Saint the village temporarily exercises its dominance over the city. Abdel-Aziz notes with pride that his people 'would impose themselves, their breath, and the clattering of their sandals on this city for a week'.[36] Once the festival is underway, the peasants, rendered as a communal body through the performance of the *dhikr*, inflict themselves upon the space of Tanta:

> The whole mosque was shaken to its foundations by the pounding of feet and the hoarse barking sounds rising from the men's throats . . . The heart of Tanta was a slaughtered animal beneath all those naked feet. The body of the city – thousands of old buildings, twisting alleys, and ornamented streets – was being crushed beneath this rumbling flesh.[37]

The physical, corporal image of the peasants is cast as a body flattening the city of Tanta beneath its copious flesh. As he walks the streets, Abdel-Aziz imagines the villagers invading the slaughtered 'corpse', 'wandering through the veins of the city, through all its tiny capillaries and to its nerve ends', in a description that brings together the language of love and violence.[38] The countryside as 'rumbling flesh', as a body with 'thousands of arms' embraces and envelops the city, at once powerful and grotesque.[39] The strength of the villagers is short-lived, however, and the dominance of the urban is reasserted and reinforced by the display of the power of the state, represented in the presence of the police. As the villagers arrive at the Tanta train station, fences restrict their movement and the officers guarding the station violently attack them as they make their way through the gates, 'battering with their sticks whoever or whatever got in their way'.[40]

The connection between the rural and the urban extends beyond the *mawlid*. Abdel-Aziz traces the history of Tanta back to its rural roots. The canal that once split Tanta's streets lies buried beneath the asphalt, a memory of the city's rural origins:

> There had been a canal here too. But it had been buried, and this splendid layout of pruned trees and tall buildings had replaced it. He could hear the echoes of the voices far beneath his feet, the women and their little battles along the banks of the Tanta canal.[41]

Badr argues that Abdel-Aziz's musings of the past depict a time when 'the world of the village was more deeply rooted and established in the city . . . and when the city itself was closer to the village'.[42] While Tanta may have buried the evidence of its rural roots, it is not the urban sanctuary that Abdel-Aziz imagines it to be.[43] A 'film of dusty gray' covers the buildings and the cars fill the streets with smoke.⁴⁴ The islands of grass in the middle of the streets are 'ravaged' by the feet of the pedestrians and garish shop signs clutter every corner.⁴⁵ The transformation of the village, captured in the image of the buried canal, is the death of the rural, its absorption into the urban. It mirrors the death of Sufi ritual increasingly threatened by the end of the novel.

Dying Worlds

The last chapter in Qasim's novel, '*al-Ṭarīq*' (The Path), returns the reader to the village where the narrative began. This section, the seventh and final part of the Sufi ritual, marks the end of the brotherhood's journey on its spiritual path and the death of Hagg Karim. When Abdel-Aziz returns to care for his dying father and take up his role as head of the family, the world of the village has been transformed. The end of the brotherhood is the end of the community and solidarity that helped the villagers survive the difficulties of their everyday lives. Hagg Karim's family has lost all its land, sold to pay for the yearly preparations of the *mawlid* and the pilgrimage to Tanta. In a remarkable scene in which Abdel-Aziz tends to the little tract of land that the family still possesses, he suddenly embraces the soil in recognition that 'this is his land and his people'.⁴⁶ The power of this realisation is immediately undermined, however, with the collapse of his buffalo, the only other possession of worth that the family still owns. Unable to treat its broken leg, the men of the village, now headed by Abdel-Aziz's uncle, decide to sell the animal to the butcher. One of the brothers, Ahmed Badawi, explains that in the past Hagg Karim 'would slaughter the animal with his own hand, distribute the meat, collect the money, and buy a buffalo better than the one that had fallen'.⁴⁷ Abdel-Aziz's uncle and his men are, however, unlike Hagg Karim and his brothers, 'there was a sternness in their faces, and their laughter was loud and strong'.⁴⁸ The reader is thus invited to connect these three events – the death of Hagg Karim, the collapse of the water buffalo, and the loss of the land – to the transformation of rural life and the disappearance of the world of Sufi ritual.

This transformation is encapsulated in the appearance of the village café as the alternate space of community, replacing the circle of the brotherhood that convened in Hagg Karim's *dawwār*, and spelling the end of the mystic, collective experience of the Sufi circle. Instead, we see the imposition of the outside world, exemplified in the blasting radio that reverberates through the café. In a vivid scene, Abdel-Aziz watches the men engrossed in conversation, playing cards and smoking pipes. We are told how 'in the old days the men used to speak slowly and deliberately. They lived without all this bedlam. But these were boisterous, exasperated men. They talked about politics, cooperatives, feudalism, oppression, Kennedy and Khrushchev. Abdel-Aziz felt he had to leave.'[49] Evident immediately is the introduction here of the linear time of the outside world, absent thus far from the depiction of the life of the village. The cyclical movement that is captured in the ongoing rituals of Sufi practice and the yearly preparations for the *mawlid* of Sayyid Badawi, is displaced here by the reference to a particular historical moment, through the reference to Kennedy and Khrushchev. The alternative relationship to time has disappeared with the gradual disappearance of the space of Sufi ritual.

The change that has occurred to the village men is noted by Ahmed Badawi whose own experiences are testament to this transformation. The marginalisation of Hagg Karim's circle suggests a reading of this change as part of the establishment of a new world order. Selim suggests that, because of the role played by Abdel-Aziz's uncle in the closing scenes, there is no transition from one world to the next, from the old to the new, but rather that the end of the novel reveals the 'coexistence' of the two worlds all along. However, she goes on to say that

> in this alternate community, the loud political space of the coffee-house once and for all replaces the fragile dream-world of the past, and reflects the real pressures and interventions of a historical time that is common to both the village and the city.[50]

The placement of this scene in the café following the death and displacement of the members of the Sufi order speaks, I would argue, to the violent replacement of one world with another, and not with the sudden appearance of a side of village life that existed all along.[51] The representation of the café and its role in the lives of the villagers is intended to be met with ambivalence on the part of the reader. While Abdel-Aziz appears to find a community in which he can momentarily immerse himself, amidst the noise and clamour of the café culture, the men of Hagg Karim's old circle seem isolated in this new world. The younger men of the village are 'strong and bitter, full of frustration and anger'.⁵² Though the café may, as Selim argues, represent the space of the political, in which the men of village angrily oppose their position of oppression and marginalisation, it is not necessarily the space of action. What is stressed in the scene is the continuous *talking* of the men: 'Abdel-Aziz found himself speaking, quietly at first, but then excitedly at the top of his voice. As the broadcast continued its struggle with the boisterous voices of the men, his excitement increased. Everyone was talking.'⁵³ The reader is thus left wondering whether the power of the small room is the power of action or of speech alone, for as al-Musawi states, the 'noise recalls the noise of 1967, where there is excitement and rhetoric with no action'.⁵⁴ Despite the transformation of the village, represented in the replacement of the space of Sufi ritual with that of the political space of the café, the community remains marginalised at the end of the novel. The introduction of a new order must come at the expense of the brotherhood. Ultimately, the efficacy of the space of the political in affecting change in the lives of the villagers is by no means certain.

Darkness Descends on the Minisi Farm

Yusuf al-Qaid's novel *Akhbar ʿIzbat al-Minisi* (News from the Minisi Farm, 1971), the second novel in the author's extensive oeuvre, is emblematic of the author's literary and political preoccupations.⁵⁵ Written during his time as a conscript in the Egyptian army (1965–74), the novel focuses on a farm in Itay al-Barud, al-Bihira, in the region of the Nile Delta. The novel begins with the official notice that launches the investigation into the murder of the watchman's daughter Sabrin. From there we move backwards (and forwards) in time, charting the events that led to the killing. This, like the majority of al-Qaid's works, is a rural novel; others include *al-Hidad* (Mourning, 1969), *Ayyam al-Jafaf* (Days of Drought, 1973), *al-Bayat al-Shitwi* (Hibernation, 1974), *Yahduth fi Misr al-ʾAn* (Happening in Egypt Now, 1976), *Harb fi Barr Misr* (*War in the Land of Egypt*, 1978), *Thulathiyyat: Shakawi al-Misri al-Fasih* (The Trilogy: Complaints of an Eloquent Egyptian, 1981–5) and *Qitar al-Saʿid* (The Saʿid (Upper Egypt) Train, 2001).⁵⁶

News from the Minisi Farm recalls Tawfiq al-Hakim's earlier novel *Yawmiyyat Naʾib fi al-Aryaf* (*Maze of Justice: Diary of a Country Prosecutor*, 1937) that also tracks the murder of a young girl in the Egyptian countryside.

Both novels revolve around themes of honour, violence and revenge.[57] Significant as an example of popular fiction that draws upon the genre of the detective story, al-Hakim's novel is based upon the act of investigation, the tools and tricks that the public prosecutor (*nāʾib*) must employ to discover the perpetrator.[58] Despite this emphasis, al-Hakim's novel does not end with a resolution to the crime and the mystery remains unresolved. In the case of al-Qaid's novel, however, while the identity of the killer is known by the end of the novel, the narrative does not closely follow the investigator himself. By and large the voices we hear are those of the villagers and not, as with Hakim's text, that of an outside investigator. Instead, al-Qaid employs the mystery as a way to explore village life itself, providing space for the voices of the villagers to be heard. Ultimately, solving the crime brings about little resolution to the inhabitants of the Minisi farm.

In an introductory preamble entitled '*Mashhad Iftitāḥī*' (Opening Scene) the narrator describes the geography of the farm and its surroundings:

> Here is Hajj Hebat Allah al-Minisi's farm. To the west, where the sun sets every day at dusk, is the village of Dimisna, which everyone calls 'town'. To the east, lies al-Muwarda's farm, huddled against the bridge of the great river. Behind the bridge the sun emerges everyday from the dark underground. The river, a branch of Rashid, lies between the high bridge and the interior from which the sun emerges. To the south, where the bus passes daily on its way from Kafr al-Zayat, is the village of al-Sawalim al-Bahari. To the north, where the bus travels at the end of the day to Damanhur, signaling with its mournful horn, are the villages of Kafr ʿAwana and Niklat al-ʿinab. Amidst the fields, the farm appears as a muddy heap kneeling on the ground, thick and messy. A few buildings have been painted in white plaster. These are the pigeon towers, Hajj Hebat Allah al-Minisi's mansion, and the chief clerk's office. Here and there, scattered, is a palm tree, a sycamore tree, or a mulberry tree watching over the farm. Only the tops of the trees appear to the onlooker, hiding the dreary grey farm life. Here, gentlemen, is Hajj Hebat Allah Abd al-Jabbar al-Minisi's farm.[59]

This opening immediately establishes the exact geographic location of the farm, situating it vis-à-vis the neighbouring villages. The locale connects the farm to al-Qaid's own biography, this being the area of the author's birth and early life. Al-Qaid, often referred to as '*muʾarrikh al-qarya al-miṣriyya*' (the historian of the Egyptian village), was born and raised in the village of al-Dahriyya in Itay al-Barud, al-Bihira, also the setting of his first novel *al-Hidad* (Mourning, 1969).[60] The connection to his own experience is made explicit in the dedication addressed to his father, which states that 'these things are about our village'.[61] This attention to geography and place is intentional in all of al-Qaid's works and the strategy of naming is purposeful; as the author explains, place

> has a special presence in my consciousness and therefore I am very careful to specify by name the places where the events of the novels occur. So I don't say 'it happened in village x or city y' like many novelists, because that would diminish the vivid presence of place and transform it to just a hollow symbol void of meaning and connotations.[62]

This opening scene is one of six short descriptions with which the novel begins, suggesting that the farm be viewed as a central character, not unlike Hajj al-Minisi or the people of the farm, both of which also receive their own introductions. The passage is descriptive in a way that implies that the narrator is familiar with the intricacies of the Minisi farm; the direction of the sun, the route of the daily bus, and the appearance of the buildings and trees to a first-time onlooker. Here the voice of the storyteller emerges and intersects with that of the author/narrator. The 'gentlemen' in the closing line points to an audience to whom the narrator/storyteller is directing this introduction. This evokes the potential that the readers are also being addressed. The technique of addressing and even engaging the reader in the development of the narrative is one that is more fully developed in many of al-Qaid's later works.[63]

Descriptions of the fields abound in the novel, and nature intersects and often reflects the emotional.[64] It is perhaps more than anything the 'dreary grey farm life' (*rumādiyyāt al-ḥayāh fī al-ʿizba*) that is described and documented throughout the novel. This is particularly the case in passages that signal the coming of night over the farm: 'this moment brings nothing but despair. The particles of darkness descend, the hazy, grey color. Every individual withdraws inside himself the moment night falls on the farm.'[65] Similar descriptions are echoed throughout the novel, with the obscurity and gloom of nightfall a constant refrain; 'in this moment, night creeps over the vast distance'.[66]

While many of the novel's events occur under the cover of night, the light of day is no less harsh. The toil and labour undertaken by the farm labourer take place under a scorching sun, reminiscent of the scenes described in Qasim's novel. In a later chapter entitled '*al-Rudūkh*' (The Surrender), the chronological predecessor of '*al-Taḥqīq*' (The Investigation), emphasis is placed upon the noontime sun that beats down upon the workers:

> The heat and aridity are columns weighing down on man's back every passing moment. The silent void of the fields surrounds the farm from every side, sheltered by clouds of sorrow that increase its depth and density. The distant, dull, grey fields are sheltered by a dome of heat and silence.[67]

This silence and sorrow is interrupted once a year during the cotton harvest season, which brings 'unexpected joy' to the workers.[68] This temporary joy is melancholy, captured in the haunting songs which Sabrin sings in the fields, 'a sad song, in it you can smell the scent of the fertile land, the coming night'.[69] Fertility connects Sabrin to the land – this being the chapter in which her 'surrender' to Safwat al-Minisi, the son of Hajj al-Minisi, takes place. And yet hers is a fertility that eventually destroys her. Following her desires brings her only pain and suffering: forced to abort her child she is then killed for her transgressions. Similarly, the fertility of the land and its cotton harvest bring only temporary joy to the workers. It is not just that their desires are continually withheld, but also, as the narrator reminds us repeatedly throughout the novel, 'this land is his . . . the houses, the alleys, the firewood on the roofs, the pigeon towers, the single grocery, the mosque, the farm-yard all belong to Hajj Hibat Allah al-Minisi'.[70] The farmers, cultivators in a system of land sharing, remain unconnected to the land, unable to reap the benefits of their labour. They are also detached from the official governing bodies that control their lives, the cooperative society, members of parliament, the village mayor, or the police, who all deal exclusively with Hajj al-Minisi.

The separation of the workers and their isolation from any form of government extends to the farm's position vis-à-vis the nation. While the novel's events take place during the lead up to the 1967 war, the enormity of such events is registered in the narrative only by way of radio broadcasts that are barely acknowledged by the characters. The similarities to Qasim and Abdallah's novels are striking, and yet here al-Qaid references the war repeatedly throughout the narrative and not just in the closing pages. The first time is in the opening chapter 'The Official Investigation', which is marked with the date 23 May 1967, just a month before the outbreak of the war. Walking past Abul Futuh's store, Abdel Sattar sees the 'group of men gathered around the radio, at this time every night'.[71] This newscast relays both the movement of the armed forces in Sinai and the declaration of the state of emergency. And yet both announcements are all but ignored by Abdel Sattar, the men and the narrator. We are told only that the men 'answered back his greetings but he neither heard the rest of their words, nor the talk on the radio'.[72] The farm of al-Qaid's workers, like many of the rural villages he depicts in his novels, is largely disconnected from the outside world. While the personal calamity of Sabrin's murder resonates with the national calamity of the 1967 defeat, the villagers themselves barely acknowledge the events unfolding on the national stage. For the people of Minisi farm, suffering and degradation precede the war. Thus, the defeat of 1967 is not cast here as a definitive turning point. Like in the works of Qasim and Abdullah, the post-revolutionary Egyptian village remains separate from the rest of the nation, marginal and marginalised, unchanged by the policies and promises of the Nasserist regime, and principally governed by the feudal norms of earlier decades.

Mythical Transformations

The Minisi farm, with its scorching daytime sun and nights of despair, is temporarily transformed by Sabrin's death. While the first chapter of the novel begins with an official notice from the investigator regarding the murder, and a familiar description of the bleak nights that descend upon the farm, it closes in a strikingly different way. The watchman of Dimisna escorts Abdel Sattar to the graveyard. There the police commissioner, the mayor and the forensic physician are already in the process of digging up Sabrin's grave to conduct an autopsy. In the following scenes, the perspective shifts between the first and third person, and the past and present merge. Abdel Sattar recalls memories of his daughter's birth, her death and her burial. Sabrin is rendered a mythical figure, first by the inhabitants of the farm, and then by her father:

Sabrin was transformed into a myth told by the people here. They said they saw her sitting and weeping by the north water-wheel, and that over there, a small bush grew where she was weeping, and they named it the bush of tears.[73]

In a yet more fantastical scene, Abdel Sattar conjures up images of his daughter's marriage to Safwat, the son of Hajj al-Minisi, and the cause of her shame and eventual death:

Suddenly, he saw something unbelievable: A wedding in its entirety, with singing, drums, and flutes. The bride is Sabrin but the groom is not Abul Ghayt. (He proposed five years ago, but the wedding was delayed for financial reasons.) The groom is Safwat al-Minisi, the great Hajj's son. A dancer dances, a singer sings. On the maize husks, Qamariyya sings. Sabrin laughs, smiles . . . The wedding party escapes before him, crosses the canal, the bridge, and the distant fields. The wedding ascends to heaven, vanishing into melancholy space.[74]

The farm, and its fields, are transformed into a mythical space, one in which Sabrin is reimagined and recast as the bride she never was. As we have seen with other writers of this generation, the mythic and the fantastic are used to disrupt the realist narrative, and here the official investigative tools of the state are undercut by Sabrin's resurrection. A scene intended to reveal the truth regarding the murder, via formal autopsy, is instead transformed into a display of mythic celebration, an episode that renders Abdel Sattar's dreams a reality.

Just as fantastical perhaps is the transformation of the farm itself; we are told that the connection between the inhabitants of the farm and the outside world is significantly changed in the aftermath of Sabrin's death:

After Sabrin's murder, they began to establish new relations with their daily life. This even developed to a degree no one could have imagined, coming to include their view of the land, the farm, Hajj Hebat Allah, their view of themselves as human beings, individuals, connected to Hajj Hebat Allah as people, as human beings. This defined their position on life and death, hopes and expectations, shared farming, the Socialist Union, the mayor (*al-ʿumda*), Egypt, and the war.[75]

The workers began to engage with their own lives, so that when they met they 'stopped, exchanged opinions, discussed everything, connecting dispersed ideas and thinking about them'.[76] This passage is not unlike the café scene in Qasim's novel (or the intervention of the external nationalist rhetoric in Abdullah's work). And yet this transformation is short-lived; the workers' reflections are soon replaced by a resignation about their position in life. The closing of the novel, '*Mashhad Khitāmī*' (A Final Episode), ends with the repetition of the question weighing on the minds of the people of Minisi farm, '*tayyib wa ʾīh al-ʿamal?* (So what's to be done?)'.[77] This question, posed in the colloquial like all of the dialogue of the novel, is seemingly attributed to no one and everyone, and is ultimately left unanswered, suggesting acquiescence on the part of the people of the farm. Any focus on the connection between the local and the national is abandoned in favour of the pressing concerns of daily life:

> People here are certainly different, but the topic of their concern was one. It was not Sabrin's murder; it was something else: the land, the house, each one's life, his existence, his wife, his children, their dealings with one another, their relationship with the Chief Clerk, their relationship with Hajj Hebat Allah al-Minisi and the farm.[78]

Hajj al-Minisi continues to be the dominant figure in their lives, and thus power relations are essentially unchanged in post-revolutionary Egypt. And while the farmers momentarily engage with the events unfolding on the national stage, this cannot be read as a transformation of their political agency. They remain disconnected from the rest of the country, with even the 1967 defeat, as noted earlier, acknowledged only in passing.

Reimaging the Rural: Cycles of Narrative

Al-Qaid, in this and many of his works, manipulates the form of the realist novel. Here, while the time and place of the narrative are clear to the reader, the author alters the chronological progression of the work. The novel opens, as stated earlier, with an introductory scene intended to familiarise the reader with the Minisi Farm, emphasising its geographical location. The initial narrator is reminiscent of a folkloric storyteller, what Marie-Therese Abdel-Messih refers to in her introduction to the English translation as a 'ballad narrator'.[79] Addressing the listeners/readers, the 'gentlemen' of the introduction, al-Qaid's storyteller/narrator sets the scene for a cycle of stories concerning the farm and its inhabitants. The storyteller then presents a number of significant characters to the reader/listener: Hajj al-Minisi, the Chief Clerk, the inhabitants of the farm and the mosque leader. This opening scene is not, however, relegated to a particular moment but seems to occupy something of an eternal present, the reader imagining that this is the way the farm has always been.

The narrative then shifts with the following chapter signalling a change in narrator and tone. The official notice of 23 May 1967 orders the investigation into Sabrin's death, which we learn occurred on 13 April of the same year. No longer then is the narrative only an oral tale told by a folkloric storyteller. Instead, the inclusion of the official notice marks the first intrusion of official forms of documentation, and thus the authoritative voice of the state. This is not unlike the form of al-Ghitani's work discussed in Chapter 1. It also, as al-Bashir argues, links al-Qaid's work to the external world, affirming a connection to historical time.[80] The movement back and forth through time operates throughout the entire novel, structuring the narrative's chronology. Each of the three following cycles is titled after a principal event that takes place in the chapter and is accompanied by the date of the action: *al-Rudūkh* (The Surrender: Tuesday 13 September 1966); *al-Kibriyāʾ* (Pride: Monday 23 September 1962); and *al-Qatl* (The Murder: Thursday 13 April 1967).[81] Thus, while the novel opens in May 1967, with each chapter we move further back in time, leaping forward to April 1967 only in the last chapter. The dated titles are a reminder that this record is part of an official investigation, carried out to uncover the individual responsible for Sabrin's death. And yet the form and content of each chapter complicates the nature of this designation, filled as they are with the musings and memories of the individual characters that invade the narrative with little warning, connecting us to oral folk narratives and cycles of stories, rather than the official texts of the investigation. Finally, the novel closes as it began, this time with a chapter entitled 'A Final Episode' that describes the farm after Sabrin's death and again dedicates segments to each of the principle characters. The reader is ultimately transported to the novel's beginning and is once again reminded of the cyclical nature of al-Qaid's work.

This circularity suggests the intersection between the official and the folkloric and is one of the ways in which al-Qaid brings the narrative devices of the oral tradition to bear upon the novel. The significance of the folkloric is further emphasised by the dominance of the character of al-Adham, who casts a wide shadow over al-Minisi farm. Adham al-Sharqawi – known in popular folklore as al-Adham – is the modern-day Robin Hood of the Nile Delta, renowned for his bravery and honour.[82] Born in 1898 in the village of Zubayda in Itay al-Barud, al-Adham was best known for seeking vengeance for the murder of his uncle, challenging government forces and the colonial British authorities. He was eventually captured and killed by the Egyptian police.[83] It is no surprise then that al-Adham, as a native son of Itay al-Barud and a seeker of vengeance, is held in such high esteem by the people of Minisi. Abdel Sattar's inability to punish his daughter for her indiscretions, and his acceptance of Hajj al-Minisi's financial assistance in obtaining an abortion for Sabrin, reveal his shortcomings as a heroic figure, the very antithesis of the vengeance-seeking al-Adham. As we will see, he is remarkably similar to Mustafa in Abdullah's novel. Lamenting his fate and his existence in a world with no place for the heroic, Abdel Sattar contrasts the present world with that of the past: 'Ours are not the times of great men. Where have those days gone, the days of al-Adham, al-Zanati Khalifa, Zahran al-Rifaʿi? Ours, are days of starvation, of fire and drought.'[84] Significantly, it is his son, al-Zanati, who also bears the name of another popular heroic figure, who comes to see himself as al-Adham, 'the real man', dispensing justice for his sister's transgressions.[85] And yet, the reader of al-Qaid's novel is left questioning the heroism of a character who murders his sister instead of assisting her in her time of need. Masculinity understood through this form of vengeance, and enacted on the female body, is not celebrated in the novel. Not only is Sabrin the victim of the narrative, but Abdel Sattar is left bereft and heart broken, 'actually dead', and al-Zanati is charged with murder and imprisoned for his crime.[86] And so the 'mystery' at the heart of *News from the Minisi Farm* is solved by the novel's end, but this resolution brings little by way of justice for the slain Sabrin. The reader is all too aware of the injustice in a world where the wealthy and powerful escape unscathed. Safwat al-Minisi is ultimately unaffected by his treatment of Sabrin. The violence of such killings, as we shall see, is once again the centre of the rural narrative in Yahya Taher Abdullah's *The Collar and the Bracelet*.

The Collar and the Bracelet: The Rural as Mythic Space

Yahya Taher Abdullah's novel *The Collar and the Bracelet* (1975) is set in the Upper Egyptian village of al-Karnak and tells the generational story of a family's struggle to survive. Hazina, the mother and matriarch, is left to care for her family after the death of her husband Bikhit al-Bishari. Alone with her daughter Fahima, the two women long for the return of Mustafa, the son living away from Egypt, working first in Sudan and then in Palestine. The tragedies that befall the family are part of a larger world of suffering and affliction. Fahima marries al-Haddad after her father's death, only to discover he is impotent. Hazina's attempt to help her daughter, by having another 'man' impregnate her, only ends in misery, with the return of Fahima to her family home. The cycle is repeated with the following generation; Fahima's daughter Nabawiya becomes pregnant out of wedlock and pays for her transgression with her life.

The repetition of cycles of violence and transgression takes place against the backdrop of the Upper Egyptian village, a landscape that Abdullah transforms into a mythic space, dominated by the house and the temple, both sites of violence and confinement. Samah Selim reads the space of the village in this novel as a 'mythic landscape' arguing that this work

> encodes this bleak vision of rurality in a dramatically new narrative language, thereby fully disengaging the village from the conventional and symbolic structures of representation through which is has been articulated from the foundational period onwards. The opacity of the novel's abbreviated, poetic language and the elision of conventional narrative point-of-view embed the novel in a competing folk narrativity.[87]

While I agree with Selim's analysis of Abdullah's extensive use of forms of 'folk narrativity', I suggest that the representation of the village should also be read in light of the socio-economic and political transformations of the period. The rural as mythic space is used by Abdullah to emphasise the ongoing marginalisation of the Upper Egyptian village of al-Karnak in relationship to the Egyptian nation, ultimately calling into question the transformative possibilities of revolutionary action. Writing in 1975, Abdullah returns the reader to the 1952 revolution, only to cast doubt upon the efficacy of this moment, which precipitated agricultural reforms intended to improve the lives of the rural population.

The Collar and the Bracelet is significant as one of the first novels to take place in an al-Karnak, with authors more often choosing the villages of the Nile Delta over those of Upper Egypt. In describing the centrality of the rural world to his work, Abdullah establishes a connection between the position of the individual and that of the village:

> I am the son of the village and I will remain that way. My experience is almost all in the village . . . and the obvious life of the village is that of al-Karnak in Luxor or Old Tiba and I think that what befell the nation befell it. It is a small, forgotten, exiled village, in the same way that I am exiled and forgotten . . . And I don't live except in its lower world . . . and when I meet with them [my people] we meet as *ṣaʿayda* (people from Southern Egypt) and as children of al-Karnak and we live together our Egyptian pain, and our Arab calamity, and our distance from the age as alienated individuals.[88]

Abdullah's words capture the centrality of the rural world and the experience of its people to his life and work. The sense of alienation experienced by the individual, that he is 'exiled and forgotten' is echoed in the position of the village vis-à-vis the rest of the nation. The 'lower world' to which Abdullah refers is the not the rural world with which the reader is familiar, the world of fields and agricultural land, of labourers and farmers. Instead the landscape is dominated by the ancient temples of the Pharaohs, strongly connecting this village to its historic, and mythic, past. It is a land where 'the hills are black and the sand on either side is yellow. Kings walk the country. Sun passes through sky and water. In the water is a moon and in the sky is a moon.'[89] We do not encounter 'optimistic heroes from among the downtrodden' but rather 'men and women [who] struggle with a heavy destiny that seems eternal owing to its excessive weight on their souls'.[90] The characters of his novel are not only landless, and thus tenant farmers (like those of the Minisi farm), but some do not even work on the land as labourers and therefore must find employment in the surrounding hotels. This is a significant departure from Abdullah's earlier works which focus upon rural families that own land and enjoy a position of power and privilege. This is the case particularly in his two earlier short story collections *Thalath Shajarat Kabira Tuthmiru Burtuqalan* (Three Big Trees that Bear Oranges, 1970) and *al-Daff wa-l-Sunduq* (The Tambourine and the Chest, 1974), stories featuring the wealthy family of Shaykh Fadil.

As with other writers of the sixties generation, Abduallah's sense of alienation marks his literary production, colouring the representation of space in his literary works. The rural world that we encounter in *The Collar and the Bracelet* is the world of a village on the periphery, marginal and marginalised, dominated by the house and the temple, and not the fields and farms.

House of Death

In his analysis of the relationship between myth and literature, Northrop Frye argues that mythic structures revolve around cycles of life and death.[91] It is these cycles that form the basis of Abdullah's narrative, though it is death more than anything else that dominates this world. Loss pervades the house of Fahima and Bikhit al-Bishari, the space that is central to the novel and that seems to stand alone amidst the rural world of al-Karnak. It is also where the story begins and ends, creating a sense of repetition and circularity that is echoed in the title of the work. The house as a space of confinement resonates with the *tawq* (collar) and the *iswira* (bracelet) of the title, which convey ideas of continuity, but also of entrapment. The opening of the novel presents the now invalid Bikhit as he passes his days outside the house, marking the passage of time by the movement of the sun. He has in many ways become an extension of the structure of the house. Laid out on the bench, he is reliant upon his wife and daughter to move him from one spot to another. He longs to escape both the house and his life, wishing for the sleep that will carry him straight to God. His wish is eventually granted:

> Hazina uncovered his face. There, she saw three colors – black, blue, and yellow – and she divined the approach of death . . . Hazina heard and Fahima heard and Shaykh Fadil heard the door close behind the Angel of Death with the soul of Bikhit al-Bishari in his arms.[92]

It is only through death that members of the family leave the confines of the home – any other attempts that are made by the characters are ultimately thwarted. While Mustafa is able to escape the home and village struggling to overcome the poverty and destitution of life in al-Karnak, he must eventually return.[93] And when he does, he is destined to suffer the same fate as his father – he spends the end of his days paralysed, alone with his mother Hazina in the family home. This is just one of many generational repetitions that produce the circularity and continuity that structure the novel. Fahima too is only able to leave the home temporarily. Her marriage to al-Haddad, and the move to his home, is short-lived; when her husband divorces her, she finds herself back in the familial home, this time with her daughter Nabawiya. Again, like her father, she can only escape the confines of the home through death. The scene of her passing is described in the same language as that of Bikhit al-Bishari. Hazina once more tends to the dying: 'Terror struck her when she saw her daughter's face turn the three colors: yellow, black, and blue.'[94]

The home as the space of death and imprisonment is best captured in the experience of Fahima's daughter Nabawiya, who is raised by her grandmother following her mother's passing. In love with Shaykh Fadil's son, she aspires to break through the boundaries of her world, a transgression for which she is punished. She is also pursued with zeal by her cousin al-Saʿdi who wishes to marry her. With the return of her Uncle Mustafa, however, Nabawiya is confined to the house. And yet her tragedy does not end there. The discovery of her pregnancy spells the end of her life. In the most tragic scene of Abdullah's novel, Nabawiya is beaten and buried alive by her uncle, who insists she reveal the identity of her lover:

> Enraged Mustafa meted out the searing blows to Nabawiya and turned the lovely face into a swollen pulp. He gathered up the raven hair in two strong hands bulging with purple veins and threw the body desired by men onto the ground. He dragged her along, kicking the sinful belly over and over with his feet, then he left her there for a moment – a heap of broken bones, flesh moaning at the foot of the wall – in order to dig the pit.
>
> He tossed the hoe aside, lifted Nabawiya and stood her up in the pit. Then he shoveled the earth back in over the body up to the neck, leaving the head exposed and the hair grazing in the dirt.[95]

What is so powerful about this description is the way Nabawiya literally becomes part of the grounds of the house, enveloped in the earth outside her home. Her paralysis surpasses that of her father's, and her containment in the house ultimately leads to her death. Refusing to reveal the identity of her lover she remains buried in the grounds of her home, with only her head above the earth.

When al-Saʿdi learns of her transgression he puts an end to her life in a scene that even surpasses Mustafa's brutality:

> Al-Saʿdi kicked in the door of Bikhit al-Bishari's house with a ferocious blow ... He drew, from beneath the folds of his torn robes, the sharp-toothed scythe and seized the grimy bundle of lunatic black hair as he would grab hold of a bundle of clover, and he sheared [*ḥaṣada*] off the long proud neck. The dovecote tottered, the doves took flight, and the wolf howled at the sight of the spurting blood soaking his garments and running, snake-like in the dirt. Howling he carried off the head, its eyes still shining with life.[96]

Here Nabawiya is a part of the land, her hair a bundle of clover, which al-Saʿdi brutally attacks with his scythe. This is the materialisation of Nabawiya's earlier utterance that she is '*al-arḍ*' (earth/land) and Shaykh Fadil's son is '*al-samāʾ*' (sky).[97] In the Arabic original the word used to describe al-Saʿdi's actions is the verb *ḥaṣada*, meaning to reap, harvest, or as appears in the English translation, to shear. It is used in two earlier instances of striking significance. In the chapter ominously entitled '*Aladhī la yaqdir ʿalā manʿihi aḥad*' (What no one can prevent) the villagers mistakenly dismiss the significance of the relationship between Nabawiyya and Shaykh Fadil's son, referring to them repeatedly as brother and sister, when the two in fact soon consummate their relationship. In the description of the development of the two children we are told that Shaykh Fadil's son (who is never named) calls to Nabawiyya in a voice that has become 'rough like the scythe of the reaper working in the clover'.[98] The phrase in Arabic, *minjal al-ḥāṣid* (the scythe of the reaper), here connects both the scythe and the act of shearing to Shaykh Fadil's son, who is ultimately absent from the final scenes of vengeance, but is largely responsible for Nabawiya's fate.

The sexual overtones of the imagery of the scythe working its way violently through the clover recalls an earlier scene in which the Hazina confronts her daughter about al-Haddad's impotence. Addressing Fahima, she says 'a man tills his land ... plows it, throws in the seeds, and continues to water it ... then he reaps [*yaḥṣid*] the harvest. Does al-Haddad till his land?'⁹⁹ Here again, Abdullah uses the verb *yaḥṣid*, from the same root as *ḥaṣada*, in describing the sexual act between al-Haddad and Fahima. Ironically of course, al-Haddad is impotent and thus unable to impregnate Fahima, just as he has no actual land to till. In this mythic, desolate landscape, we see no fields, no tilling or reaping of harvests. The characters have no land to farm. Instead production and procreation are transposed onto the female body, as land and earth, with tragic consequences. If Abdullah draws upon the metaphor of women as land, he does so in order to expose the impotency and infertility of the men, and the demise of the women in the rural communities they inhabit. Just as in al-Qaid's novel, here too violence is wrought upon the female body, with men (particularly the rich) escaping unscathed from their transgressions.

The Temple: The Mythic as the Site of Violence

Abdullah's village is a mythic landscape, amidst which stand only the house of Bikhit and Hazina and the ancient Pharaonic temple. The latter brings together the world of the human and the divine in a scene that recalls the mythic tales of the past. After discovering her husband is impotent, Fahima solicits the help of her mother Hazina. When the latter's remedies fail to restore al-Haddad's sexual potency, Hazina takes her daughter to the ancient temple to discover whether she is the cause of the problem:

> Here is the ancient massive-stoned temple, ruined by impudent time. The seven gates of the temple are still intact, however. Above every gate sits a winged sun disk guarded by two interlaced snakes.
>
> There inside, is the hall of columns where the people of old used to offer their prayers. In this hall they burned piles of incense brought from the farthest reaches of the civilized world. Inside, trapped in his narrow chamber lurks the naked-loined god of procreation. The unfinished obelisk – the sonorous obelisk – and the sacred pond lie beyond. Its waters neither rise nor fall in spite of the springs that weep ceaselessly into its small basin.¹⁰⁰

The temple, the 'breach between the real and the legendary', is one of the few detailed descriptions of physical space that are given in the entire novel.¹⁰¹ It is also one of the ways Abdullah produces what Richard Jacquemond describes as 'an Egyptian version of Latin American magic realism', against and in response to the realist mode that dominated the literary field until the middle of the 1950s.[102] Abdullah invokes elements of the ancient Egyptian mythic tradition in creating a scene in which Fahima is impregnated by 'the god of procreation'.[103] The reality of this situation is not called into question but presented as entirely plausible within the world of the novel; Abdullah here, to follow Warnes' definition of the magical realist narrative strategy, 'naturalizes the supernatural, integrating fantastic or mythical features smoothly into the otherwise realistic momentum of the narrative'.[104]

The mythic here is used in a scene of brutality and force rendering the temple a space of violence. Alone in the dark, dank chamber Fatima is impregnated by the 'naked black giant' with the 'two red eyes glowing like coals'.[105] And from this encounter Fahima's daughter Nabawiya is conceived, the daughter who will be the cause of Fahima's divorce and return to her family home. She, like her mother, will also conceive an illegitimate child that will bring about her downfall. The temple remains in Fahima's mind a site of violence and brutality. As she walks with her mother over the burial grounds of the dead, Hazina re-tells the story of the workers who died in the old temple. This story of the confrontation between the Arab workers and the French antiquities inspector takes on similar mythic proportions, serving to connect the colonial and postcolonial moments in the mind of the reader. Refusing to listen to the workers' complaints about the condition of the old temple, the foreman compels them to keep working. As a result, 'the earth groaned by its Lord's command and the world turned upside down. It happened at midday and the men's bodies were removed just before sunset.'[106] Following the accident, the French inspector drowns in the Nile and the foreman's wife keeps giving birth to babies that die in their first month.

In listening to this story, Fahima cannot help but be taken back to her own experiences in the temple, though she struggles to keep her memories at bay: 'Voices croaked in Fahima's ears, dogs howling, cats screeching, frogs croaking, flesh crackling and grindstone grinding, a grindstone rhythmically, incessantly grinding, and to this regular continuous beat the naked black man comes closer, his stone feet pounding on the stone floor.'[107] Immediately following this scene, Fahima collapses and dies. Here the connection is made explicit. The temple as a site of mythic violence is first where the land literally opens up and swallows the Arab workers, punishing the colonial overlords for their transgressions. It is later the site of Fahima's abduction and eventual death. In both cases magical events take place against the backdrop of the mythic landscape of al-Karnak.

Time, Space and the Nation

The village of al-Karnak, isolated and marginalised, is the exiled space of which Abdullah speaks. This is emphasised by the way in which time operates in the novel, once again through circularity and repetition. Within the context of the narrative the reader marks the passage of time by the generational cycle of the family of Bikhit and Hazina, whose members seem destined to repeatedly suffer the same fate. Nadia Yaqub argues that Abdullah's novel draws on techniques from the Arabic popular epic (*sīra*), principally in the use of epic time, which contrasts to the historic time associated with the realist novel. She thus notes, for example, that 'like the characters of the *sirah*, Fahimah and Hazinah live in a world which is characterised by recurring cycles, in which events repeat themselves in familiar patterns'.[108]

The form of the work also suggests an alternative to the linearity of the realist novel; the novel is made up of fifteen chapters which are in turn composed of shorter sections, some a few lines long, some extending for several pages. Some sections are given their own titles, suggesting their existence as independent tales. It is the cumulative effect of the individual sections that moves the reader through the narrative, as if the novel itself were composed of a succession of short stories or folk tales.[109] In his analysis, Badawi compares the short tales that make up the novel to the Egyptian *mawwāl* (popular folk song) of '*Hasan wa Naʿima*' or '*Shafiqa wa Mitwwali*'. He argues that as opposed to the story cycle of the Arabian Nights, which ultimately ends with the possibility of happiness for the principal characters, here the narrative begins as it ends, with a sense of foreboding and defeat, both for the characters and the larger community.[110] Critics have gone as far as to argue that this is not a novel at all; in his analysis of Abdullah's work, Sabry Hafez argues that it should be seen as a '*qiṣṣa qaṣīra ṭawīla*' (a long short story).[111] Furthermore, Hafez notes that Abdullah begins his work with several short stories previously published in other collections. The story '*al-Shahr al-Sadis min al-ʿAm al-Thalith*' (The Sixth Month of the Third Year) and a modified version of '*al-Mawt fi Thalath Lawhat*' (Death in Three Scenes) appeared in his earlier collection *al-Daff wa-l-Sunduq* (The Tambourine and the Chest, 1974). For Hafez, the reappearance of these stories marks a conscious strategy on the part of the author to connect his long and short works.

The circularity both in form and content contrasts with the linear time that operates outside of the limits of the village. While the novel tells the story of the family of Bikhit and Hazina, it also tells the story of the anti-colonial struggles in the Arab world. This is the only means for the reader to identify the narrative with an actual historical moment. The world outside the village is experienced only through the travels of Mustafa, the exiled son whose presence in the novel is largely marked by his absence from the village. The lands of Sudan and the Levant exist as faraway destinations, significant only as places from which letters from Mustafa come back to his family. The loss of Palestine in 1948 brings Mustafa back to Egypt to work in the British Camps in the Canal Zone. It is from there that he launches attacks on the British officers, leading a rag-tag group of men. And yet Mustafa, his activities and the context of the anticolonial struggle seem divorced from the reality of village life, removed as it is from the nationalist moment and the events taking place in the rest of the country.

The historical events of the novel reach their height around the moment of revolution in 1952. The experience of national fervour finds its way into the world of the village through the experience of Shaykh Fadil and his friends, who listen to the songs of Umm Kulthum and write articles proclaiming their patriotic commitment. Here we see the brief appearance of the character of the journalist Muhammad Ahmad al-Sharqawi in the narrative, who brings together a multitude of 'exemplary verses and some popular sayings' in order to write an article about the revolutionary moment, entitled 'The Sea of the Past Flows into the Sea of the Present but the Sea is Not Yet Full'.[112] Selim notes that the language of the texts cited by the journalist is 'a generic, declamatory language constructed by an urbane, elite class and bordering on empty cliché' that has little to do with the 'lived experience of the long-suffering liminal community which it perhaps claims to represent'.[113]

The journalist's words also place an emphasis upon the textual, at the expense of the oral, a distinction which Abdallah himself has called into question on numerous occasions. In discussing his work, he states:

> If I speak and speak well I will find those who will listen to me and this is what I do . . . I have to speak and not write because my nation doesn't read . . . And when I speak my listeners increase because people are not deaf. I don't think that addressing intellectuals is an issue of importance . . . I asked myself: Who am I writing for? I found that the people that I am writing about don't read my art . . . and they are exiled, alienated, and dispossessed . . . For this reason I think that speaking is better and the stories that I write I have already told a hundred thousand times to a hundred thousand people . . . For this reason also I say that I don't exert much energy in writing my stories because I record what I say in my gatherings and exchanges.[114]

Abdullah's own biographical experience encourages a connection between the written and the oral. He was known to be a remarkable storyteller and performances of his work were famous throughout the literary circles in Cairo during the 1960s and 1970s. He composed his stories in his head, reciting them from memory for his audience and only writing them down for publication.[115] If the journalist in *The Collar and the Bracelet* connects the written word to the discourse of nationalism, Abdullah challenges this connection in drawing upon the oral tradition. Writing in the decades that followed national independence Abdullah returns to the moment of change, but rather than positing it as a moment of optimism, it is recast as one that even in its origin was built upon the exclusion of the rural village, here represented by the Upper Egyptian village of al-Karnak. At the height of the nationalist moment, the village of al-Karnak is wholly disconnected from the rest of the nation. In stressing this isolation and separation, Abdullah calls into question the possibilities of revolutionary transformation and the vision of national unity with which it was associated.

Conclusion

Abd al-Hakim Qasim, Yusuf al-Qaid and Yahya Taher Abdullah all represent interesting cases within the writers of the sixties generation for their focus upon the space of the rural in Egypt. Their originality lies in their move away from the social realism that dominated the depictions of rural narratives in the previous decades, and their turn to alternative modes of representation. All three writers produce cyclical narratives that work to unsettle the time and space of the rural novel. In this chapter I have shown that Qasim, al-Qaid and Abdullah reimagine the rural as mystical and mythical space, and in doing so draw attention to the way in which the villages they depict stand apart from the rest of the nation. No longer the terrain of political revolution, the peripheries of the Egyptian countryside are the purview of the downtrodden and forgotten. All three writers also represent the figure of the rural intellectual as distinct from his/her urban counterpart, depicting the rural realities of their respective origins. In doing so they also contend with the possibility of engaging the oral and textual traditions in their works. Thus, Qasim recreates the time and space of Sufi ritual in chapters which mirror the preparations and journey that precede the yearly pilgrimage to the shrine of the Sufi saint. Al-Qaid disrupts the official tools of the state, merging the authoritative voice of the investigator with that of the memories, recollections and speech of the rural villagers. And finally, Abdullah tells his story of generational struggle through a novel that in its composition echoes the folk tales of the oral tradition. In this reimagination of the rural space of Egypt the writers call into question the position of the rural vis-à-vis the nation, particularly in terms of revolutionary possibility and change. This focus upon peripheral spaces is extended and expanded in the following chapter in which we move to exilic spaces beyond the boundaries of the nation.

Notes

1. Abdullah, *al-Kitabat al-Kamila*, p. 491.
2. Abd al-Hakim Qasim, in a letter to Naji Najib (26 February 1973). See Shaʿir, *Kitabat Nubat al-Hirasa*, p. 35.
3. All three writers would eventually move to Cairo. This rural to urban migration had been ongoing since the first half of the twentieth century. As Waterbury explains, 'rural overpopulation and land hunger fed a steady exodus to the cities. Mobilization of able-bodied men during the Second World War accelerated the process, and Cairo's population grew at 4.8 percent per annum between 1937 and 1947. Probably half of the 800,000 new Cairenes of those years were of rural origins, and many of the recruits among them stayed in the city after demobolization.' Waterbury, *The Egypt of Nasser and Sadat*, p. 208.

This exodus to the city continued in the decades that followed. As was explored in Chapter 1, housing projects such as those described in Aslan's novel were built to cater to the increasing numbers of rural migrants from Upper and Lower Egypt. This also speaks to the continued dominance of Cairo as the cultural and intellectual capital.

4. Siddiq, *Arab Culture and the Novel*, p. 100.
5. Ibid. p. 100.
6. Ansari, *Egypt: The Stalled Society*, pp. 57–69. It is also a part of the literary representations of the rural question, most famously rendered in Muhammad Husayn Haykal's novel *Zaynab* (1914).
7. Ansari, *Egypt: The Stalled Society*, p. 79.
8. Waterbury, *The Egypt of Nasser and Sadat*, p. 281.
9. Ansari, *Egypt: The Stalled Society*, p. 4.
10. Ibid. p. 7.
11. Waterbury, *The Egypt of Nasser and Sadat*, p. 48.
12. Ansari, *Egypt: The Stalled Society*, p. 5.
13. Waterbury, *The Egypt of Nasser and Sadat*, p. 304.
14. Al-Sharqawi, *al-Ard*. Desmond Steward translates the title as *Egyptian Earth*. The novel was also made into a film of the same title, directed by Youssef Chahine in 1969, and nominated for the Grand Prix du Festival International du Film at the Cannes Film Festival in 1970.
15. For excellent analyses of Sharqawi's novel, see Badr, *al-Riwaʾi wa-l-Ard*, pp. 113–55; and Selim, *The Novel and the Rural Imaginary in Egypt*, pp. 159–85.
16. In relation to Qasim's work, see Selim, *The Novel and the Rural Imaginary in Egypt*, p. 186; al-Musawi, 'Beyond the Modernity Complex', pp. 22–45; and Mehrez, 'Introduction', p. xiii. For Abdullah's work, see al-Saʾigh, *Thunaʾiyyat al-Makan*.
17. The chapters are entitled as follows: '*al-Ḥadra*' (The Evening Gathering); '*al-Khabīz*' (The Baking); '*al-Safar*' (The Journey); '*al-Khidma*' (The Lodgings); '*al-Layla al-Kabīra*' (The Big Night); '*al-Wadāʿ*' (The Farewell); and '*al-Ṭarīq*' (The Path). I take the translations of the chapter titles from the English translation, *The Seven Days of Man*. For an excellent discussion of the novel, see Allen, *The Arabic Novel*, pp. 167–77.
18. Mehrez, 'Introduction', p. xii. He reappears, for example, in Qasim's later novella *al-Mahdi*. For a reading of the novel that focuses on the development of the protagonist, see al-Musawi, 'Beyond the Modernity Complex'.
19. These two novellas appear in the English edition *Rites of Assent*. Qasim did,

however, also write city novels – *Muhawala li-l-Khuruj* (An Attempt to Get out, 1980) and *Qadar al-Ghuraf al-Muqbida* (The Fate of the Oppressive Rooms, 1982). I borrow the translations of titles of the novels from Kilpatrick. For a comprehensive list of all Qasim's published works see Kilpatrick, ''Abd al-Hakim Qasim and the Search for Liberation', p. 51.
20. Badawi, *al-Riwaya al-Haditha fi Misr*, p. 26.
21. Qasim, *The Seven Days of Man*, pp. 1–2.
22. Ibid. p. 2.
23. Ibid. p. 100.
24. Ibid. p. 168.
25. Ibid. p. 168.
26. Ibid. p. 3.
27. Although the nightly gatherings are restricted to the men of the village, the women experience a similar sense of solidarity and community in the gathering that takes place for the baking of the bread for the journey to Tanta. These scenes are described in the second chapter of the novel, 'al-Khabīz' (The Baking).
28. Qasim, *The Seven Days of Man*, p. 5. The Bani Hilal epic (*sīra*) tells the story of the Bani Hilal tribe's migration from the Arabian Peninsula, through Egypt, and their conquest of North Africa, sometime between the tenth and twelfth centuries. The epic appears again in al-Qaid's novel discussed later in this chapter (see note 84). The *Burda* poem (*Qasīdat al-Burda*), the 'Poem of the Mantle', is a panegyric poem composed by the Egyptian poet al-Busiri (d. 1295/6) in praise of the Prophet Muhammad. The poem was written to celebrate the poet's miraculous recovery from paralysis which he attributed to the Prophet. For more. see Sedghi and Abbas, 'al-Būṣīrī'.
29. Qasim, *The Seven Days of Man*, p. 6.
30. Al-Kharrat, *al-Hassasiyya al-Jadida*, p. 12.
31. Qasim, *The Seven Days of Man*, p. 34. The *dhikr* (remembrance of God) is enacted through the repetition of the names of God. It is a service or ceremony common to mystical groups in Islam. In Qasim's novel, the Sufi brotherhood perform the *dhikr* or *hadra* through the repetition of the names of God, the recitation of the Qur'an and the readings of poetry. See Gardet, 'Dhikr'.
32. Qasim, *The Seven Days of Man*, p. 34; Selim, *The Novel and the Rural Imaginary in Egypt*, p. 204.
33. Qasim, *The Seven Days of Man*, p. 117.
34. Ibid. pp. 176–8.

35. Ibid. p. 178.
36. Ibid. p. 131.
37. Ibid. p. 153.
38. Ibid. p. 155.
39. Ibid. p. 155.
40. Ibid. p. 112.
41. Ibid. p. 102.
42. Badr, *al-Riwaʾi wa-l-Ard*, p. 209.
43. For more on Abdel-Aziz's internal conflict, as represented by the conflict between the city and the village, see al-Musawi, 'Beyond the Modernity Complex'; and Selim, *The Novel and the Rural Imaginary in Egypt*, pp. 185–205.
44. Qasim, *The Seven Days of Man*, p. 103.
45. Ibid. p. 104.
46. Ibid. p. 197.
47. Ibid. p. 205.
48. Ibid. p. 204.
49. Ibid. p. 207.
50. Selim, *The Novel and the Rural Imaginary*, pp. 204–5.
51. See, for example, Khashaba, 'Jil al-Sittinat fi al-Riwaya al-Misriyya'; Hafez, 'The Egyptian Novel in the Sixties'; and Badawi, *al-Riwaya al-Haditha fi Misr*, pp. 25–50.
52. Qasim, *The Seven Days of Man*, p. 217.
53. Ibid. pp. 217–18.
54. Al-Musawi, *Islam on the Street*, p. 115.
55. Al-Qaid, *Akhbar ʿIzbat al-Minisi*. The translations from the Arabic are my own.
56. A notable exception is *Laban al-Asfur* (Pigeon's Milk, 1994) that takes place in Cairo.
57. Similar preoccupations are central to al-Qaid's first novel *al-Hidad* (Mourning, 1969), which also takes place in a village in the Egyptian Delta, not far from the Minisi farm. In *News from the Minisi Farm*, Hajj al-Minisi expresses sadness at the death of Hajj Mansur Abu Allayl, the *ʿumda* (village chief or mayor) of al-Dahriyya and a central character in the previous novel. This is one of the only explicit instances in which connections are drawn between the two novels.
58. For an excellent discussion of al-Hakim's novel and its critique of Egypt's legal system, see Colla, 'Anxious Advocacy'.
59. Al-Qaid, *Akhbar ʿIzbat al-Minisi*, p. 20.

60. Ashhabun, 'Riwayat Yusuf al-Qaid-*Qismat al-Ghurama*'', p. 130. For more on al-Qaid's biography, see al-Kafuri, *Yusuf al-Qaid*, pp. 23–37.
61. Al-Qaid, *Akhbar ʿIzbat al-Minisi*, p. 3.
62. Al-Qaid, quoted in Mahmud Amin al-ʿAlim, 'al-Tarikh wa-l-Fan-wa-l-Dalala fi Thalath Riwayat Misriyya', p. 27.
63. This is particularly the case in *Yahduth fi Misr al-ʾAn* (1977) and *al-Harb fi Bar Misr* (1978) where the author/narrator often addresses the reader directly as a co-creator. For a discussion of this conflation in *Yahduth fi Misr al-ʾAn*, see Radwan, 'A Place for Fiction in the Historical Archive'; and al-Bashir, *Tajdid al-Riwaya al-ʿArabiyya*, pp. 361–411.
64. Al-Qalamawi, 'Muqadimma', p. 8.
65. Al-Qaid, *Akhbar ʿIzbat al-Minisi*, p. 32.
66. Ibid. p. 39.
67. Ibid. p. 68.
68. Ibid. p. 75.
69. Ibid. p. 75.
70. Ibid. p. 21.
71. Ibid. p. 39.
72. Ibid. p. 40.
73. Ibid. p. 64.
74. Ibid. p. 65.
75. Ibid. p. 195.
76. Ibid. pp. 195–6.
77. Ibid. p. 211.
78. Ibid. p. 212.
79. Abdel-Messih, 'Introduction', p. 17.
80. Al-Bashir, *Tajdid al-Riwaya al-ʿArabiyya*, p. 91. While al-Bashir is largely discussing the novel *Yahduth al-ʾAn fi Misr*, many of the claims regarding the manipulating of realist time apply to *News from the Minisi Farm* and other works by al-Qaid.
81. 'The Surrender' recounts Safwat's failures, both romantic and academic, in Alexandria, culminating in his seduction of Sabrin upon his return to the farm and her eventual submission. 'Pride' focuses primarily upon the night of Sabrin's marriage to Abul Ghayt; though the marriage contract is signed, their wedding ceremony is delayed for financial reasons. And finally, 'The Murder' charts Sabrin's fate following her submission to Safwat's advances. This chapter opens and closes with a death: the first being of Sabrin's baby who

she is forced to abort, and the second being of Sabrin herself, poisoned by her brother al-Zanati.

82. While the oral tradition lauds al-Adham for his bravery, casting him as a noble thief who helped the poor and lived by a strict moral code, the historical figure that emerges from the official archives is a criminal, a murderer and a thief who terrorised his rural community before being killed by the police. It is the popular folk hero that is celebrated by the characters in al-Qaid's novel. For more on al-Adham, as both hero and criminal, see Ezzeldin, 'History and Memory of Bandits in Modern Egypt'; Salih, 'Adham al-Sharqawi, Batal am Mujrim?'; and Hassan, 'Majala ᶜUmruha 88 Aman Tarsim Surat Adham al-Sharqawi'.

83. His story is immortalised in the *mawwāl* (popular folk song) sung by the famous Muhammad Rushdi and was also the subject of several radio, television and cinematic productions. The full text of the *mawwāl* in (transliterated) Arabic and English translation is cited in Larkin, 'A Brigand Hero of Egyptian Colloquial Literature'. The poet Mahmoud Ismail Gad wrote a version of the story for the radio, produced by Yusuf al-Hattab in 1964. Hussam al-Din Mustafa's 1964 film *Adham al-Sharqawi* was celebrated at least partially for the inclusion of songs sung by the famous Abdel Halim Hafiz, and a television show aired in 1985 sparked controversy after complaints by the Sharqawi family about the portrayal of al-Adham. See Ezzeldin, 'History and Memory of Bandits in Modern Egypt', pp. 61–4.

84. Al-Qaid, *Akhbar ᶜIzbat al-Minisi*, p. 57. Al-Zanati Khalifa, the historical ruler of the Berbers in Tunis, is also the principal enemy in *Sirat Bani Hilal* (The Bani Hilal Epic), and the ruler who must be defeated in order for the Bani Hilal bedouin tribe to rule Africa. The tribe's migration from the Arabian Peninsula, their crossing through Egypt, their conquest of North Africa and ultimate defeat are historical events that occurred between the tenth and twelfth centuries. The epic is, as has been noted, also central to Qasim's novel. See Reynolds, *Heroic Poets, Poetic Heroes*, pp. 13–20.

85. Al-Qaid, *Akhbarᶜ Izbat al-Minisi*, p. 162.

86. Ibid. p. 199.

87. Selim, *The Novel and the Rural Imaginary in Egypt*, p. 228. For more on mythic space as characteristic of the writing of the sixties generation, see Hafez, 'The Transformation of Reality and the Arabic Novel's Response', p. 106. The rural as mythic space can also be seen in Muhammad al-Bisati's first novel *al-Tajir wa-l-Naqqash* (The Merchant and the Painter, 1976).

88. Abdullah, *al-Kitabat al-Kamila*, p. 491. This is taken from an interview that took place between the author and the journalist Samir Gharib and was first published in the journal *al-Mustaqbal al-ʿArabi*.
89. Abdullah, *The Collar and the Bracelet*, p. 6.
90. Badawi, *al-Riwaya al-Haditha fi Misr*, pp. 53–4.
91. Frye, 'From Fables of Identity: Studies in Poetic Mythology, p. 134.
92. Abdullah, *The Collar and the Bracelet*, pp. 14–15.
93. In the scene in which Mustafa's return home is described – 'The Meeting that Follows a Long Absence' – the family house is tellingly described as a tomb in which 'The ghost of Bikhit al-Bishari, the father and husband, whispered in the air. Fahima's ghost, daughter and sister, whispered in the air'. Abdullah, *The Collar and the Bracelet*, p. 58.
94. Ibid. p. 39.
95. Ibid. p. 68.
96. Ibid. p. 69. For the Arabic original, see Abdullah, *al-Tawq wa-l-Iswira*, p. 147.
97. Abdullah, *al-Tawq wa-l-Iswira*, p.140. My translation.
98. Ibid. p. 114. My translation.
99. Ibid. p. 42. My translation.
100. Abdullah, *The Collar and the Bracelet*, p. 24.
101. Hafez, 'Qisas Yahya al-Taher Abdullah al-Tawila', p. 197.
102. Jacquemond, *Conscience of the Nation*, p. 91. He cites Muhammad Mustaghab and Saʿid Kafrawi as other examples of writers developing this form of writing.
103. Abdullah, *The Collar and the Bracelet*, p. 25
104. Warnes, *Magical Realism and the Postcolonial Novel*, p. 151.
105. Abdullah, *The Collar and the Bracelet*, p. 25.
106. Ibid. p. 38.
107. Ibid. p. 39.
108. Yaqub, 'The Tale of Those Who Did Not Travel', p. 128.
109. Badawi, *al-Riwaya al-Haditha fi Misr*, pp. 53–5.
110. Ibid. pp. 58–61
111. Hafez, 'Qisas Yahya al-Taher Abdullah al-Tawila', p. 196.
112. Abdullah, *The Collar and the Bracelet*, p. 51.
113. Selim, *The Novel and the Rural Imaginary in Egypt*, p. 226.
114. Abdullah, *al-Kitabat al-Kamila*, p. 491.
115. For more, see 'Introduction' to *al-Kitabat al-Kamila*, p. 5. Selim focuses upon the role of the oral storyteller, both in terms of the novelist himself and with

regards to the narrator of *al-Tawq wa-l-Iswira*, showing the way Abdullah seems to have bridged the gap between the writer and the traditional storyteller. Selim, *The Novel and the Rural Imaginary in Egypt*, pp. 216–17.

4

The Politics and Economics of Exile

I go beyond, or my imagination goes beyond [the Egyptian border] to an imaginary Emirate, following those simple, sad souls forced to leave, escaping hunger, in pursuit of their livelihoods.

Muhammad al-Bisati[1]

When you carry your exile upon your shoulders!

Bahaa Taher[2]

Egyptian novelists and short story writers have long drawn on national, regional and international spaces in the construction of the literary landscapes of their works. In the early decades of the twentieth century, writers regularly transgressed the borders of the Egyptian nation state in novels and short stories that moved beyond the space of the homeland. Works such as Taha Hussein's *Adib* (*A Man of Letters*, 1935), Tawfiq al-Hakim's *ʿUsfur min al-Sharq* (A Bird from the East, 1938) and Yahya Haqqi's *Qindil Umm Hashim* (*The Lamp of Umm Hashim*, 1944) all depict characters who travel to the West for their education.[3] Such literary texts betray the complexity of the relationship between Egypt and Europe during the period of colonial rule and with the legacies of *nahḍa* thinkers very much in circulation.[4] Europe in these works serves a largely metaphorical purpose, as Egypt's other and the place from which protagonists can evaluate and assess the progress of their native country. It also reflects a historical reality, and an overlapping of autobiography and fiction, with many writers and intellectuals having studied in Europe; Hussein and al-Hakim to name only two. In some instances, a physical journey is not even required. The encounter with the Western other, and the transformation of the protagonist that results, can be accomplished through an intellectual journey and a process of reading, such as the one experienced by Hussein in *al-Ayyam* (*The Days*) prior to his departure from Egypt. In this case the literary, cultural and intellectual sources that serve as the Arab writer's Western interlocutor bring about a change similar to the one that takes place during actual encounters.[5]

As El-Enany shows in his study of Arab representations of the West in literary production, this encounter has in modern times always been characterised by 'ambivalence'.[6] Rather than adhering to a binary of demonisation or emulation, Arab writers have grappled with the complexities of the Western other; 'To Them the European other was simultaneously an object of love and hate, a shelter and a threat, a usurper and a giver, an enemy to be feared and a friend whose help is to be sought'.[7] It is within the context of this Egyptian narrative tradition that one must situate the work of the writers of the sixties generation. Here we witness a change in the spaces represented; Europe as the space of education and progress is transformed, becoming instead that of political exile, or displaced by the Arab Gulf as the space of economic migration and exploitation. This change reflects the socio-economic and political reality of the postcolonial period, addressing the economic and political dislocation that took place under the regimes of Sadat and Mubarak. It is also a reminder of the failure of unities, both regional and international, attempted and imagined under Nasser. Muhammad al-Bisati and Bahaa Taher belong to a generation of writers that strongly supported the establishment of regional and international solidarities, particularly during the height of anti-colonial movements in the Arab world, Africa and Latin America. The transgression of national borders in their fiction thus occasions a broader critique of the failures of postcolonial regimes to create and maintain lasting alliances on a local or global scale. The move beyond the boundaries of Egypt is central to Taher's *al-Hubb fi al-Manfa* (*Love in Exile*, 1995) and al-Bisati's *Daqq al-Tubul* (*Drumbeat*, 2006), two works that manipulate the form of the realist novel to question the ideological and political valence of the nation. The two novels foreground the relationship between migration, labour and community in the contemporary world.[8] Taher calls into question the realism of his work by using both the lyrical and the documentary; the elevated, dream-like language of the descriptions of nature provide a glaring contrast to the techniques of recording and reporting used to document the horrors of war. Al-Bisati creates a fantastical situation that undermines the reality of life in the Emirate, providing possibilities of revolt and liberation. In addressing their critiques of the Egyptian state, both writers represent alternative homelands, and in doing so unsettle national and regional forms of belonging.[9]

In thinking about movement within the new global context, Arjun Appadurai suggests a relationship between five main 'scapes': ethnoscapes, technoscapes, financescapes, mediascapes and ideoscapes. The ethnoscape resonates with the worlds that are captured in the two novels. In explaining the term Appadurai states:

> By ethnoscape I mean the landscapes of persons who constitute the shifting world in which we live: tourists, immigrants, refugees, exiles, guest workers, other moving groups and persons constitute an essential feature of the world and appear to affect the politics of (and between) nations to a hitherto unprecedented degree. This is not to say that there are no relatively stable communities and networks, of kinship, of friendship, of work, and of leisure, as well as of birth, residence, and other filiative forms. But it is to say that the warp of these stabilities is everywhere shot through with the woof of human motion, as more people deal with the realities of having to move or the fantasies of wanting to move.[10]

For Appadurai the movement through global culture, the 'world of disjunctive global flows', is often uncertain, destabilizing and chaotic.[11] It is also a world in which the primacy of the nation state cannot be taken for granted; according to Appadurai 'the relationship between states and nations is everywhere an embattled one'.[12] The authors examined in this chapter contend with the ever more prominent 'landscapes of persons' who are moving, or forced to move, between nations, and the ongoing attempt to create and maintain different forms of community. Their works are literary renderings of the spaces of exile, dislocation and exploitation, capturing both the longing for, and the fantasy of, movement and the disappointments and struggles such actualisations can bring.

Taher's Community of Exiles

Bahaa Taher's *Love in Exile* is set in a nameless European capital. The opening of the novel presents the time and space of the narrative, explained through the relationship between the nameless protagonist (and first-person narrator) and the young Brigitte, and thus follows the 'well-worn technique of presenting the parties of the encounter through a male figure standing for the East and a female for the West'.[13] The two central characters of the novel, both exiles from their homelands, struggle to make a home for themselves in a foreign city:

> I was a Cairene whose city had expelled me to exile in the north. She was like me, a foreigner in that country. But she was European and with her passport she considered the whole of Europe her hometown. When we met by chance in that city, 'N', to which I was tied by work, we became friends.[14]

In Taher's earlier short story *Bil-Ams Halumtu Biki* (Yesterday I Dreamt of You, 1984), the protagonist also works in a nameless city in northern Europe, entering into a relationship with the foreign Anne Marie. As El-Enany argues, Taher's work presents

> a vision of tolerance and human fraternity hitherto unencountered in Arab representations of the West, a vision that transcends both the violent clashes of the past and the political differences of the present in order to concentrate on the ultimate concord of human beings on the individual level, their ultimate unity in suffering, in fragility before the cruelty of the human condition, be they from East or West.[15]

In *Love in Exile*, the protagonist, a middle-aged journalist and staunch supporter of Nasser, suffers increasing marginalisation with the coming of Sadat to power. Becoming as he calls it 'the consultant no one consulted', he chooses to leave Egypt and settle in Europe, where he works as a correspondent forced to write inconsequential articles.[16]

The protagonist's circumstance recalls the fate of writers and intellectuals in the aftermath of Sadat's ascension to power in 1970, which was followed by purges in both the political and cultural spheres. The 'Corrective Revolution' instigated by Sadat in 1971 effectively toppled his political opponents and marginalised the left wing of the Arab Socialist Union (ASU). Beginning that same year, Sadat took steps to dismantle the cultural edifice established under Nasser: literary magazines were shut down, and writers and intellectuals deemed hostile to the regime were removed from their positions and prevented from publishing. This policy continued throughout the 1970s, up until a month before Sadat's assassination, when in September 1981 over 1500 intellectuals were arrested. The antagonism exhibited by the state towards members of the intellectual and cultural establishment led many to leave Egypt: both Taher and al-Bisati left the country during this time.[17]

Brigitte, the other central character of the novel, is a young woman from Austria, who leaves her country after she and her African husband suffer a racist attack that results in her miscarriage. The third exile is the protagonist's old colleague Ibrahim, also an Egyptian journalist and communist, who is imprisoned under Nasser, endures persecution with the purges instituted by Sadat, and leaves Egypt to Iraq, Syria, finally settling in Beirut.[18] The three characters are unexpectedly united in this foreign city, meeting at a human rights conference on Chile, and come to constitute a temporary community of exiles.

I read these characters as exiles based on the notion that the state of exile refers to both forced and chosen departure from the homeland, allowing for expansive understandings of the notion and its literary renderings. According to Bettina L. Knapp:

> Exile may be involuntary (one is banished or expelled from one's native land by authoritative decree), or voluntary (one escapes persecution, evades punishment or stressful circumstances, or carves out a new existence for oneself). The fact or state of being deported, expelled, proscribed, expatriated, or simply leaving one's homeland implies prolonged separation from one's native country.[19]

The characters of the novel are examples of this second form of exile, one that is undertaken voluntarily, largely because of persecution in one's homeland.

Why then does this community of exiles meet in a nameless city, the city N?[20] On the one hand, the reader is told that the city is in Europe, allowing a connection to be made to a real geographical location. On the other hand, the absence of an actual location, a nationally defined space, suggests the possibility of the existence of a 'supranational community' based upon a form of 'internationalist solidarity'.[21] This community, as we shall see, proves untenable, a reflection of the failure of the internationalist movements of the earlier decades, and an unrealistic possibility within the current context. It also makes an interesting point of comparison with the nameless protagonist, though as Jabir ʿAsfur notes, while we know a great deal about the character's history, we learn very little about the city.[22] This I would suggest only serves to solidify its separation from the outside world. It also recalls, but does not directly mirror, the events of the author's own life. Like the protagonist of his novel, Taher worked as a journalist, joining the Egyptian Radio Service following his graduation from university in 1956. During this time, he helped establish the Second Program, the radio's cultural station, where he worked producing dramatic plays for radio. He was forced to leave his job in 1975 when he was targeted by Sadat's purge of left-leaning intellectuals. His unemployment was accompanied by difficulties in publishing his fiction. This drove him to leave Egypt for Geneva, where he lived and worked as a translator for the United Nations (1981–95). It is during this time of self-imposed exile that he wrote *Love in Exile*.[23]

Lorenzo Casini, in his reading of the novel, focuses upon the sense of estrangement experienced by the protagonist and Brigitte. While the former experiences marginalisation in the workplace and separation from his family, the latter cuts herself off from the world following the attack which results in her miscarriage. This causes Casini to see the idea of exile in Taher's novel referring 'not so much to the physical location in which the love story (*al-ḥubb*) between the Egyptian protagonist and an Austrian woman (Brigitte) takes place (an unnamed European city) as to the existential condition experienced by both lovers'.[24] Casini also notes how the words for exile in Arabic (*manfā* and *ghurba*) bring together these ideas of exile and estrangement. During the 1960s in Egypt, the idea of exile as estrangement gained traction with the influence of writers such as Camus, Sartre and Kafka. The term *ightirāb* (from the root which also means to be/feel a stranger/alienated) was used within this context to convey a sense of estrangement, often associated with existentialism. In the decades that followed, the term *ghurba* came to be more closely associated with the term *manfā*, to convey a meaning of banishment or exclusion from the nation or homeland.[25] While this sense of estrangement is certainly the cause of an existential anxiety for both characters, I would argue that the exile is both existential and physical. The estrangement recalls the condition of writers and intellectuals of Taher's own generation, whose work captures this sense of alienation. But the protagonist's attempt to escape this condition of estrangement is manifest in the novel as a form of physical escape, resulting in a foregrounding of the space of the city.

City of Salvation

Love in Exile brims with descriptions of the natural beauty of the city, encouraging a reading of this exilic space as a refuge. As Mahmud Amin al-ʿAlim states, 'gardens and water are always in our path throughout the novel'.[26] Descriptions of the mountain, the woods and the river suggest a peace and tranquility that the protagonist craves. They also mark the progression of time in the narrative. From the appearance of the trees and the flowers the reader discovers it is summer; the narrative time of the plot is only between the summer and autumn. While this is not a complete break-down of linearity, Taher manipulates the progression of time here to further separate the city of exile from the outside world. On one of many excursions the protagonist takes, he stops to admire the beauty of the woods, the 'radiant green, almost diaphanous' trees, and the 'little yellow and white wildflowers that adorned the land in the summer'.[27]

The lyricism of such language renders the city magical, a space that transcends the here and now. This is not to say that Taher does not produce a realist novel, but that he undercuts this realism in various ways, one of them being in his elevation of nature and the potential it holds for salvation. It is primarily through the free (direct and indirect) discourse of the narrator, as exemplified in the descriptive passages, and through his dialogue with other characters that the events of the novel are relayed. The internal thoughts of the protagonist do not, however, just focus on his feelings. Al-Kharrat, in discussing the innovative contributions of Taher as part of the sixties generation, notes that the first-person narrator is 'very careful to describe what he sees and narrate what happens'.[28] For al-Kharrat this results in the transformation of the first-person discourse into part of the larger dialogue that dominates much of Taher's work. It is noteworthy in this context that the discourse and dialogue are used first to present descriptions of the striking beauty of the city and later to convey the horrors of the events in Lebanon. The scenes of violence and destruction are described through conversations between the characters (one of whom is a witness to the events), or through the thoughts of the protagonist as he watches the events unfold on television. Such thoughts dominate the second half of the novel, taking the place of his reflections on the beauty of nature.

Situated amidst the river and the mountains is the café, the communal space for the characters; here the protagonist meets daily with his new love Brigitte and with his old colleague Ibrahim. The protagonist describes the 'oval-shaped café jutting into the river like a shell cast on the rocky tongue of land. A long path lined on both sides with beds of well-tended flowers led to its quiet location on the riverbank.'[29] It is not only that the café is a space that exists in harmony with nature, but also that it is a space of tranquility and peace that invites forgetting, an example of Lefebvre's 'representational spaces', spaces that are 'alive' that 'speak[s],' and that 'embrace[s] the loci of passion, of action and of lived situations, and thus immediately impl[y] time'.[30] The characters of this novel are intent on living in a present that is both perpetual and removed from the rest of the world, and it is in the café, a space of no small significance within the Arabic literary context, that the three exiles meet time and again to experience their permanent present.[31]

Nature as a distraction and an escape is further emphasised by the presence of the protagonist's 'secret garden', an enclave in the city to which he retreats when in need of solace. Following Ibrahim's confession that he no longer has any interest in visiting historical sites during his travels, but prefers to see the 'trees and the green' in any city he visits, enjoying anything that reminds him of his 'childhood, of the Nile, and the sycamores and the willows', the protagonist takes him to his 'secret garden'.[32] As they walk among the 'high poplars with their thick green foliage and the chestnut trees that had begun to bear their round green nuts' and the roses and pansies 'in the youthful flush of early summer', nature offers the two men momentary respite from their troubles.[33]

The protagonist's need to escape is built into his relationship with Brigitte, which is represented, like the city, as a haven from the world. It is because of a promise to Brigitte that he detaches himself from the world, refraining from writing articles or reading the news. In thinking about their relationship, the protagonist envisions it as a means for them both to evade the misery of past and present: 'I wish I could soar above this thick, massive, wall-filled world, and you with me to another world, soft and transparent . . .

a world that rectifies all the past and erases it, a world that fixes the present, keeping nothing but joy' he declares.³⁴

City N versus Cairo

City N as refuge appears in opposition to Cairo, the protagonist's home, and the city from which he flees. Cairo is first described as the city that 'expelled' the protagonist into exile. However, as we learn from the narrative, he chooses exile because of the increasing marginalisation he faces under Sadat's regime. After refusing to write an article in support of the new president, the professional success he enjoyed under Nasser comes to an end. While lyrical descriptions of city N are abundant, Cairo is never described in material, physical terms. Rather, its function is largely symbolic, representing the socio-economic and political transformations of post-revolutionary Egypt. The collapse of Nasser's regime is an extension of the protagonist's failure, professional and personal, and both are entangled with Cairo as representative of the homeland. So it is that Nasser comes to be the source of many disagreements with his wife Manar, and the President's death echoes the collapse of the marriage. The protagonist's estrangement at work is mirrored in his divorce and separation from his family; he explains 'that was one of the reasons I left the country. It was difficult for me to be in the same city with my children but apart from them, making appointments [to see them] like friends or strangers.'³⁵

Likewise, Taher presents the transformation of Egyptian society through changes in the family. The protagonist's ex-wife Manar abandons her secular, feminist ideals and embraces religious conservatism, donning the veil and writing articles on *sharīʿa*. His son Khalid cites a fatwa to justify abstaining from an international chess tournament and tries to exercise increasing control over his younger sister Hanadi. In numerous conversations Ibrahim mistakenly refers to Khalid as Nasser, ironic given that Khalid represents the changes to Egyptian society that the protagonist resents and that he associates with the passing of Nasser. Hanadi embodies the consumerism and burgeoning private investment associated with Sadat's economic policies, demanding expensive gifts in every conversation with her father. Thus, the novel 'exploits the shift in space occasioned by forced exile and physical dislocation from Egypt to reflect on the identity of the homeland'.³⁶ It is from this changed society, from Cairo, his homeland, and his failed position within it that the protagonist is so desperate to escape.

The Impossibility of Escape

Taher's exilic city initially offers the possibility of escape, a place for the protagonist to flee from the disappointments of the past and present. However, this temporary peace is destroyed by the devastating events that unfold in Lebanon and return the reader to the 'real world'.[37] This also introduces real or historic time into the narrative, placing us firmly in the summer and autumn of 1982, during the Siege of Beirut. From his exile, the protagonist is tormented by the paralysis of the Arab regimes in the face of the violence and destruction that are unleashed on the people of Lebanon. The events culminate in the Sabra and Shatila massacre.[38] The novel describes the bloodshed in explicit detail:

> In the refugee camps naked children and mothers wearing plastic slippers ran, slapping their own faces in the midst of huts whose roofs had slid down on their walls to create jagged piles of rubble, of dust and bricks and twisted iron rods amid black and white smoke ... overturned tables, children's toys stained with blood, photographs, and small statues of the Virgin Mary smashed on the floor in the midst of fires and corpses lying on their backs and others doubled on their sides.[39]

Ibrahim, having returned to Lebanon, is a witness to the events that unfold, and it is from him that the protagonist first learns of the tragedy. Calling the protagonist from the refugee camp in Beirut, Ibrahim struggles to describe the horrors he has seen. He tells of the 'smell of death and the vast swarms of flies' and the 'wet lime on the ground covering a large pit and from the pit peered smashed heads and blackened arms and legs'.[40] In Ibrahim's narrative the blood and the corpses of the victims combine with the rubble of smashed buildings to form a new landscape, one born of death and destruction. The descriptions of the horrors of the refugee camp stand in stark contrast to the lyricism and poetry of the earlier passages describing the city, though in both cases there is a sustained attention to the physical; the lyrical passages completely disappear from the novel following Ibrahim's disclosure of the details of the massacre. Once again, the space of the novel is not confined to the nameless European city, but rather Taher purposefully traverses borders to extend the narrative to other nations within the Arab world.

The descriptions of Sabra and Shatila bring together the use of dialogue and observation that are one of the innovative hallmarks of Taher's writing. The atrocities are presented first through the conversation between Ibrahim and the protagonist, during which he dictates part of the article that he wishes the protagonist to publish on his behalf. Then the reader observes the events as if he/she, like the protagonist, were watching the report on television: 'After that the camera moves around in silence. It moves through narrow alleys in the midst of destroyed houses ... Piles of corpses strewn over the ground. Corpses behind corpses and corpses next to corpses.'[41] Taher draws upon eyewitness accounts and testimonies, the tools of journalistic investigation and writing, in recreating the events of 1982.[42] Al-ʿAlim reads the use of testimonies as part of the novel's attempt to present 'a documentary picture of our current age'.[43] While I disagree with al-ʿAlim's assertion that these accounts undermine the centrality of the protagonist's narrative, I argue that the desire to document is very much a part of Taher's literary project and speaks to the overlapping roles of fiction and journalism as suggested by this novel. Given that journalism in the Arab world, particularly in the first half of the twentieth century, played a significant role both in the circulation of ideas of reform and opposition, and in the development of Arabic narrative discourse, Taher's use of journalistic accounts suggests a continuation of a tradition that brings together the two genres of fiction and journalism, both here invested in documenting the violence of the state.[44]

Discussing the 'self-reflexive novel' of the 'post-Mahfouzian' period, al-Musawi notes that such works often include sources from 'the news, journalistic reports, rumors and transmitted information' that allow for the reexamination of reality and 'all it contains in terms of the violation of the rights of people, communities, and the writer himself'.[45] In an interview, Taher explains the difficulty in undertaking such a task:

> This novel has a long story. Its writing took ten years or more but I wasn't writing regularly. I began it after 'Sabra and Shatila'. I was violently defeated and agitated about these massacres but I said: it is a lie to write about an experience you haven't seen or participated in. So I stopped. Despite this,

there remained within me something urging me to write to fulfill an obligation to those martyrs.[46]

Taher's words here help us understand the use of factual accounts in his narrative to come to terms with the horrors that have taken place and to do justice to the victims of such violence. In an afterword citing the real sources used in the novel, the author closes with the chilling revelation that the interviews and articles are as real as 'the blood of the martyrs'.[47]

The intersection between journalism and fiction is foregrounded in both the form and content of the novel; evident immediately is that the protagonist and the other main characters are all journalists, struggling to come to terms with the role and efficacy of their profession. The political role of the journalist, the sense that he/she is committed to the struggle for freedom, equality and democracy is one that is shared with the writer of fiction – this recalls the analysis of the task of the intellectual in Chapter 1. Here too, Taher's protagonist strives to enact change in a world in which he is increasingly marginalised and ever more irrelevant. The political power of writing resonates through the figures that populate the novel; Ernest Hemingway, Federico García Lorca and Pablo Neruda all appear in the novel as reminders of the political and artistic role of the literary writer. They also bring the literary inspirations of the sixties generation to the fore. This is striking when read against the work of the Arab exilic poets themselves, who include the very same figures in their poetry. For example, al-Musawi argues that these figures come to populate the literary landscape of the exilic poems of the Iraqi modernist poet Abdel Wahab al-Bayati forming a 'new homeland, a poetic space of forebears and ancestors who hold many things in common and who offer him lineage and filiation'.[48] Taher creates a similar 'textual homeland' in his novel, a space that is occupied by the protagonist and a community of literary exiles, while also bringing the interlocutors of the sixties generation to centre stage.[49]

The events in Lebanon spell the death of the internationalist community, formed at the start of the novel, by the community of exiles. It is also the death of the Arab nationalist dream to which the protagonist defiantly clings, even after the death of Nasser. As Dirgham notes 'this war, from the point of view of the novel, would not have taken place in such a glaring manner if the nationalist direction of Abdel Nasser had continued'.[50] Following the massacres of Sabra and Shatila, political protests are organised on the streets of city N, which is momentarily recast in the novel as the space of political activity and resistance and seems to emerge briefly as Lefebvre's 'differential space', that of opposition and dissent.[51] The characters note that what cannot take place in Cairo and other Arab capitals (namely public demonstrations denouncing Israel's policies) is instead taking place in this European city. And yet the efficacy of this expression of resistance is highly suspect. Europe as a site of political action is greatly undermined by the difficulties of immigration and questions of human rights that are raised in the novel. The conference with which the novel opens, and the lack of interest it generates, undercuts any form of international solidarity, undoing the idea of Europe as a space of political revolution. 'Who did you want to come? Who cares now, here or anywhere else?' the protagonist asks himself.[52] International solidarity thus emerges as a thing of the past, part of the struggle for democracy, social and economic equality, intended to bring together the peoples of Latin America, Europe and the Arab world. This clearly no longer has any viability in the world of Taher's novel.

Despite the struggle undertaken by the protagonist, he is unable to affect any real change, either through his writing or the political activism of the street demonstrations. The novel closes with an overwhelming sense of failure and foreboding; the protagonist's refusal to cooperate with the Arab Prince, in the establishment of an Arabic newspaper, ultimately results in the loss of his and Brigitte's jobs. Unemployed and defeated Brigitte decides to return to her home in Austria. The fate of the protagonist is even more precarious. Travelling to the Prince's castle to confront him, the protagonist stumbles upon Pedro (a Chilean refugee from the human rights conference) now selling drugs to make ends meet. This encounter takes place 'at a small park on the riverbank, a deserted park in the midst of the fog and the cold'.[53] Momentarily, Taher returns to the lyricism of the novel's beginning. The protagonist's collapse, and suggested death, is rendered in highly poetic language, reminiscent of the earlier scenes of natural beauty:

> I wasn't tired. I was sliding into a calm sea, carried on my back by a soft wave and the melody of a pleasant flute . . .

The wave was carrying me away.
It was undulating slowly and rocking me. The flute was accompanying me, with its long, plaintive melody, to peace and tranquility.[54]

The episodes of escapism associated with the contemplation of the natural sites of the city, the river, mountain and gardens, all culminate in this final scene. The city as a space of salvation and retreat is undermined once the events in Lebanon force the protagonist to confront the current political reality. As a writer and intellectual there is no possibility for Taher's protagonist to remain isolated from the world. Death is ultimately the only escape.

Drumbeat: Spatial Inequality and an Emirate Divided

Muhammad al-Bisati's *Daqq al-Tubul* (*Drumbeat*, 2006) tells the story of a nameless Arab Emirate, emptied of its native inhabitants in the wake of the World Cup football tournament. Leaving the migrant workers in control, the locals travel to Europe to support their national team. As an urban narrative it is something of an anomaly within al-Bisati's oeuvre; along with *al-Khaldiyya* (*Over the Bridge*, 2006) and *Layali Ukhra* (*Other Nights*, 2000), *Drumbeat* is the only other city novel amongst his thirteen novels.[55] It is also important as one of the few Egyptian novels to explore the issue of economic migration to the Gulf. The other notable example is Ibrahim Abdel Meguid's *al-Balda al-Ukhra* (*The Other Place*, 1991).[56] *Drumbeat* was well received by critics upon its publication and was awarded the Sawiris Literary Award for the novel in 2009, one of the most highly regarded independent literary awards in Egypt.

Al-Bisati's shift in space speaks to changes within the Egyptian national context that resulted in increased labour migration to the Gulf. While migration for educational purposes was encouraged in the 1960s, Sadat's 'Open Door' policy actively promoted labour migration as part of a development strategy, authorising temporary and permanent migration in 1971 and lifting all restrictions on labour migration in 1974. Although this included migration to the West, Iraq, Libya and the oil-rich countries of the Gulf increasingly attracted growing numbers of Egyptians.[57] In discussing migration policies under the regimes of Nasser and Sadat, Ralph Sells argues that pan-Arabism made labour migration socially acceptable, framing the process as one in which Egyptians were helping their Arab brothers. This remained the official position even after Sadat re-directed Egypt's strategic orientation away from the Arab world.[58] Sells goes on to explain that whatever the impact of Nasser's pan-Arabism, these sentiments were largely overwhelmed by later developments: 'In classic fashion capitalist development complemented demographic forces in the creation of surplus labor through the simultaneous creation of consumer desires and structural under-employment'.[59] This caused the continued outflow of Egyptian workers in the decades that followed, particularly given that Sadat's successor, Mubarak, adopted a similar position towards labour migration.[60] Despite the recognition of the economic and demographic forces at play, Sells ends his article (published several decades before this novel) with the suggestion that perhaps 'the Arab nationalist dream of oil capital and Egyptian people' would eventually lead to better working conditions and rights for the migrant population.[61] This is clearly not the case in *Drumbeat*, a novel that raises questions about political and economic solidarity and the pan-Arabism upon which it was based.

In the opening of the novel the (again nameless) Egyptian protagonist alludes to a moment in the past when the transformation of the Emirate began, driven by the oil boom:

> The discovery of oil here many years ago had changed everything overnight. Modern sky-scrapers shot up, sheathed in smoked-glass façades to repel the scorching sun. Huge multistoried malls proliferated with their banks of gleaming escalators ... As construction boomed and the city sprawled, suburbs were born: complexes of grand and ornately embellished villas, each with its own swimming pool and set in spacious gardens, every tree, bush, and flower of which had been nurtured from seedlings flown in from abroad.[62]

The emerging skyscrapers and booming malls mark symbolically and materially the birth of the urban landscape, in a detailed description that reinforces the realism of al-Bisati's text.[63] And yet, this realism is undercut by the distance that al-Bisati creates between this world and an actual sense of time and space. Here, as in Taher's novel, there is reference to a real geographic location, but not an actual country. This serves to distance the space of the Emirate from the real world, but also from the author's own experience. Al-Bisati spent a number of years working in Saudi Arabia (1980–5) and though the novel is not strictly autobiographical, it certainly resonates with his experience.[64] More importantly al-Bisati's Emirate straddles the boundaries between the real and the imaginary; while the reader is reminded of any number of places within the Arabian Gulf, one cannot determine which one, if any, serves as the basis for this novel. That the World Cup is being held in France (which is revealed as the locals make their exodus) provides some means to date the events of the novel. France hosted the World Cup only twice, in 1938 and 1998. And in 1998 Saudi Arabia was a participant. Given that Saudi Arabia is a kingdom, and not an emirate, the exact identification between real and imaginary country does not hold, but the similarities between monarchy and emirate as forms of government are no doubt on al-Bisati's mind.[65]

It is the discovery of oil that brings workers from around the world. The separation between the locals and the migrant workers is manifest in the division between the old and new quarters of the city, further emphasising that the construction of space is ultimately a 'product of power relationships'.[66] The upper echelons of the local population inhabit the new suburbs, with their lavish villas and swimming pools, as described in the earlier passage. Separated from these suburbs by large expanses of green 'scrub bush' are the old neighbourhoods with their mud houses, simple structures that have 'weathered countless years since they first served to gather in the indigenous inhabitants from their far-flung tents in the desert'.[67] These buildings too have undergone changes with the 'modernisation' that has taken place; the houses are connected to the sewage system, fitted with new floors, air conditioning units and fans.[68] The old neighbourhoods thus come to occupy an indeterminate space between the traditional and the modern. With the expansion of the new suburbs, discussions arise about the removal of the older neighbourhoods. It is decided, however, that they should remain as symbols of the past, as 'ancestral homes' which people might wish to visit from time to time.[69] Care is taken to preserve 'their historic character' through the antique lamp posts hanging in the streets, the palm trees in the court yards, and the pigeon towers on the roofs of the houses.[70] The foreign workers take up residence in the older neighbourhoods, favouring the low rents and the atmosphere that allows them to 'live at ease amid their familiar din'.[71] The local population regard these neighbourhoods, preserved for their 'historical' charm, as tourist attractions. They bring their foreign guests to dine there, enjoying the music and entertainment of these quarters.[72] The neighbourhoods are renovated and preserved to allow them to fulfil a cultural function, as symbols of the Emirate's past. As Khalaf notes in his study of the changes to the Gulf city, 'since the 1990s, the Gulf municipalities have renovated and preserved many traditional quarters as heritage monuments'.[73]

The division between local and foreigner, manifest in the division between the old and new sections of the city, is mirrored in the homes of the Emiratis themselves. Not all the foreigners live in the old neighbourhood – many reside in the homes where they work. Within these homes they are required to operate with as little visibility as possible. The narrator explains that the Emiratis prefer to employ workers from the Philippines because they are known for their hard work *and* because they are 'small and compact and so do not take up much room'.[74] The novel's narrator, an Egyptian who works as a driver, lives in Abu Amer's house, a wealthy sheikh. He, along with the other workers of the household, live in 'annex[es]' attached to the vast villa of Abu Amer.[75] While they clean and tend to the grounds of the villa, 'trimming shrubbery and cleaning the swimming pool', they neither live in nor enjoy these spaces, but only maintain them for their employers. And thus, on the level of both public and private, Emirate and home, space is segregated and divided according to socio-economic and national hierarchies.

Fantasy Football

The divided world of al-Bisati's Emirate is temporarily turned on its head with the beginning of the World Cup tournament; the Emir asks all the citizens to fly to France in support of the national team. What ensues as a result is a situation that is quite outside the realm of the ordinary; with all the nationals gone the country is temporarily in the hands of the foreign workers. This transformation of the Emirate into an exceptional space, removed from the rest of the world, can be connected to what al-Kharrat describes as one of the markers of the 'new sensibility' which defines the work of this generation. One of the main trends he identifies is that of magical realism, noting how writers use elements of 'fantasy and embellishment' in their work as a means to undermine the division between the real and the imaginary.[76] Here, the author creates a fantastical situation which blurs the boundaries, bringing together the worlds of dreams and reality. It is not unlike al-Ghitani's magical impotency curse and Abdullah's mythical impregnation discussed in previous chapters. This is also reminiscent of al-Bisati's later novel *Over the Bridge*, the story of a protagonist who builds an architectural model of his ideal city, only to have his fictional creation come to life before his very eyes. In both novels, the opportunity to create a utopian society free of social and economic inequality is momentary, and the protagonists' cities inevitably recreate the disparities of the real world.

The narrator of *Drumbeat* immediately recognises that this unusual situation has created the opportunity for the subversion of the existing order. Here too, Jackson's assertion that the fantastic has the potential to enable a subversive or transformative strategy is instructive.[77] After dropping off Abu Amer and his family at the airport, the narrator notes that the 'whole country was now in the hands of the foreign workers . . . If they took over the Emirate' he imagines, 'closed the ports, and broadcast an impassioned message to the world demanding recognition for their new regime, on the grounds that everything in the country was built with their toil and sweat, they could well receive some international recognition'.[78] This is a reminder that the nationals are vastly outnumbered by the foreign population. As Khalaf states 'only the Gulf oil city has up to 80% of its population as transient guest workers with few equal legal rights and privileges as compared to the nationals'.[79] Here the disproportionate division of the population occasions the imagination of a moment of radical transformation. The narrator then proceeds to tell of an example that took place in the neighbouring emirate, where the prince staged a coup against his father, when the latter left the country for medical treatment. While the workers in this novel do not stage an insurrection against their absent 'fathers', they engage in acts of resistance, encroaching on spaces ordinarily denied them.

Once Abu Amer's family has left, the workers immediately jump in the swimming pool. The narrator returns from the airport to find them in the garden in the midst of a pool party, 'the Filipinos were in their swimming suits, frolicking loudly in the pool, splashing water in all directions'.[80] The lavish pool, a symbol of wealth and power, thus becomes the site of subversion: the workers lay claim over the houses they occupy but do not inhabit. Similarly, Rishim, Abu Amer's maid, who is forced to lie about her marital status to acquire and retain her employment, can temporarily live with her husband,

and chooses to do so in Abu Amer's bedroom, undermining the segregation of living space.

Other examples of limited acts of rebellion take place within the larger context of the Emirate. The police officers let the prisoners out of their cells, provided they 'report for roll call every morning' and return to their cells the day before the Emiratis return.[81] Stores are left unattended with signs asking customers to leave payment for their purchases.[82] Acts such as these suggest a controlled display of subversion, small gestures of sedition that remain within a restricted realm: the opportunity for an uprising is never realised, nor even attempted. Ultimately, the existing system of hierarchy and control is not overturned. The prisoners do in fact return every morning and the customers note that the stores 'have hidden cameras that can pick up a cockroach moving', thus reminding us that the system of surveillance and control still operates even in the absence of the Emiratis themselves.[83]

A potential moment of liberation exists in the football stadium, a space that is transformed into one of celebration and festivity, a possible moment of release from the suffocating climate of the Emirate. Here the workers gather each night to watch the tournament, with each national group setting up its own tent in the stadium, serving its cuisine and enjoying its own music and dance; 'I wove through the babble of languages toward the stadium', the narrator describes, 'inhaling the aromas of cuisines from around the world as I passed by one food stand after another surrounded by midnight snackers.'[84] There is a sense that the possibility exists here for the growth of a cosmopolitan existence, a coexistence of different ethnic and national identities, outside of the system of hierarchy. In some ways this is the idea of the Gulf city that Khalaf describes:

> The urban culture of the Gulf city is rather a constellation of urban subcultures representing multiple ethnic groups and life ways. It can be argued here that it is indeed this cultural diversity that has become a distinguishing feature of the Gulf oil city culture, which manifests itself in the simultaneous performance of multiple ethnic characters. This generates a cultural kaleidoscope of urban lifeways and identities, all with their different nationalities, religions, physical types, dress, food, music, smells, and even localized suburban environment.[85]

Despite the idealism of Khalaf's description, he is cognisant of the fact that these subcultures exist under the shadow of the dominant national culture. In al-Bisati's novel this shadow looms large; workers from the large villas refuse to mix with other groups and separation by national identity is not transgressed. Instead, what we see is the replication of the existing system of division and stratification. The possible unity that the narrator envisions at the very start of the novel, a unity of foreign migrant workers in opposition to the local elite, is once again undermined.

The gathering that takes place in the football stadium is, after all, in support of the Emirate's team, and thus the allegiance of the different national and ethnic groups to the team reinforces the disparity and inequalities inherent in the social structure.[86] The foreign workers support with a passion and ferocity the team of a nation of which they can never hope to be nationals. This is all too familiar in the case of migrant workers in the Arab world. Migrants to countries such as Kuwait, Saudi Arabia and the United Arab Emirates do not gain any kind of citizenship rights.[87] The reminder of the dominance of the national culture seems to undermine the possibility of the cosmopolitan collectivity suggested by the descriptions of the groups occupying the stadium. Rather, the reader comes to identify the situation more with what Diane Singerman and Paul Amar have termed 'petro-cosmopolitanism', the system of exploitation that 'dispenses with the concept of citizenship' while maintaining a system of 'guest-worker apartheid'.[88]

The celebrations and street parades that follow the team's victories recall forms of political expression, as 'a medley of different nationalities' take to the street in a public display of solidarity with the players.[89] Particularly striking is the narrator's observation that 'this had to have been the first time in the history of the Emirate that women ever appeared in a march', representing another transgression of the gendered segregation of space.[90]

> An Egyptian carried on others' shoulders was the most zealous cheerer in their segment of the parade. 'With our soul, with our blood we support you!' he bellowed, pausing to let the others echo the chant after him, fists punching the air.[91]

The chant of 'With our soul, with our blood we support you' (*bil rūḥ bil dam*) is a political slogan repeated during protests. Its use here, in reference to the Emirati football team, suggests that such international sports events are an opportunity for the assertion of national identity, and an alternative to meaningful political participation within a social structure that is predicated upon a clear distinction between national and foreigner.

With the defeat of the national team and the impending return of the Emiratis, the re-establishment of the status quo is all but guaranteed. The potentially liberating situation created by the absence of the Emiratis cannot continue. The end of the novel tells of the preparations that are undertaken by the workers in anticipation of the nationals' return:

> The streets were decked with victory arches made of flowers. Each was crowned with a photo of one of the members of the national soccer team, intercepting the ball with the edge of his foot . . . The prisoners were back behind bars. Their arms reached through the windows waving miniature national flags . . . I stood with the throngs that packed the sides of the road leading from the airport to the capital. We were waiting to cheer the returning team.[92]

Abu Salem's Villa and the Manifestation of Inequality

Al-Bisati's *Drumbeat* imagines a moment of revolutionary possibility in the Emirate; the protagonist's early vision that the foreign workers take over the Emirate frames the events that ensue. However, what becomes increasingly clear is that this libratory opportunity is not fully seized by the foreign population. The continuation of the system of discrimination and inequality is at the heart of the story of the Egyptian worker Zahiya. Beside Abu Amer's house is the home of Abu Salem and his wife; the latter, now bedridden because of her excessive weight, hires Zahiya to act as her helper and companion.

Passing by the house one evening the narrator is invited in by Zahiya who proceeds to tell her story during the nights that follow. That the narrator is able to enter Abu Salem's villa and get to know Zahiya at all is a direct result of the Emiratis absence. The segregation of men and women is discussed at length in the novel. The male workers, fearful of any accusation of inappropriate behaviour, which could lead to their deportation, avoid even looking at a woman –national or foreigner. The narrator tells us how this constant suppression of desire has led to a condition of impotency rife amongst the foreign workers. This is largely related to the 'Drumbeat' of the novel's title; famous throughout the city is the 'African', the one man who has escaped this cursed condition and who performs in a café by exposing himself to the sound of music. Here of course the reader is aware of the way al-Bisati draws upon the existing racist stereotypes of 'Africans' as virile and sexually dominant. However, what is also suggested is the relationship between political, economic and sexual repression. The sexual impotency of the men is a manifestation of their lack of any form of political or economic agency given their status as foreign migrant workers in the Emirate. This also connects to the discussion of the sexual as the site of agency in Chapter 1.

Structurally, the narrative of Zahiya's life and her experience in Abu Salem's house runs parallel to the larger narrative of the Emirate and the unusual circumstances of the football tournament. Both characters suffer the same fate; unable to provide for their families in Egypt, they must endure separation to make ends meet. The position of the two characters, the only two whose voices we hear, represents al-Bisati's implicit critique of the failure of the postcolonial Egyptian state to provide for its citizens. Given the reality of the system of inequality and discrimination under which Zahiya and the narrator find themselves living, the failure of the Arab nationalist dream of the past is laid bare. While the critique is not as explicit as in Taher's novel, the system of exploitation in place in the Emirate is symptomatic of the demise of the unity and solidarity dreamt of by Taher's protagonist. The dream of regional Arab unity and cooperation has been replaced by a system of economic exploitation and inequality that is a part of the larger system of global capitalism.[93]

Zahiya's experience cements this idea. Her nationality does not safeguard against the forms of exploitation endured by the foreign workers of the Emirate. Coming to the house of Abu Salem as his wife's companion, she spends her days listening to Umm Salem recount stories of her childhood. Zahiya's circumstances change for the worse when Umm Salem, in a desperate attempt to limit her husband's sexual indiscretions, concocts a plan for Zahiya to become his mistress. Powerless to object to the situation, Zahiya is forced to comply with Umm Salem's wishes. Her circumstances continue to deteriorate when she discovers she is pregnant with Abu Salem's child, who she is coerced into pretending is not her child but that of Umm and

Abu Salem (themselves unable to conceive). As a result, Zahiya finds herself trapped both in Abu Salem's house and in the Emirate, any decision to return to Egypt tantamount to abandoning her child.

Zahiya's experience of Salem's house, even in their absence, is one of confinement. While the rest of the Emirate celebrates, Zahiya remains in the house, never leaving the grounds of the villa. Not only that, but unlike the workers in Abu Amer's villa, Zahiya does not take the opportunity to enjoy the spaces ordinarily off limits to her. Rather she remains in Umm Salem's bedroom, alone except for the nightly visits of the protagonist. During the first visit, Zahiya explains that she remains inside as she has nowhere to go: 'They've all gone out. I was about to, too, but then I thought, where would I go? My job is to sit and keep her company. That's what I've grown used to. I don't know anybody outside these grounds.'[94] Zahiya's sense of isolation and seclusion can be read as a form of alienation. Scholars researching the experiences of migrant workers in the Gulf have argued that their experiences can be understood as exile as far as social, economic and emotional alienation are concerned.[95] This sense of imprisonment, as a result of the misery Zahiya has endured, is understood and relayed by the narrator. Alone, having left her after one of his nightly visits, he describes her moving through the empty villa, imagining what she *could* do, 'She could roam through its dozens of rooms, sit on whatever balcony suited her mood, or stroll among the trees in the garden, clutching her robe around her.'[96] And yet what Zahiya does is no different than usual:

> All alone in the vacant house, she goes out of one room and into the next, passes through corridors, opens some doors and takes a peek, night after night, until she finally ends up in the room she's grown used to. She sits on the armchair next to the bed. The image of Umm Salem sprawled out on the bed appears to her.[97]

Zahiya's experience of the villa, in as far as it is captured by the narrator's imagination, does not change despite the libratory moment created by the absence of Umm and Abu Salem. Rather, she continues to exist in her solitary world, remaining inside the villa walls, aimlessly wandering its rooms. If anything, her previous isolation seems to have found its full expression in the now completely empty house. The house of Abu Salem, as the continued site of confinement, seems to stand in opposition to the potential presented in the house of Abu Amer, the streets of the city, and the football stadium. The limited acts of subversion that take place in each of these spaces are entirely absent from the villa. And yet, given that the novel ends with the impending return of the Emiratis from abroad and with Zahiya's ongoing seclusion, the libratory promises of the exceptional circumstances are entirely aborted by the end of al-Bisati's novel.

Conclusion

Bahaa Taher's *Love in Exile* and Muhammad al-Bisati's *Drumbeat* both register a movement outside of the space of the Egyptian nation state, and in doing so alert us to the socio-economic and political changes of the postcolonial period. As I have shown in this chapter, these two novels demonstrate a shift in space that is markedly different from their predecessors. Taher represents the space of political exile, and al-Bisati depicts that of economic and political dislocation. Both novels contain an implicit critique of the postcolonial Egyptian state for failing to provide political and economic stability and security for its citizens. They are also critiques of the Arab nationalist project of the earlier decades, and a recognition of the end of any hope of solidarity in the region. The violence that is documented in these works, through the Lebanese civil war and the exploitation of worker populations in the Gulf, renders the Arab nationalism of the past a dream. While both authors also suggest a more inclusive internationalist community as an alternative to national and regional forms of belonging, ultimately the potential of either Taher's society of exiles or of al-Bisati's community of workers is not realised. Both authors provide possibilities of transgressing the limitations of national identity, suggesting, to return to Appadurai, that the ever-fluctuating ethnoscape of migrants and exiles is a serious challenge to the primacy of the nation state. And yet this challenge remains unfulfilled.

Notes

1. Shukri, 'al-Riwaʾi al-Misri Muhammad al-Bisati'.
2. Taher, *al-Siraʿ fi al-Manfa*, p. 5.
3. See Uthman, 'A Storied Exile: Poetics of Displacement in Modern Arab/ic Novels'.

4. Ideas of reform and modernisation were fundamental to the discussions of the *nahḍa* (awakening/enlightenment) period of the late nineteenth and early twentieth centuries. It is Muhammad Ali (1805–48) who is most famous for sending student educational missions to Europe. The first mission to Paris was sent in 1826, under the spiritual leadership of Rifaʿa Rafiʿ al-Tahtawi. This was part of a concerted effort to open Egypt up to Western ideas and to 'modernize' the country through encounter with the European other. Under Ali's rule the army and navy were transformed, taxation and administration were centralised, and professional schools were established. Students were sent to Europe, translating technical works upon their return. This stance towards the West continued well into the nineteenth and early decades of the twentieth century. Numerous intellectuals during the early *nahḍa*, also members of the social and economic elite, travelled abroad for their education; Ahmad Lutfi al-Sayyid, Ahmad Fathi Zaghlul and Qasim Amin among them. Later, Taha Hussein, Tawfiq al-Hakim and Salama Musa would all do the same. For more, see Hourani, *Arabic Thought in the Liberal Age 1798–1939*, pp. 34–102; El-Ariss, *Trials of Arab Modernity*, pp. 1–52; and Selim, *The Novel and the Rural Imaginary in Egypt*, pp. 1–24.
5. For an extensive discussion of this issue and the complexity of the Western encounter, see al-Musawi, *Islam on the Street*, pp. 41–71, and *The Postcolonial Arabic Novel*, pp. 163–205; and El-Ariss, *Trials of Arab Modernity*, pp. 88–113.
6. El-Enany, *Arab Representations of the Occident*, p. 2
7. Ibid. p. 2. El-Enany's extensive study focuses upon writers from across the Arab world and their representations of the Western other, be it Europe, the Soviet Union or the United States. El-Enany uses the following divisions: pre-colonial, colonial and postcolonial. The latter is divided into proud and humbled encounters.
8. Several works within the Arab literary context contend with similar issues. Ibrahim Abdel Meguid's *al-Balda al-Ukhra* (*The Other Place*, 1991) is one of the most notable Egyptian examples. Writers across the Arab world have long addressed the changing dynamics of labour and migration. Prominent examples include Ghassan Kanafani's *Rijal fi al-Shams* (*Men in the Sun*, 1962), Sahar Khalifeh's *al-Sabbar* (*Wild Thorns*, 1976), Saud Alsanousi's *Saq al-Bambu* (*Bamboo Stalk*, 2012) and Abdel Rahman Munif's quintet *Mudun al-Milh* (*Cities of Salt*, 1984–9).
9. An interesting comparison can be made here to Muhammad Mansi Qandil's novel *Qamar ʿala Samarqand* (*Moon Over Samarqand*, 2004) in which the author uses the post-Soviet space of Uzbekistan as a mirror for Egypt, to present

the abuses of the authoritarian regimes of Nasser and Sadat. For an excellent discussion of this novel, see Litvin, 'Egypt's Uzbek Mirror'.
10. Appadurai, 'Disjuncture and Difference', p. 32.
11. Ibid. p. 45.
12. Ibid. p. 37.
13. El-Enany, *Arab Representations of the Occident*, p. 135. And yet, as El-Enany argues, the two characters are not mere stereotypical, cultural types but complex individuals.
14. Taher, *Love in Exile*, p. 3.
15. El-Enany, *Arab Representations of the Occident*, p. 135.
16. Taher, *Love in Exile*, p. 28.
17. For more, see Stagh, *The Limits of Freedom of Speech*; Jacquemond, *Conscience of the Nation*; and ʿIsa, *Muthaqqafun wa ʿAskar*.
18. Nasser's persecution of the communists in Egypt is discussed in Chapter 1. The struggle between Nasser and the communists plays itself out in the novel in the discussions that take place between the protagonist (a staunch Nasserist) and Ibrahim (a committed communist).
19. Knapp, 'Introduction', p. 1.
20. Taher, *Love in Exile*, p. 3. Similarly, in Gamal al-Ghitani's novel *Shath al-Madina* (City Roaming, 1992), a nameless protagonist also finds himself in a nameless city. He is viewed with suspicion by the inhabitants of the metropolis and the protagonist seems to experience a similar sense of estrangement to that of Taher's characters. In both cases the reader encounters an alienated Nasserite intellectual in a world which no longer contains a shared sense of communal belonging. For a reading of the novel within the context of postcolonial Arabic narrative tradition, see al-Musawi, *The Postcolonial Arabic Novel*, pp. 292, 330–1 and *Infirat al-ʿAqd al-Muqaddas*, p. 80.
21. Casini, 'Beyond Occidentalism', pp. 11–12.
22. ʿAsfur, 'Naqd al-Thanaʾiyya al-Qadima', pp. 128–9.
23. Some critics thus assume that the novel takes place in Switzerland, but this is never stated. See, for example, al-Raʿi, *al-Riwaya fi Nihayat al-Qarn*, p. 194. For an in-depth biographical account of this period in Taher's life, see Fayyad, 'Burtrih Malik Hazin', pp. 15–25.
24. Casini, 'Beyond Occidentalism', p. 10.
25. Ibid. p. 12.
26. Al-ʿAlim, 'Mulahazat ʿala Hamish *al-Hubb fi al-Manfa*', p. 123.
27. Taher, *Love in Exile*, pp. 5–6. Al-ʿAlim takes note of the beauty of the language

that is used in descriptions such as the one of the forest, going as far as to compare them to the poetry that is read and quoted by the characters. See al-ʿAlim, 'Mulahazat ʿala Hamish *al-Hubb fi al-Manfa*', p. 121.
28. Al-Kharrat, *al-Hassasiyya al-Jadida*, p. 183.
29. Taher, *Love in Exile*, pp. 24–5.
30. Lefebvre, *The Production of Space*, p. 42.
31. The role of cafés in Cairo as sites of intellectual, artistic and literary exchange is well-known. Establishments such as Riche, Isevitch, al-Hurriyya, Odeon and Le Grillon have long served as places for writers and other intellectuals to gather, share work and connect. Cafés are also at the heart of neighbourhood communities and appear in novels from Mahfouz onwards; they are discussed in relation to Aslan's novel in Chapter 1. For more on the cultural cafés of Cairo specifically, see Jacquemond, *Conscience of the Nation*, pp. 167–81.
32. Taher, *Love in Exile*, p. 86.
33. Ibid. p. 87.
34. Ibid. p. 163.
35. Ibid. pp. 97–8.
36. Siddiq, *Arab Culture and the Novel*, p. 90. Along with *al-Hubb fi al-Manfa*, Siddiq also cites Sonallah Ibrahim's *Najmat Ughustus* (August Star, 1974) and *Beirut Beirut* (Beirut, Beirut, 1984), and Ibrahim Abdel Meguid's *The Other Place* as examples of novels that deploy this shift in space in a similar way.
37. Sami, '*al-Hubb fi al-Manfa*: Butulat al-la Batal', p. 143.
38. The Lebanese Civil War (1975–90) is ongoing during the events of the novel. In June 1982, Israel invaded Lebanon with troops reaching as far as Beirut. The siege of the city resulted in the eviction of the PLO (Palestine Liberation Organization) from Lebanon. Taher focuses on the Sabra and Shatila massacre (16–18 September 1982) that was carried out by the Christian Phalanges, with what is largely acknowledged as support from the Israel Defense Forces. While the Phalanges claimed to be rooting out PLO fighters, thousands of civilians were killed, predominantly Palestinians and Lebanese *shiʿa*.
39. Taher, *Love in Exile*, pp. 135–6.
40. Ibid. p. 237.
41. Ibid. p. 236.
42. In the author's note, Taher explains that the descriptions of the experiences of Sabra and Shatila and the invasion of Lebanon are based on eyewitness accounts. He also uses actual articles published in the newspapers. Taher, *Love in Exile*, p. 279.

43. Al-ʿAlim, 'Mulahazat ʿala Hamish *al-Hubb fi-al-Manfa*', pp. 119–20.
44. Hafez, *The Genesis of Arabic Narrative Discourse*.
45. Al-Musawi, *Infirat al-ʿAqd al-Muqaddas*, p. 75.
46. Taher, 'Qariban min Baha Tahir: Hiwar maʿa al-Bahaʾ Husayn', p. 171. My translation.
47. Taher, *Love in Exile*, p. 278.
48. Al-Musawi, *Arabic Poetry*, p. 192.
49. Ibid. p. 193.
50. Dirgham, *Fi al-Sard al-Riwaʾi*, pp. 51–2. It is also important to consider that this war not only presents the violence of Israel against the Palestinians, but also of Arabs against each other.
51. Lefebvre, *The Production of Space*, p. 52.
52. Taher, *Love in Exile*, p. 10.
53. Ibid. p. 276.
54. Ibid. p. 277.
55. Nancy Roberts translates the title as *Over the Bridge*. Presumably this is because the word *Khaldiyya*, used to denote a generic name of the imagined town at the heart of the novel, is not familiar to readers of English.
56. Another example is that of Muhammad Abdel Salam al ʿUmari's *Ihbitu Misr* (Descend to Egypt, 1997) which also takes place in an imagined country understood to be in the Gulf region. For a reading of the novel, see al-Musawi, *Infirat al-ʿAqd al-Muqaddas*, pp. 317–20.
57. Sells, 'Egyptian International Migration and Social Processes', pp. 87–108.
58. Ibid. pp. 87–108.
59. Ibid. p. 92. See also La Towsky, 'Egyptian Labor Abroad'; and Zohry and Harrell-Bond, 'Contemporary Egyptian Migration'.
60. For more on labour migration in the 1980s and 1990s, see Roy, 'Egyptian Emigrant Labor'; and Feiler, 'Migration and Recession'.
61. Sells, 'Egyptian International Migration and Social Processes', p. 103.
62. Al-Bisati, *Drumbeat*, p. 1.
63. The opening of al-Bisati's novel is remarkably similar to non-fictional accounts of the history of the oil-rich Gulf countries and the changes that have taken place in the twentieth century. See Khalaf and Alkobaisi, 'Migrants' Strategies of Coping and Patterns of Accommodation in the Oil-Rich Gulf Societies', p. 272.
64. According to the author, he wrote nothing during his time away from Egypt. Shukri, 'al-Riwaʾi al-Misri Muhammad al-Bisati'.
65. I am grateful to Professor Brent Edwards for bringing these issues of date and

place to my attention. For further discussion of this technique of disguise, this time in relationship to Abdel Rahman Munif's *Mudun al-Milh*, see El-Enany, '*Cities of Salt*', pp. 214–15.
66. Berquist, 'Introduction', p. 8.
67. Al-Bisati, *Drumbeat*, p. 2.
68. Ibid. p. 2
69. Ibid. p. 3
70. Ibid. p. 3.
71. Ibid. p. 3.
72. The state of living conditions of migrant workers in the Gulf countries has been explored by scholars in different fields. See, for example, Khalaf and Alkobaisi, 'Migrants' Strategies of Coping and Patterns of Accommodation in the Oil-Rich Gulf Societies', p. 292.
73. Khalaf, 'The Evolution of the Gulf City', p. 252.
74. Al-Bisati, *Drumbeat*, p. 2.
75. Ibid. p. 6.
76. Al-Kharrat, *al-Hassasiyya al-Jadida*, p. 19.
77. Jackson, *Fantasy: The Literature of Subversion*, p. 34.
78. Al-Bisati, *Drumbeat*, p. 15.
79. Khalaf, 'The Evolution of the Gulf City', p. 251.
80. Al-Bisati, *Drumbeat*, p. 19.
81. Ibid. p. 48.
82. Ibid. p. 47.
83. Ibid. p. 47.
84. Ibid. pp. 58–9.
85. Khalaf, 'The Evolution of the Gulf City', pp. 259–60.
86. For more on the way national identity is reinforced through sports, see Alabarces, Tomlinson and Young, 'Argentina versus England at the France '98 World Cup', pp. 547–66; and Tomlinson and Young, 'Culture, Politics, and Spectacle in the Global Sports Event', pp. 1–13.
87. See Zohry, 'Egyptian Irregular Migration to Europe', pp. 1–34.
88. Singerman and Ammar, 'Introduction', p. 30.
89. Al-Bisati, *Drumbeat*, p. 44.
90. Ibid. p. 72.
91. Ibid. p. 44.
92. Ibid. p. 122.
93. Theorists have argued that the international movement of wage labour can be

seen as the unequal exchange of different modes of production. Within this context, the exploitation of foreign migrants is understood as generating profit for the capitalist system. See Cardoso and Faletto, *Dependency and Development in Latin America*; and Khalaf and Alkobaisi, 'Migrants' Strategies of Coping and Patterns of Accommodation in the Oil-Rich Gulf Societies'.
94. Al-Bisati, *Drumbeat*, p. 30.
95. Khalaf and Alkobaisi, 'Migrants' Strategies of Coping and Patterns of Accommodation in the Oil-Rich Gulf Societies', p. 296.
96. Al-Bisati, *Drumbeat*, p. 86.
97. Ibid. p. 87.

5

Beyond the Sixties

The writers of the sixties generation, once the newcomers on the literary scene, were to become the established members within the cultural field in Egypt. While writers and critics questioned their significance as an emerging movement upon their appearance, it quickly became clear that this was not a group to be cursorily dismissed, but rather that the literary contribution of its members would have a profound impact upon cultural production in Egypt. Their experience of the political and social upheavals of the 1960s incited literary innovation that transformed the aesthetic norms of narrative fiction, as far as both the short story and the novel were concerned, creating a wave of change that continued in the decades that followed. While the majority of the writers of this generation began publishing their fiction in the second half of the 1960s, many would continue producing literary works in the following years, maintaining what Mattias Bolkeus Blom refers to as 'a sustained publishing trajectory'.[1] This is certainly true for the writers whose work has been at the heart of the analysis undertaken in this book, and who are some of the most prolific members of this generation, producing numerous novels, novellas, autobiographies, short story collections and works of literary criticism.[2]

The generation's continued literary output and the foothold they gained in the cultural field meant that the label of sixties generation (*jīl al-sittīnāt*) became highly desirable. It also meant that writers who perhaps did not start writing in that decade, but shared the group's aesthetic, political and ideological directions, became members of this group. This is true for a number of writers, among them Radwa Ashour and Ibrahim Abdel Meguid. It also meant, as Jacquemond shows, that several women writers in the 1970s, including Salwa Bakr, Sahar Tawfiq, Siham Bayyumi and Ibtihal Salim, began 'to publish along lines opened up by the very masculine generation of the sixties'.[3]

Acceptance in the cultural field meant that the literary innovations of the sixties generation were acknowledged as the dominant direction of Egyptian narrative fiction. This brought with it increased attention and consideration from literary critics and scholars writing in both Arabic and English. While the group garnered attention at the time of its appearance, as evidenced by the discussion in the Introduction, the following decades resulted in more sustained consideration of its literary output, both as a generation and as individual writers.[4] The writers of this generation would come to be the focus of scholarly works; special editions of literary and cultural journals; dissertation theses; conferences and symposia. Muhammad Badawi, in his 1993 study, would go as far as to state that '*riwāyat al-sittīnnāt hiya ḥāḍir al-riwāya al-ʿarabiyya fī Miṣr*' (the sixties novel is the current Arabic novel in Egypt).[5] Scholars in the field concentrated on classifying the spectrum of aesthetic directions in what al-Kharrat would call '*al-ḥassāsiyya al-jadīda*'. Finally, it is no small matter that their emergence onto the scene resulted in broader discussions surrounding generational terminology, literary critical terms, and the larger cultural field in Egypt.

The recognition of the group's literary innovations was accompanied by their consecration in the cultural field. According to Bourdieu, the 'consecrated writer is the one who has the power to consecrate and to win assent when he or she consecrates an author or a work – with a preface, a favorable review, a prize, etc.'[6] I use the term consecration here to refer to the recognition of these writers as important players within the cultural sphere, occupying positions within the literary and cultural establishment, and hence able to consecrate others. It is also reflected in the reception and translation of their works and in the conferral of awards, both sources of material and cultural acclaim.[7] All of the writers discussed in the previous chapters have had numerous works translated into English (and many into French and other world languages).

All of the writers have also been the recipients of awards, administered by both the state and independent organisations, though many of these did not come until the 1990s and the 2000s.[8] Al-Bisati, al-Ghitani, al-Kharrat, Taher, Abdullah, Aslan, Abdel Meguid and al-Qaid were all acknowledged by the state.⁹ Al-Bisati also received both the al-Owais Prize (2000–1) and the Sawiris Literary Award (2009). Aslan was the recipient of the Constantine Cavafy Prize for Literature (2005) and the Sawiris Literary Award (2006). Taher won the International Prize for Arabic Fiction in its inaugural year (2008). Al-Ghitani received the al-Owais Prize (1996–7), the Sheikh Zayed Book Award (2009) and was named Chevalier de l' Ordre des Arts et des Lettres in 1987. Ashour received the Constantine Cavafy Prize for Literature (2007), the Tarquinia Cardarelli International Criticism Prize (2009), the al-Owais Award (2010–11), and the first part of her Granada Trilogy won first prize at the first Arab Women's Book Fair (1995). She is also one of only twelve female writers to make it onto the Arab Writers' Union list of the top 105 novels; all the writers of this book (except Abdullah) also appear on this list. Al-Kharrat won the al-Owais Prize (1994–5), the Constantine Cavafy Prize for Literature (1998) and the Naguib Mahfouz Medal for Literature (1999). Al-Qaid won the al-Owais Award (2014–15) and Abdel Meguid won the Naguib Mahfouz Medal for Literature (1996), the Sheikh Zayed Book Award (2014) and the Sawiris Literary Award (2012). Ibrahim, known for his distance from state institutions, refused to accept the prize for the novel at the Second Cairo Conference on the Arab Novel in 2003. He has, however, accepted the al-Owais Award (1992–3) and the Ibn Rushd Prize for Freedom of Thought (2004). The untimely deaths of Abdullah and Qasim may account for their lack of official recognition, although Abdullah did posthumously receive the State Encouragement Award in 1981.

Aslan, Abdullah, al-Qaid and Ibrahim have all had their works adapted for cinema and television, thus reaching a broader audience. Dawud Abdel Sayyid's *al-Kit Kat*, based on Aslan's *Malik al-Hazin*, was released in 1991 and became an immediate hit. The sequel *ᶜAsafir al-Nil* was directed by Magdi Ahmad Ali in 2010. Abdullah's *al-Tawq wa-l-Iswira* was adapted by Khayri Bishara in 1986, and Ibrahim's *Zaat* was adapted for television, becoming very popular when it ran during the month of Ramadan in 2013. A number of al-Qaid's works have been adapted for television and cinema including *Ziyarat al-Sayyid al-Raʾis*, *Qitar al-Saᶜid*, *al-Muwatin al-Masri* and *ᶜIzbat al-Minisi*. This is also true for Abdel Meguid; *La Ahad Yanam fi al-Iskandariyya* and *Qanadil al-Bahr* were both adapted for television, and *Sayyad al-Yamam* was made into a film.

The members of this generation also came to occupy noteworthy positions within the cultural and literary establishment, serving as literary editors and series editors, and establishing various periodicals and cultural magazines. Al-Ghitani was the founder and editor of the well-known *Akhbar al-Adab* for over ten years. Abdel Meguid occupied several positions in the Ministry of Culture, beginning in 1976, and also served as editor-in-chief of the series *Kitabat Jadida* published by the General Egyptian Book Organization. Aslan served as editor for the series *Muhktarat al-Fusul*, the cultural section of *al-Hayat*, and of the series *Afaq al-Kitaba* published by the Ministry of Culture until the explosion of the famous Haydar Haydar affair.[10] Al-Bisati served as editor-in-chief of the series *Aswat Adabiyya* until his resignation from the Ministry of Culture over disputes regarding censorship.[11] Taher was one of those suggested for the position of Minister of Culture after Faruq Husni's resignation in 2011, but he declined, maintaining his detachment from political power.[12]

The process of consecration did not prevent ongoing confrontations from emerging between the writers of the sixties generation and the various institutions of the state. As has been traced throughout the chapters of this book, the decade of the 70s proved to be particularly challenging for writers and intellectuals in Egypt. Almost immediately after taking power, Sadat began to dismantle the cultural establishment instituted under Nasser, closing down journals and newspapers, withdrawing state support from the arts, and cracking down on leftist oppositional critics, forcing many writers and journalists into retirement. This reached its zenith with arrests that took place in September 1981, when critics of the Camp David agreements were imprisoned on the pretext of instigating unrest.[13] This policy of persecution and marginalisation pushed many writers into exile during these years. With the coming to power of Mubarak there was a reversal of the cultural policies of the state, with greater emphasis once again placed upon establishing links between intellectuals and the institutions of power. It is during Mubarak's time that many of the members of this generation were recognised by the state. This policy did not, however, avert conflicts between writers and the state surrounding issues of censorship, domestic and foreign policy and the limits of dissent. Each member of this generation has negotiated this position in different ways, with some writers, like Ibrahim, insisting upon a complete separation from the regime of power.[14] Others have tried to maintain links with the state while nevertheless taking important stands against government policy at various points in their careers. Al-Ghitani occupied the position of editor-in-chief of the state-run *Akhbar al-Adab* but continued to voice objections to government policy concerning issues of foreign policy and spoke in defense of various artists and intellectuals during numerous censorship scandals.[15] Al-Bisati, Aslan and Abdel Meguid all worked in the Ministry of Culture at various junctures of their careers but either refused to comply with the state's attempt to limit their independence or resigned from their positions in protest. Taher largely remained separate from state institutions, while al-Qaid agreed to serve in the post-revolutionary parliament in 2015, as a non-elect MP, appointed among others by the President. Ashour helped form a number of groups in strict opposition to government positions: the National Committee against Zionism in Egyptian Universities and the March 9 Movement, which called for the independence of Egyptian Universities under Mubarak.[16] Such choices have of course affected the position and recognition of each writer within the literary field.[17]

The struggles that took place over categorisation throughout the 1960s and 1970s did not ultimately alter the dynamics of the field, but largely subsided once the legitimacy of the sixties generation was no longer in question. This is further attested to by the fact that an innovative movement in narrative fiction that caused a comparable stir on the literary scene in the decades that followed came to be known as the nineties generation. This is in line with what W. J. van de Akker and Gillis J. Dorleijin label as the 'idea of alternate generations', such that 'once a generation has established itself, it is succeeded by a new one'.[18] The nineties generation includes May Telmissany, Ibrahim Farghali, Miral al-Tahawy, Nura Amin, Mustafa Zikri, Samir Gharib Ali, Somaya Ramadan, Mona Prince and Ahmed Alaidy. Evident immediately is what Mehrez terms 'gender equality in literary production', with female writers occupying a more prominent position within this generational group.[19] This is all the more striking given the overwhelmingly male composition of the sixties generation. The emergence of this group onto the cultural scene in Egypt was met with much of the same consternation that accompanied the appearance of their predecessors. As Sabry Hafez notes, the members of literary and cultural establishment in Egypt did not by and large welcome the innovations of this group; 'the young writers were accused of poor education, nihilism, loss of direction, lack of interest in public issues and obsessive concentration on the body; of stylistic poverty, weak grammar and inadequate narrative skills and sheer incomprehensibility'.[20] Once again questions were asked about the legitimacy of their literary and artistic production and the significance of their appearance on the cultural scene in Egypt. Furthermore, like the sixties generation before them, the members of this group have maintained precarious relationships to state institutions. Preferring not to publish with the state-controlled publishing houses, the writers of this generation largely benefited from the appearance of independent publishers namely *Dar Sharqiyyat* and *Dar Merit*; they are in fact often referred to as the Sharqiyyat generation.[21]

The nineties generation, much like their predecessors, emerged from and sought to respond to a particular socio-economic and political context. These are largely the children of Sadat's *infitāḥ* period and Mubarak's emergency laws, and inheritors of the corruption, privatisation and inequalities of the neo-liberal order established in Egypt.[22] The decline in the standard of living for much of the Egyptian population has gone hand-in-hand with the decline of the country's standing as a regional power. Largely acquiescing to US-Israeli interests in the region, the government has responded to the people's outrage over successive military ventures in the region by cracking down on activists and demonstrators. The overwhelming sense of impotency in the domestic realm has exacerbated this generation's outrage at witnessing violence and war erupt across the Middle East; in Lebanon, Palestine, Iraq and Afghanistan.[23]

Within this context, the writers of the nineties generation emerged onto the cultural scene, producing works that sought to break with the aesthetics and directions of the sixties generation, which had since become the established norms in the literary field. Given the hierarchical nature of the cultural field, it should come as no surprise that the newcomers once again positioned themselves in opposition to their predecessors; this generative opposition once more allowed a nascent movement to foreground its innovations in productive ways. One of the principle ways that the new generation sought to separate itself was through a reimagining of the political. While they were attacked for not attending to '*al-qaḍāyā al-kubrā*' (the big issues), and instead focusing on the mundane, and the everyday, this strategy was not in fact a renunciation of the political.[24] Rather it speaks to the group's desire to move away from the position of '*iltizām*' (commitment) so strongly embraced by the sixties generation. As Yousef Rakha explains, the politics and aesthetics of the previous generation were seen as inseparable; 'now that the Sixties' political points are no longer fresh, their style frequently seems stale as well'.[25] Rakha's engagement with the 'vexed legacy' of the sixties generation is echoed by May al-Tilmasani, for whom the 'commitment' of her predecessors was no longer appealing.[26] 'We think about writers as "committed writers," and no writer can escape this' al-Tilmasani says. In response, she continues, came a desire to be 'committed to my writing and nothing else'.[27] While this position was taken by the established figures as a sign of the new generation's renunciation of the political and of the public, as Elsadda rightly argues the 'personal is political', and hence the focus on the individual and on the everyday is as much a rejection of their contemporary reality as anything else.[28]

The rearticulation of the political was accompanied by a number of significant literary and aesthetic innovations, many of which have been classified by critics in the field as they contend with the experimental contributions of this generation of writers. Chief among these are the focus on the individual (as opposed to the collective); the use of colloquial and the language of the everyday; polyphony; intertextuality; and the breakdown of linear time.[29] In many ways these experimentations emanate and depart from the work of their predecessors. This is not to suggest that the innovations of the nineties generation are not significant, but rather that the move away from realism so central to the work of the sixties generation continued to propel a great deal of literary innovation in the decades that followed. As the analysis in the chapters of this book has shown, the sixties writers began to undo the linearity and cohesion of the realist text by foregrounding circularity, multiplicity and polyphony, while often also drawing attention to the construction of their own works of fiction. And yet, as Hafez argues, while the sixties generation ultimately had a 'burning desire to change the world', the ever more marginalised nineties generation did away with this as a central tenant of their fiction.[30] Striving to represent their isolation and alienation, the nineties writers produce 'fragmented, self-reflexive' texts.[31] These include 'ghosts, psychotic breaks, unrealistic and fantastical turns of events'.[32] In doing so these writers have clearly pushed the literary directions of the Egyptian novel in new and innovative ways.

The innovations of the nineties generation have also been tied to the spatial representations in their work. Hafez argues that the members of this generation are the children of what he calls the 'third city', the ʿashwāʾiyyāt, the informal slums that have developed around and within the city of Cairo in response to the shortage of housing and the governments continued negligence.[33] Even those who are not the direct product of these areas Hafez argues, are 'children of its imagination, its time, and its rhythm'.[34] As such the impact of the haphazard, marginalised, often suffocating neighbourhoods can be read in the aesthetic transformations undertaken by the nineties writers. This is in many ways an expansion of the focus on marginalised areas undertaken by writers of the sixties generation (as discussed in the first chapter of this book, writers like Ibrahim Aslan engaged with the district of Imbaba and its ʿashwāʾiyyāt).

Hafez's argument regarding the importance of the urban transformation of Cairo to the aesthetic project of the nineties generation is part of growing scholarly attention being paid to spatial representations in the work of this more contemporary generation; other notable works include those by Hishmat and Mehrez.[35] Hafez also explores some examples of the appearance of the rural in this fiction, and Hishmat makes important connections between the urban and the rural. Such works are in line with the underlying premises of this book. As I have argued throughout *Space in Modern Egyptian Fiction* the representation of urban, rural and exilic space in the work of the sixties generation speaks to the socio-economic and political changes that so strongly influenced the work of this group. It is also one of the principle ways to read the aesthetic innovations for which this generation was celebrated, and that altered the literary direction in Egypt for decades. By expanding the consideration of this literary generation beyond the boundaries of a single decade, I have tried to shed light on a pivotal moment in modern Egyptian literary and cultural history. This group of writers transformed the literary landscape and have continued to impact the cultural field in a multitude of ways. Becoming the established figures in the field has meant that emerging generations, like the nineties generation, have sought to position themselves in opposition to the writers of the sixties generation. Despite the differences in political and ideological positions, the struggles of the writers of the sixties generation are not wholly divorced from those of their successors. They too were a generation contending with the aftermath of revolutionary change, the realities of the failings of democratic projects, and the role of artists and intellectuals in confronting the injustices of the state. As *Space in Modern Egyptian Fiction* has argued, with the sixties generation came the disappearance of the idealised Egyptian nation in the novel. The works of their successors continue to grapple with its aftermath.

Notes

1. Blom, 'Tracing Literary Careers', p. 371.
2. See, for example, al-Kharrat, *al-Hassasiyya al-Jadida* and *al-Kitaba ʿAbr al-Nawʿiyya*; and Ashour, *Gibran and Blake, al-Tariq ila al-Khayma al-Ukhra* and *al-Hadatha al-Mumkina*.
3. Jacquemond, *Conscience of the Nation*, p. 190.
4. For consideration of the sixties generation as a group, see al-Kharrat, *al-Hassasiyya al-Jadida*; Badawi, *al-Riwaya al-Haditha fi Misr*; Mehrez, *Egypt's Culture Wars*, Jacquemond, *Conscience of the Nation*; Kendall, *Literature, Journalism and the Avant-Garde*; and Hafez, 'The Egyptian Novel in the Sixties'. The literary criticism focusing on the individual members is abundant and too numerous to cite here.
5. Badawi, *al-Riwaya al-Haditha fi Misr*, p. 8.
6. Bourdieu, *The Field of Cultural Production*, p. 42.
7. And yet, as Bourdieu argues, in the 'autonomous sector of the field of cultural production' there is often a reversal of ordinary economic rules so that the 'loser wins'. Bourdieu, *The Field of Cultural Production*, p. 39. Mehrez uses this in a compelling way to read Sonallah Ibrahim's symbolic success in the field. Mehrez, *Egypt's Culture Wars*, pp. 25–41.
8. For a more extensive account of the awards received by the members of the sixties generation, see the Appendix. The websites for the various organisations also list past recipients.
9. For a comprehensive list of the recipients of the state awards for literature between 1958 and 2006, see Jacquemond, *Conscience of the Nation*, pp. 291–6. For recipients after this date, from 2009 to the present, see the website of the Supreme Council of Culture, scc.gov.eg.
10. In March and April 2000 attacks were launched on the Ministry of Culture for

the re-issuing of the novel *Walima li-Aʿshab* (Banquet for Seaweed, 1983) as part of the series *Afaq al-Kitaba*, edited by Ibrahim Aslan. The author was accused of blasphemy and in the months that followed the uproar intensified, with debates in the National Assembly, rulings by al-Azhar, the official questioning of Aslan, and the eventual halting of the series. For more on the Haydar Haydar affair, see Hafez, 'The Novel, Politics and Islam'.

11. In January 2001, the Minister of Culture Faruq Husni banned three novels published by the General Organization for Cultural Palaces (GOCP). The works by Tawfiq Abdel Rahman, Yasser Shaʿban and Mahmoud Hamid were all published as part of the series *Aswat Adabiyya*, edited by al-Bisati. While al-Bisati had already resigned as a result of disputes with the administration, he, Ali Abu Shadi (head of the GOCP) and Girgis Shukri (managing editor of the series) were all interrogated regarding the novels in question. All three men were dismissed from their positions. For more on this, see Mehrez, 'Take Them Out of the Ballgame' and Rakha, 'Floating Bureaus'.

12. Rashwan, 'Bahaa Taher: Rafadt Mansib Wazir al-Thaqafa baʿd al-Thawra Mubasharatan'.

13. For more, see Stagh's *The Limits of Freedom of Speech* and Harlow, 'Egyptian Intellectuals and the Debate on the "Normalization of Cultural Relations"'.

14. See Mehrez, *Egypt's Culture Wars*, pp. 25–41. While Ibrahim has long been commended for his autonomy and principled positions, he did come under attack following comments that he made in support of Abdel-Fattah al-Sisi in 2013.

15. See Mahmoud *et al.*, 'Q&A with Gamel El-Ghitani'.

16. Al-Qasas and Rabiʿ, 'Radwa Ashour: Jisr min ʿAta Ibdaʿi Bayn al-Mutakhayyal wa-l-Waqiʿi'.

17. See the Appendix.

18. Van de Akker and Dorleijin, 'Talkin' 'Bout Two Generations', p. 11.

19. Mehrez, *Egypt's Culture Wars*, p. 126. See also Elsadda, *Gender, Nation, and the Arabic Novel*, pp. 151–2; and Hafez, 'Jamaliyyat al-Riwaya', p. 214.

20. Hafez, 'The New Egyptian Novel', p. 49.

21. See Mehrez, *Egypt's Culture Wars*, pp. 125–6; Elsadda, *Gender, Nation and the Arabic Novel*, p. 146; and Hafez, 'The New Egyptian Novel', p. 50.

22. For more, see Hafez, 'The New Egyptian Novel', p. 48.

23. Ibid. p. 48.

24. Badawi, quoted in Elsadda, *Gender, Nation, and the Arabic Novel*, p. 145.

25. Rakha, 'Empty Feeling'.

26. Ibid.
27. Al-Tilmasani, quoted in Anishechenkova, 'Feminist Voices of the 1990s Generation', p. 101.
28. Elsadda, *Gender, Nation, and the Arabic Novel*, p. 145.
29. For excellent studies on the contribution of the nineties generation, see Hafez, 'The New Egyptian Novel' and 'Jamaliyyat al-Riwaya'; Anishchenkova, 'Feminist Voices of the 1990s Generation'; Mehrez, *Egypt's Culture Wars*, pp. 123–69; Elsadda, *Gender, Nation, and the Arabic Novel*, pp. 145–213; and Jacquemond, *Conscience of the Nation*.
30. Hafez, 'Jamaliyyat al-Riwaya', p. 203.
31. Hafez, 'The New Egyptian Novel', p. 56.
32. Rakha, 'Empty Feeling'.
33. Hafez, 'The New Egyptian Novel', p. 60, and 'Jamaliyyat al-Riwaya al-Jadida'.
34. Hafez, 'Jamaliyyat al-Riwaya', p. 195.
35. Hishmat, *al-Qahira fi al-Adab al-Misri al-Hadith wa-l-Muʿasir*, particularly chapters 4, 5 and 6. See also Mehrez, *Egypt's Culture Wars*, pp. 144–67.

Appendix

Ibrahim Abdel Meguid (b. 1946)

Abdel Meguid was born in Alexandria. After graduating from the University of Alexandria with a BA in philosophy in 1973, he moved to Cairo, where he would take up the first of many positions in the Ministry of Culture, beginning with Consultant for Cultural Matters at the Popular Culture Council in 1974. He published his first novel *Fi al-Sayf al-Sabiᶜ wa-l-Sittin* (In the Summer of '67) in 1979. His Alexandria Trilogy is one of his most famous works; the first part, *La Ahad Yanam fi al-Iskandariyya* (*No One Sleeps in Alexandria*, 1996), won best novel at the Cairo International Book Festival in 1996, and the final installment, *al-Iskandariyya fi Ghayma* (*Clouds Over Alexandria*, 2014), was nominated for the International Prize for Arabic Fiction. His other novels include *al-Masafat* (*Distant Train*, 1983), *Laylat al-ᶜIshq wa-l-Dam* (*The Night of Love and Blood*, 1982), *Bayt al-Yasmin* (*House of Jasmine*, 1987), *al-Balda al-Ukhra* (*The Other Place*, 1991), *Qanadil al-Bahr* (*Jellyfish*, 1993) and *Huna al-Qahira* (*Here is Cairo*, 2016). His short-story collections include *al-Shajara wa-l-ᶜAsafir* (*The Tree and the Birds*, 1986), *Ighlaq al-Nawafiz* (*Closing the Windows*, 1990), *Fadaʾat* (*Spaces*, 2001) and *Sufun Qadima* (*Old Ships*, 2001). He has also published works focusing on his experience as a writer and critic, including *Ana wa-l-Cinema* (*Me and Cinema*, 2018) and *Ma Waraʾ al-Kitaba: Tajribati maᶜa al-Ibdaᶜ* (*What Lies Behind Writing: My Experience with Creativity*) which won the Sheikh Zayed Award in 2016. Abdel Meguid was the inaugural recipient of the Naguib Mahfouz Medal for Literature (1996) for *al-Balda al-Ukhra*. He has also received the State Prize for Excellence (2003), the State Grand Prize (2007), the Sawiris Prize (2012) and the Katara Prize for the Arabic Novel (2015).[1]

Yahya Taher Abdullah (1938–81)

Abdullah was born in al-Karnak, Luxor, where he completed his education, obtaining a diploma in agriculture. He worked in the Ministry of Agriculture for a short period, moving to Qina in 1959, where he first met the poets Abdel Rahman al-Abnudi and Amal Dunqul. He wrote his first short story *Mahbub al-Shams* (The Sun's Beloved) in 1961. In 1964 he moved to Cairo, joining al-Abnudi and Dunqul, and completing his first short story collection *Thalath Shajarat Kabira Tuthmir Burtuqalan* (Three Big Trees that Bear Oranges), which was published in 1970.[2] This collection includes the story *Tahunat al-Shaykh Musa* (Shaykh Musa's Mill), which first appeared in the magazine *Ruz al-Yusuf* in 1962, and *Jabal al-Shay al-Akhdar* (The Mountain of Green Tea, 1968), which appeared in *al-Katib* and *Gallery 68*.[3] He credited Yusuf Idris with helping him publish his first short-story collection. After moving to Cairo, he pursued no other profession but writing. He was imprisoned in October 1966 with other writers from his generation during Nasser's crackdown on writers and intellectuals, and released the following April. He died suddenly on 9 April 1981 in a car crash on the road between Cairo and al-Wahat. He was awarded the State Encouragement Prize that same year. His other works include the short-story collections *al-Daff wa-l-Sunduq* (The Tambourine and the Chest, 1974) and *Hikayat li-l-Amir Hata Yanam* (Stories to Send the Prince to Sleep, 1978). His complete works were published in 1983 by Dar al-Mustaqbal al-ᶜArabi. He has perhaps not received the symbols of recognition due to his premature death but is widely regarded as one of the key figures of the sixties generation, particularly celebrated for his experimentation with the short story.[4]

Ibrahim Aslan (1935–2012)

Born in the city of Tanta, Aslan lived in Imbaba, Giza, for much of his life, working for the postal and telegraph services. He published his first short story in 1965. His short-story collections include *Buhayrat al-Masaʾ* (The Evening Lake, 1972), *Yusuf wa-l-Ridaʾ* (Yusuf and the Dress, 1987), *Wardiyat Layl* (Nightshift, 1991) and *Hikayat Min Fadlallah ᶜUthman* (Stories from Fadlallah Uthman, 2003). Two of his novels have been adapted for the big screen. *Malik al-Hazin* (*The Heron*, 1981), perhaps Aslan's most popular work, was made into a very successful film *al-Kit Kat* (1991) directed by Dawud Abdel Sayyid. *ᶜAsafir al-Nil* (*Nile Sparrows*, 1999) was also made into a film (of the same name) in 2010 and was directed by Majdi Ahmad Ali. His final novel *Hujratayn wa Sala: Mutataliya Manziliyya* (Two Rooms and a Hall: A Domestic Suite) was published in 2009. He also published *Khalwat al-Ghalban* (Poor Man's Hermitage, 2003), a collection of essays, and *Shayʾun min Hadha al-Qabil* (Something like That, 2007), a collection of his newspaper columns originally published in *al-Ahram* and *al-Karama*. He served as Editor of the series *Mukhtarat Fusul* between 1987 and 1995, and as Editor of the cultural section of the London-based *al-Hayat* newspaper from 1992. He also served as Editor of the series *Afaq al-Kitaba* between 1997 and 1999. He was awarded the Taha Hussein Prize for Literature (1989), the State Grand Prize (2003), the Cavafy International Prize (2005), the Sawiris Prize (2006) and the Nile Prize for Literature (2012).[5]

Radwa Ashour (1946–2014)

Born in Cairo, Ashour received a BA in English literature at Cairo University (1967) and an MA in comparative literature from the same institution (1972). She received a PhD in African-American literature from the University of Massachusetts in 1975. Returning to Cairo, she was a professor at Ain Shams University where she taught English and Comparative Literature. She dedicated much of her life to activism, helping found the National Committee against Zionism in Egyptian Universities, and the March 9 Movement which called for the independence of Egyptian Universities. One of the most prolific members of this generation, Ashour published over fifteen works of fiction, memoir and criticism. Her novels include *Hajar Dafiʾ* (A Warm Stone, 1985), *Khadija wa Sawsan* (Khadija and Sawsan, 1989), *Qitᶜa min Uruba* (A Piece of Europe, 2003) and the Granada Trilogy, which included *Gharnata* (*Granada*, 1994) and the second and third installments *Maryama wa-l-Rahil* (Maryama and the Departure, 1995). Her autobiographical works include *al-Rihla: Ayyam Taliba Misriyya fi Amrika* (The Journey: Days of an Egyptian Student in America, 1983), *Athqal min Radwa: Maqatiᶜ min Sira Dhatiyya* (Heavier than Radwa: Excerpts from an Autobiography, 2013) and *al-Sarkha: Maqatiᶜ min Sira Dhatiyya* (The Scream: Excerpts from an Autobiography, 2015). She also published works of criticism in English and Arabic, including *al-Tariq ila-l-Khayma al-Ukhra: Dirasa fi A^{c}mal Ghassan Kanafani* (The Road to the Other Tent: A Study of the Works of Ghassan Kanafani, 1977), *al-Tabi^c Yanhad: al-Riwaya fi Gharb Afriqiya* (The Subaltern Rises: The Novel in West Africa, 1980) and *Gibran and Blake* (1978). She edited *Arab Women Writers: A Critical Reference Guide 1873–1999* with Ferial Ghazoul and Hasna Reda-Mekdashi (an abridged version of the Arabic *Dhakira li-l-Mustaqbal: Mawsu^{c}at al-Katiba al-^{c}Arabiyya*, 2004) and supervised the translation of part nine of the *Cambridge History of Literary Criticism* in 2005. The General Egyptian Book Organization awarded her the prize for the best novel at the first Arab Women's Book Fair, for *Gharnata*, in 1995. She was also awarded the Constatine Cavafy Prize for Literature (2007) and the al-Owais Award (2010–11).[6]

Muhammad al-Bisati (1937–2012)

Al-Bisati was born in in the village of al-Jamaliyya, overlooking Lake Manzala, in the governorate of Sharqiyya. He moved to Cairo where he attended Cairo University earning a degree in commerce in 1960. He then worked as an accountancy inspector for the government until his retirement. He published his first short story, *al-Hurub* (The Escape), in 1962 after winning the Taha Hussein Prize for Literature. His stories appeared in *al-Majalla*, *al-Masa'* and *Gallery 68*. His first novel, *al-Tajir wa-l-Naqqash* (The Merchant and the Painter), was published in 1976. He is among the most prolific members of his generation publishing nine short-story collections and thirteen novels many of which have been translated. His short-story collections include *al-Kibar wa-l-Sighar* (The Old and the Young, 1968), *Hadith min al-Tabiq al-Thalith wa Qisas Ukhra* (Conversation from the Third Floor and Other Stories, 1970), *Munhana al-Nahr* (The River's Bend, 1990) and *Daw' Da^{c}if la Yakshif Shay' an* (A Dim Light that Reveals Nothing, 1993). A collection of his short stories, *A Last Glass of Tea and Other Stories*, was translated by Denys Johnson-Davies and published in 1994. His novels include *Buyut Wara' al-Ashgar* (*Houses Behind the Trees*, 1993), *Sakhb al-Buhayra* (*Clamor of the Lake*, 1994), which won the Cairo International Book Fair's award for the Best Novel, and *al-Khaldiyya* (*Over the Bridge*, 2006). His novel *Ju^c* (*Hunger*, 2007) was short-listed for the International Prize for Fiction (2008–9). He served as Editor-in-chief of the literary series *Aswat Adabiyya* established by the Ministry of Culture for a number of years, but resigned from his position in 2001 after disputes with the senior management over issues of censorship.[7] Al-Bisati was awarded the al-Owais Award for his fiction in 2001 and the Sawiris Prize for his novel *Daqq al-Tubul* (*Drumbeat*) in 2009, and the State Grand Prize in 2011.[8]

Gamal al-Ghitani (1945–2015)

Gamal al-Ghitani was born in the village of Juhayna in Suhag, Upper Egypt, but moved to Cairo with his family a few years later, spending the first thirty years of his life in the neighbourhood of Jamaliyya. After completing school, he spent three years studying oriental carpet design, an experience that greatly influenced his literary style. Arrested in 1966 for his criticisms of Nasser and his involvement with the Communist Party, he was released in 1967. He worked as a war correspondent for many years, reporting from the front during the 1973 war. In 1985, he became Head of the cultural section of the state-owned *al-Akhbar*. He was Founder and Editor of the Egyptian literary magazine *Akhbar al-Adab* between 1993 and 2011. He published his first collection *Awraq Shabb ʿAsh Mundhu Alf ʿAm* (Papers of a Young Man Who Lived a Thousand Years Ago) in 1969. He published dozens of novels and short-story collections, which have been translated into a number of languages. His novels include *al-Zuwayl* (Zuwayl, 1974), *al-Zayni Barakat* (*Zayni Barakat*, 1974), *al-Rifaʿi* (Rifaʿi, 1977), *Khitat al-Ghitani* (al-Ghitani's *Khitat*, 1980), *Kitab al-Tajalliyat* (*The Book of Epiphanies*, 1983–6), *Shath al-Madina* (City Roaming, 1990), *Mutun al-Ahram* (*Pyramid Texts*, 1994), *Hikayat al-Muʾassasa* (The Story of the Institution, 1997) and *Dafatir al-Tadwin* (Archival Works, 1996–2008). He also wrote two works recording his conversations and memories with Naguib Mahfouz: *Naguib Mahfouz Yatadhakkar* (Naguib Mahfouz Remembers, 1980) and *al-Majalis al-Mahfouziyya* (*The Mahfouz Dialogs*, 2006). He was awarded the State Encouragement Prize (1980), named Chevalier de l'Ordre des Arts et des Lettres (1987), won the al-Owais Prize (1996–7), the Italian Grinzane Cavour Award (2006), the State Grand Prize (2006), the Sheikh Zayyid Award (2009) and the Nile Prize for Literature (2015).[9]

Sonallah Ibrahim (b. 1937)

Ibrahim was born in 1937 in Cairo and is one of the only writers of his generation to fully dedicate himself to the profession of writing. Abandoning his legal studies, he became involved in leftist politics in Egypt in the 1950s, joining the Marxist group al-Haraka al-Dimuqratiyya li-l-Taharrur al-Watani (The Democratic Movement for National Liberation) known as Haditu, and was repeatedly arrested for his political activities. He was imprisoned between 1959 and 1964, publishing his first novel, *Tilka-l-Ra'iha* (*The Smell of It*, 1966), after his release. He has since published numerous novels many of which have been translated into French and English. These include *Najmat Aghustus* (August Star, 1974), *al-Lajna* (*The Committee*, 1981), *Bayrut Bayrut* (*Beirut Beirut*, 1984), *Dhat* (*Zaat*, 1992), *Warda* (Warda, 2000), *Amrikanli* (2003), *al-Talassus* (*Stealth*, 2007), *al-ʿImama wa-l-Qubʿa* (The Turban and the Hat, 2008), *al-Qanun al-Faransi* (French Law, 2008), *al-Jalid* (Ice, 2011) and *Berlin 69* (2014). He made headlines in October 2003 when, during the Second Cairo Conference on the Arab Novel, he refused to accept the prize for the novel, delivering a scathing indictment of the Egyptian government and its cultural establishment, stating that he could not accept the prize from 'a government, which in [his] opinion, did not have the credibility to grant it'.[10] His distance from the official cultural establishment is perhaps one of the reasons for the dearth of awards he has received. He was, however, the recipient of the al-Owais Award (1992–3) and the German Ibn Rushd Prize for Freedom of Thought (2004).[11]

Edwar al-Kharrat (1926–2015)

Al-Kharrat was born in Alexandria and lived there for much of his early life. He studied law at Alexandria University, graduating in 1946, but was to begin writing and publishing fiction by the end of the 1950s. Between 1948 and 1950 he was imprisoned for his political activities and for belonging to a leftist organisation. He moved to Cairo in 1955, working as a translator at the Romanian embassy for four years. He was employed by the Afro-Asian Peoples' Solidarity Organization (AAPSO) beginning in 1959, and then the Afro-Asian Writers' Association, where he served as Secretary General until 1983. He also served as the Editor of *Lotus*, the journal of Asian and African literature, and founded and edited the journal *Gallery 68*. His first short-story collection *Hitan ᶜAliya* (High Walls) was published in 1958, followed by the collections *Saᶜat al-Kibriyaʾ* (Hours of Pride, 1972) and *Ikhtinaqat al-ᶜIshq wa-l-Sabah* (Suffocations of Love and Morning, 1979). His first novel, *Rama wa-l-Tinin* (*Rama and the Dragon*), was published in 1979 and would become part of the trilogy that included *al-Zaman al-Akhar* (The Other Time, 1985) and *Yaqin al-ᶜAtash* (The Certainty of Thirst, 1996). Al-Kharrat was also an established critic, publishing works of literary and artistic criticism, among them *al-Hassasiyya al-Jadida: Maqalat fi al-Zahira al-Qasasiyya* (The New Sensibility: Articles on the Narrative Phenomenon, 1994), *al-Kitaba ᶜAbr al-Nawᶜiya: Maqaalat fi Zahirat 'al-qissa-al-qasida' wa Nusus Mukhtara* (Writing Across Genres: Articles on the Phenomenon of the 'poem-story' and Other Selections, 1994), *Unshuda li-l-Kathafa* (A Hymn to Intensity, 1995), *Ma Waraʾ al-Waqiᶜ: Maqallat fi al-Zahira al-Lawaqiᶜiyya* (Beyond Reality: Articles on the Phenomenon of Anti-Realism, 1997) and *Fi Nur Akhar: Dirasat wa Imaʾat fi al-Fann al-Tashkili* (In Another Light: Studies and Intimations of the Visual Arts, 2005). He was also an established translator, producing numerous works in Arabic. He received the State Encouragement Prize (1973), the Arab-French Friendship Prize (1991), the al-Owais Award (1994–5), the State Grand Prize (1999), the Naguib Mahfouz Medal for Literature (1999) and the Nile Prize for Literature (2014).[12]

Yusuf al-Qaid (b. 1944)

Al-Qaid was born in the village of al-Dahriyya, in al-Bahira province in the Delta. In 1961, he started working as a teacher, but entered the army in 1965, serving during the wars of 1967 and 1973. In 1974, he began his career in journalism, working for *al-Musawwir*, eventually becoming Deputy editor-in-chief of the magazine, until 2000 when he decided to become an independent writer. He was among those appointed to parliament by the President in 2015. One of his most famous novels *al-Harb fi Barr Misr* (*War in the Land of Egypt*, 1978), originally banned in Egypt, was also the basis of a successful movie by the same name, starring Omar Sharif. The novel was translated into English, French, Spanish, Russian, Hebrew and German. His other works include *al-Hidad* (Mourning, 1969), *Ayyam al-Jafaf* (Days of Drought, 1973), al-*Bayat al-Shitwi* (Hibernation, 1974), *Yahduth fi Misr al-ʾAn* (Happening in Egypt Now, 1976), *Thulathiyyat: Shakawi al-Misri al-Fasih* (The Trilogy: Complaints of an Eloquent Egyptian, 1981–5) and *Qitar al-Saᶜid* (The Train of Saᶜ id, 2001). His short-story collections include *Tajfif al-Dumuᶜ* (Drying the Tears, 1981) and *al-Fallahun Yasᶜadun ila-l-Samaʾ* (Peasants Ascend to the Heavens, 1996). Al-Qaid received the State Grand Prize (2008) and the al-Owais Award (2014–15).[13]

Abd al-Hakim Qasim (1934–90)

Qasim was born in the village of al-Bandara, near Tanta, in the Nile Delta. He enrolled in the Faculty of Law in Alexandria but was compelled by family obligations to leave his studies and begin work at the Post Office in Cairo. He was arrested in 1960 for his membership of leftist political organisations and was sentenced to five years in prison in 1962, but was released after two years. During his time in prison he wrote a number of short stories and his first novel *Ayyam al-Insan al-Sabᶜa* (*The Seven Days of Man*, 1969). Increasingly marginalised by Sadat's regime, he chose to leave Egypt for a number of years. After being invited to give a lecture at the Free University of Berlin in 1974, he decided to remain there with his family until 1985. He then returned to Cairo where he worked in journalism and tried to enter the world of politics. He ran for parliament on the list of the leftist party al-Tagammuᶜ but did not succeed in getting elected. He suffered a stroke while working on the election but would continue writing until his death in 1990. His works include the novels *Muhawala li-l-Khuruj* (An Attempt to Get out, 1980) and *Qadar al-Ghuraf al-Muqbida* (The Fate of the Oppressive Rooms, 1982), the novellas *al-Ukht li-Ab* (The Half-Sister) and *Sutur min Daftar al-Ahwal* (Lines from a Logbook), published together in 1983, and the short-story collections *al-Zunun wa-l-Ruʾa* (Suspicions and Visions, 1982) and *Diwan al-Mulhaqat* (The Collected Appendices, 1990). Widely regarded as one of the most important members of his generation, his early death may account for his lack of official recognition.[14]

Bahaa Taher (b. 1935)

Taher was born in 1935 in Giza. He received a degree in history and postgraduate diplomas in history and mass media from Cairo University. He worked as a theatre director, and later as a presenter on the state-run *'al-*

Birnamij al-Thani' (The Second Program), the cultural radio station that he helped establish during the 1960s. It was there that he worked, producing drama for radio, until 1975 when he was pushed out of his job during Sadat's purging of the cultural establishment. He also had difficulty publishing his fiction during the 1970s, which led to his decision to leave Egypt for Switzerland in 1981. He lived and worked in Geneva as a translator for the United Nations until 1995, when he returned to Egypt. He published his first short-story collection *al-Khutuba wa Qisas Ukhra* (The Engagement and Other Stories) in 1972, and has since published numerous novels, short-story collections, non-fiction works and translations. His fiction has also been translated into a number of foreign languages. He was awarded the State Grand Prize for Literature (1997) and in 2000 his novel *Khalati Safiyya wa-l-Dayr* (*Aunt Safiyya and the Monastery*, 1991) was awarded the Italian Guiseppe Acerbi Prize and translated into English, French, German and Dutch. He was also awarded the International Prize for Arabic Fiction in its inaugural year in 2008, for his novel *Wahat al-Ghurub* (*Sunset Oasis*, 2007). His name was among those suggested for the position of Minister of Culture, after the resignation of Faruq Husni in January 2011, but he declined the position, maintaining his long-standing distance from the seats of power.[15]

Notes

1. For a comprehensive list of the recipients of the state awards for literature between 1958 and 2006, see Jacquemond, *Conscience of the Nation*, pp. 291–96. For recipients after this date, from 2009 to the present, see the website of the Supreme Council of Culture, scc.gov.eg. For other awards see the following websites: Sultan Bin Ali Al Owais Cultural Foundation, http://www.alowais.com; the Naguib Mahfouz Medal for Literature, http://www.aucpress.com/t-nmmdescription.aspx; the Sheikh Zayed Book Award, http://www.zayedaward.ae/; the International Prize for Arabic Fiction, https://arabicfiction.org; Katara Prize for the Arabic Novel, https://www.kataranovels.com/.
2. This collection has not been translated into English. However, a number of stories from it appear in the collection *The Mountain of Green Tea*, an English translation by Denys Johnson-Davies, of a selection of Abdullah's short stories.
3. Al-Kharrat, 'Yahya al-Taher Abdullah wa-l-Rihla ila "ma waraʾ al-Waqiʿiyya"', p. 9.
4. For more, see 'Introduction' in Abdullah, *al-Kitabat al-Kamila*, p. 5.

5. For a thorough discussion of his life and works, see Hafez *et al.*, 'Ibrahim Aslan: ᶜAman ᶜAla Rahil al-Ghalban'.
6. See 'Ashour, Radwa' in Ashour *et al.*, *Arab Women Writers*, pp. 357–8.
7. This episode is discussed in Chapter 5.
8. For more on al-Bisati's career, see, for example, Shaᶜir, 'Muhammad al-Bisati: Hikayat Siriyya min al-Sira al-Dhatiyya'.
9. See El-Desouky, 'Gamal al-Ghitani (9 May 1945–)'.
10. [Unattributed], 'al-Kalima alladhi Alqaha Sonallah Ibrahim fi Khitam Muʾtamar al-Riwaya wa-l-Madina'.
11. For more, see De Moor, 'Sonallah Ibrahim'; Naaman, 'Sonallah Ibrahim (1937–)'; and Starkey, *Sonallah Ibrahim*, pp. 17–33.
12. Amireh, 'Edwar-al-Kharrat and the Modernist Revolution in the Egyptian Novel'.
13. For more, see al-Kafrawi, *Yusuf al-Qaid*, pp. 11–20; and the entry (unattributed) for 'Yusuf al-Qaid' on the Egyptian Writers' Union website.
14. I borrow some translations of Qasim's work from Kilpatrick, ᶜAbd al-Hakim Qasim and the Search for Liberation, p. 51. For more, see Mehrez, 'Introduction', pp. vii–xx; Shaᶜir, 'Abd al-Hakim Qasim: Katib al-Ahlam wa-l-Asa'; and Phillips, 'ᶜAbd al-Hakim Qasim (1935–13 November 1990)'.
15. See, for example, ᶜUbayd Allah, 'ᶜAlam Bahaa Taher'; El-Desouky, 'Bahaaʾ Taher (13 January 1935–)'; and Fayyad, 'Burtrih Malik Hazin'.

Bibliography

Below I cite the date of publication of the edition I consulted, followed by the date of first publication in parentheses [ ] where relevant.

Abdel Baqi, Samir, 'Hakadha Yatakallamu al-Udabaʾ al-Shabab', *al-Taliʿa*, 9, September 1969, pp. 31–2.
Abdel Hakim, Muhammed Subhi, *Madinat al-Iskandariyya* (Cairo: al-Hayʾa al-Misriyya al-ʿAmma li-l-Kitab, 2007).
Abdel Meguid, Ibrahim, *al-Balda al-Ukhra* (London: Riyad al-Rayyis, 1991).
———, *Birds of Amber*, trans. Farouk Abdel Wahab (Cairo/New York, American University in Cairo Press, 2005).
———, in Jamal al-ʿArdawi (dir.), 'Ibrahim Abdel Meguid . . . al-Iskandariyya . . . ayna?', *al-Mashaʾ*, 10 March 2016, *al-Jazeera*, http://www.aljazeera.net/programs/almashaa/ (last accessed 4 June 2018).
———, in Jamal al-ʿArdawi (dir.), 'Ibrahim Abdel Meguid . . . La Ahad Yanam fi al-Riwaya', *al-Mashaʾ*, 17 March 2016, *al-Jazeera*, http://www.aljazeera.net/programs/almashaa/ (last accessed 4 June 2018).
———, *al-Iskandariyya fi Ghayma*, 2nd edn (Cairo: Dar al-Shuruq, 2013 [2012]).
———, *La Ahad Yanam fi al-Iskandariyya*, 6th edn (Cairo: Dar al-Shuruq, 2013 [1996]).
———, *No One Sleeps in Alexandria*, trans. Farouk Abdel Wahab (Cairo/New York: American University in Cairo Press, 1999).
———, *The Other Place*, trans. Farouk Abdel Wahab (Cairo/New York: American University in Cairo Press, 1997).
———, *Tuyur al-ʿAnbar*, 3rd edn (Cairo: Dar al-Shuruq, 2010 [2000]).
Abdel-Messih, Marie-Therese F., 'Introduction', in Yusuf al-Qaid, *News from The Meneisi Farm*, trans. Marie-Therese F. Abdel-Messih (Cairo: General Egyptian Book Organization, 1987), pp. 7–26.

Abdullah, Yahya Taher, *The Collar and the Bracelet*, trans. Samah Selim (Cairo/New York: American University in Cairo Press, 2008).

———, *al-Kitabat al-Kamila* (Cairo: Dar al-Mustaqbal al-ʿArabi, 1983).

———, *The Mountain of Green Tea*, trans. Denys Johnson-Davies (Cairo/New York: American University in Cairo Press, 1991).

———, *al-Tawq wa-l-Iswira* (Cairo: al-Hayʾa al-Misriyya al-ʿAmma li-l-Kitab, 1975).

Abu ʿAwf, Abdel Rahman, 'al-Bahth ʿan Tariq Jadid li-l-Qissa al-Misriyya al-Qasira', *al-Hilal*, 77:8, August 1969, pp. 80–91.

———, 'Muqaddima fi al-Qissa al-Misriyya al-Qasira', *al-Hilal*, August 1970, pp. 178–86.

Abu-Lughod, Janet L., *Cairo: 1001 Years of the City Victorious* (New Jersey: Princeton University Press, 1971).

ʿAdas, Salah, 'Azmat Nashr am Azmat Intaj', *al-Zuhur, Mulhaq al-Hilal*, 8, August 1976, pp. 8–10.

Alabarces, Pablo, Alan Tomlinson and Christopher Young, 'Argentina versus England at the France '98 World Cup: Narratives of Nation and the Mythologizing of the Popular', *Media Culture Society*, 23, 2001, pp. 547–66.

al-ʿAlim, Mahmud Amin, 'Mulahazat ʿala Hamish *al-Hubb fi al-Manfa*', in Muhammad ʿUbayd Allah (ed.), *ʿAlam Bahaa Taher: Dayf Dar Majdalawi li-ʿAm 2005* (Amman: Dar Majdalawi li-l-Nashr wa-l-Tawziʿ, 2005), pp. 119–27.

———, 'al-Tarikh wa-l-Fan-wa-l-Dalala fi Thalath Riwayat Misriyya', *al-Adab*, 2–3, February and March 1980, pp. 15–28.

Allen, Roger, *The Arabic Novel: An Historical and Critical Introduction* (Syracuse: Syracuse University Press, 1995).

Amireh, Amal, 'Edwar-al-Kharrat and the Modernist Revolution in the Egyptian Novel', *al-Jadid*, 2:9, 9 July 1996, http://www.aljadid.com/content/edwar-al-kharrat-and-modernist-revolution-egyptian-novel (last accessed 6 June 2018).

Anderson, Benedict, *Imagined Communities: Reflections on the Origins and Spread of Nationalism* (New York: Verso, 1991).

Anishchenkova, Valerie, 'Feminist Voices of the 1990s Generation: A Quest for Identity in Miral al-Tahawy's *Blue Aubergine*', *Journal of Middle East Women's Studies*, 13:1, March 2017, pp. 87–106.

———, 'Visions of Self: Filming Autobiographical Subjectivity', in V. Anishchenkova, *Autobiographical Identities in Contemporary Arab Culture* (Edinburgh: Edinburgh University Press, 2014), pp. 142–70.

Ansari, Hamid, *Egypt: The Stalled Society* (Albany: State University of New York Press, 1986).

Appadurai, Arjun, 'Disjuncture and Difference', in Jana Evans Braziel *et al.* (eds), *Theorizing Diaspora: A Reader* (Oxford: Blackwell Publishing, 2003), pp. 25–49.

ᶜAsfur, Jabir, 'Naqd al-Thanaʾiyya al-Qadima', in Muhammad ᶜUbayd Allah (ed.), *ᶜAlam Bahaa Taher: Dayf Dar Majdalawi li-ᶜAm 2005* (Amman: Dar Majdalawi li-l-Nashr wa-l-Tawziᶜ, 2005), pp. 127–35.

Ashhabun, ᶜAbdullah al-Malik, 'Riwayat Yusuf al-Qaid-*Qismat al-Ghurama*ʾ', in al-Saᶜdawi al-Kafuri (ed.), *Yusuf al-Qaid: Sabᶜun ᶜAman min al-ᶜIshq li-l-Ard wa-l-Insan* (Cairo: al-Hayʾa al-ᶜAmma li-Qusur al-Thaqafa, 2014), pp. 129–46.

Ashour, Radwa, 'Arab Prison Literature', *Minbar Ibn Rushd*, 18, Winter 2015–16, http://www.ibn-rushd.org/typo3/cms/magazine/18th-issue-winter-20152016/radwa-ashour (last accessed 4 June 2018).

———, *Blue Lorries*, trans. Barbara Romaine (Doha: Bloomsbury Qatar Foundation Publishing, 2014).

———, 'Eyewitness, Scribe and Story Teller: My Experience as a Novelist', *The Massachusetts Review*, 1:1, Spring 2000, pp. 85–92.

———, *Faraj* (Cairo: Dar al-Shuruq, 2008).

———, *Gibran and Blake: A Comparative Study* (Cairo: Associated Institution for the Study and Presentation of Arab Cultural Values, 1978).

———, *Granada: A Novel*, trans. William Granara (Syracuse: Syracuse University Press, 2003).

———, *al-Hadatha al-Mumkina: al-Shidyaq wa-l-Saq ᶜala al-Saq: al-Riwaya al-Ula fi al-Adab al-ᶜArabi* (Cairo: Dar al-Shuruq, 2009).

———, 'Hakadha Yatakallamu al-Udabaʾ al-Shabab', *al-Taliᶜa*, 9, September 1969, pp. 16–18.

———, *Qitᶜa min Uruba* (Casablanca: Al-Markaj al-Thaqafi al-ᶜArabi, 2003).

———, *al-Tariq ila l-Khayma al-Ukhra: Dirasa fi Aᶜmal Ghassan Kanafani* (Beirut, Dar al-Adab, 1981).

———, *Thulatiyyat Gharnata* (Cairo: Dar al-Shuruq, 2009 [1994–5]).

Ashour, Radwa, Ferial Ghazoul and Hasna Red-Mekdashi (eds), *Arab Women Writers: A Critical Reference Guide, 1873–1999*, trans. Mandy McClure (Cairo/New York: American University in Cairo Press, 2008).

al-ᶜAshri, Jalal, *Jil Waraʾ Jil: al-Ajyal: Liqaʾ am Siraᶜ* (Cairo: al-Hayʾa al-Misriyya al-ᶜAmma li-l-Kitab, 1987).

Aslan, Ibrahim, *ᶜAsafir al-Nil* (Beirut: Dar al-Adab, 1999 [1998]).

———, *Buhayrat al-Masaʾ: Majmuᶜa Qasassiyya* (Beirut: Dar al-Adab, 1992).

———, *The Heron*, trans. Elliot Colla (Cairo/New York: American University in Cairo Press, 2005).
———, *Hikayat min Fadlallah ʿUthman* (Cairo: Merit, 2003).
———, *Hujratayn wa Sala: Mutataliya Manziliyya* (Cairo: Dar al-Shuruq, 2009).
———, *Khalwat al-Ghalban* (Cairo: Dar al-Shuruq, 2003).
———, *Malik al-Hazin: Riwaya Misriyya* (Cairo: Matbuʿat al-Qahira, 1983).
———, *Nile Sparrows*, trans. Mona el-Ghobashy (Cairo/New York: American University in Cairo Press, 2004).
———, *Shayʾun min Hadha al-Qabil* (Cairo: Dar al-Shuruq, 2007).
———, *Wardiyat Layl* (Cairo: Dar al-Shuruq, 2005 [1991]).
———, *Yusuf wa-l-Ridaʾ* (Cairo, al-Hayʾa al-Misriyya al-ʿAmma li-l-Kitab, 1987).
ʿAwad, Luwis, 'Hadha al-Jil: Iʿsar Haqiqi am Zawbaʿa fi Finjan?', *al-Taliʿa*, 9, September 1969, pp. 69–71.
ʿAyyad, Muhammad Shukri, 'al-Qissa al-Misriyya al-Qasira', *al-Majalla*, 150, June 1969, pp. 94–7.
Badawi, Muhammad, *al-Riwaya al-Haditha fi Misr: Dirasa fi al-Tashkil wa-l-Aydiyulujiyya* (Cairo: Matabiʿ al-Hayʾa al-Misriyya al-ʿAmma li-l-Kitab, 1993).
Badr, Abdel Muhsin Taha, *al-Riwaʾi wa-l-Ard: 1870–1938* (Cairo: al-Hayʾa al-Misriyya al-ʿAmma li-l-Taʾlif wa-l-Nashr, 1971).
Bakhtin, M. M., 'Forms of Time and of the Chronotope in the Novel: Notes Towards a Historical Poetics', in M. M. Bakhtin, *The Dialogic Imagination*, trans. Caryl Emerson and Michael Holquist (Austin: University of Texas Press, 1981), pp. 84–259.
Bakr, Salwa, *al-ʿArba al-Dhahabiyya la Tasʿad ila al-Samaʾ* (Cairo: Sina li-l-Nashr, 1991).
Barakat, Muhammad, 'al-Qissa al-Qasira bayn Jilayn', *al-Hilal*, August 1970, pp. 188–200.
al-Bashir, Azid Bey Walad Muhammad, *Tajdid al-Riwaya al-ʿArabiyya: Yusuf al-Qaid Namudhajan* (Cairo: al-Hayʾa al-ʿAmma li-Qusur al-Thafaqa, 2006).
Berquist, Jon L, 'Introduction', in Jon L. Berquist and Claudia V. Camp (eds), *Constructions of Space I: Theory, Geography, and Narrative* (New York/London: T. & T. Clark, 2007), pp. 1–15.
al-Bisati, Muhammad, *Buyut Waraʾ al-Ashgar* (Beirut: Dar al-Adab, 2000 [1993]).
———, *Clamor of the Lake*, trans. Hala Halim (Cairo/New York: American University in Cairo Press, 2008).
———, *Daqq al-Tubul* (Beirut: Dar al-Adab, 2006).

―――, *Dawʾ Daʿif la Yakshif Shayʾan* (Cairo: Dar al-Sharqiyyat li-l-Nashr wa-l-Tawziʿ, 1993).

―――, *Drumbeat*, trans. Peter Daniel (Cairo/New York: American University in Cairo Press, 2010).

―――, *Hadith min al-Tabiq al-Thalith wa Qisas Ukhra* (Cairo: al-Hayʾa al-Misriyya al-ʿAmma li-l-Taʾlif wa-l-Nashr, 1970).

―――, *al-Khaldiyya* (Cairo: Dar al-Hilal, 2004).

―――, *al-Kibar wa-l-Sighar* (Cairo: al-Muʾasasa al-Misriyya al-ʿAmma li-l-Taʾlif wa-l-Nashr, 1967).

―――, *Over the Bridge*, trans. Nancy Roberts (Cairo/New York: American University in Cairo Press, 2006).

―――, *Sakhb al-Buhayra* (Cairo: Dar al-Sharqiyyat, 1994).

―――, 'al-Tajdid ... wa Majallat 68', *al Masaʾ*, 4379, 23 November 1968, p. 6.

―――, *al-Tajir wa-l-Naqqash* (Cairo: Dar al-Thaqafa al-Jadida, 1976).

Blom, Mattias Bolkéus, 'Tracing Literary Careers: Four Case Studies from the 1940 Cohort of Fiction Debut Writers in the United States', *Poetics*, 30:5–6, 2002, pp. 365–80.

Boullata, Issa J., 'New Directions in the Arabic Novel: An Interview with Jamal al-Ghitani', in Issa J. Boullata (ed.) *The Arabic Novel Since 1950: Critical Essays, Interviews and a Bibliography*. Mundus Arabicus, vol. 5 (Cambridge: Dar Mahjar, 1992), pp. 1–9.

Bourdieu, Pierre, *The Field of Cultural Production: Essays on Art and Literature*, Randal Johnson (ed.) (New York: Columbia University Press, 1993).

Bullard, Stevan, 'Informal Development in Cairo, the View from Above: A Case Study Using Arial Photo Interpretation to Examine Informal Housing in the Imbaba District of Cairo', PhD dissertation (Georgia State University, 2006).

Bulson, Eric, *Novels, Maps, Modernity: The Spatial Imagination, 1850–2000* (New York/London: Routledge, 2007).

Calvino, Italo, 'Italo Calvino On Invisible Cities', *Columbia: A Journal of Literature and Art*, 8, Spring/Summer 1983, pp. 37–42.

Cardoso, Fernando Henrique, and Enzo Faletto, *Dependency and Development in Latin America*, trans. Marjory Mattingly Urquidi (Berkeley: University of California Press, 1979).

Casini, Lorenzo, 'Beyond Occidentalism: Europe and the Self in Present-Day Arabic Narrative Discourse', European University Institute (EUI), Robert Schuman Centre for Advanced Studies (RSCAS) Working Paper 30, 2008, pp. 1–21.

Colla, Elliott, 'Anxious Advocacy: The Novel, the Law, and Extrajudicial Appeals in Egypt', *Public Culture*, 17:3, 2005, pp. 417–43.

———, 'Revolution on Ice', *Jadaliyya*, 6 January 2014, http://www.jadaliyya.com/pages/index/15874/revolution-on-ice (last accessed 1 June 2018).

———, 'Translator's Introduction', in Ibrahim Aslan, *The Heron*, trans. Elliott Colla (Cairo/New York: American University in Cairo Press, 2005), pp. v–ix.

De Certeau, Michel, *The Practice of Everyday Life*, trans. Steven Randall (Berkeley: University of California Press, 1988).

De Moor, E. C. M., 'Sonallah Ibrahim', in Julie Scott Meisami and Paul Starkey (eds), *The Encyclopedia of Arabic Literature 1* (London/New York, Routledge, 1998), pp. 386–7.

Denis, Eric, 'Urban Planning and Growth in Cairo', *Middle East Report*, 202, Winter 1996, pp. 7–12.

Denis, Eric, and Asef Bayat, 'Who is Afraid of the Ashwaiyyat? Urban Change and Politics in Egypt', *Environment and Urbanization*, 12:2, October 2000, pp. 185–99.

Di-Capua, Yoav, 'Arab Existentialism: An Invisible Chapter in the Intellectual History of Decolonization', *American Historical Review*, October 2012, pp. 1061–91.

Dirgham, ʿAdil, *Fi al-Sard al-Riwaʾi* (Beirut: al-Dar al-ʿArabiyya li-l-ʿUlum Nashirun, 2010).

Dunqul, Amal, 'Hakadha Yatakallamu al-Udabaʾ al-Shabab', *al-Taliʿa*, 9, September 1969, pp. 18–19.

El-Ariss, Tarek, *Trials of Arab Modernity: Literary Affects and the New Political* (New York: Fordham University Press, 2013).

El-Desouky, Ayman A., 'Bahaaʾ Taher (13 January 1935–)', in Majd Yaser al-Mallah and Coeli Fitzpatrick (eds), *Twentieth-Century Arabic Writers: Dictionary of Literary Biography*, vol. 346 (Farmington Hills: Cengage Gale, 2009), pp. 252–6, http://link.galegroup.com/apps/doc/PRPMGW725610478/DLBC?u=uiowa_main&sid=DLBC (last accessed 6 June 2018).

———, 'Gamal al-Ghitani (9 May 1945–)', in Majd Yaser al-Mallah and Coeli Fitzpatrick (eds), *Twentieth-Century Arabic Writers: Dictionary of Literary Biography*, vol. 346 (Farmington Hills: Cengage Gale, 2009), pp. 58–67, http://link.galegroup.com/apps/doc/PRDHHA845578658/DLBC?u=uiowa_main&sid=DLBC (last accessed 6 June 2018).

El-Enany, Rasheed, *Arab Representations of the Occident: East-West Encounter in Arabic Fiction* (New York: Routledge, 2006).

———, '*Cities of Salt*: A Literary View of the Theme of Oil and Change in the Gulf', in I. R. Netton, *Arabia and the Gulf: from Traditional Society to Modern States* (London/Sydney: Croom Helm, 1986), pp. 213–22.

———, 'Poets and Rebels: Reflections of Lorca in Modern Arab Poetry', *Third World Quarterly*, 11:4, 1989, pp. 252–64.

El Guabli, Brahim, '"The Hidden Transcript" of Resistance in Moroccan Tazmamart Prison Writings', *Arab Studies Journal*, 22:1, Spring 2014, pp. 170–207.

El Saadawi, Nawal, *Mudhakirat fi Sijn al-Nisaʾ* (Cairo: Maktabat Madbuli, 2006).

Elsadda, Hoda, *Gender, Nation, and the Arabic Novel: Egypt, 1892–2008* (Syracuse: Syracuse University Press, 2012).

Esty, Joshua, 'Excremental Postcolonialism', *Contemporary Literature*, 40:1, Spring, 1999, pp. 22–59.

Ezzeldin, Mohammed Saaid, 'History and Memory of Bandits in Modern Egypt: The Controversy of Adham al-Sharqawi', MA Thesis (Georgetown University, 2013).

Fahmy, Khaled, 'For Cavafy, With Love and Squalor: Some Critical Notes on the History and Historiography of Modern Alexandria', in Anthony Hirst and Michael Silk (eds), *Alexandria: Real and Imagined* (Aldershot: Ashgate, 2004), pp. 263–80.

———, 'Towards a Social History of Modern Alexandria', in Anthony Hirst and Michael Silk (eds), *Alexandria: Real and Imagined* (Aldershot: Ashgate, 2004), pp. 281–306.

Farahat, Muhammad Ali, 'Qaryat al-Qaid Tatasawwaf', in al-Saʿdawi al-Kafuri (ed.), *Yusuf al-Qaid: Sabʿun ʿAman min al-ʿIshq li-l-Ard wa-l-Insan* (Cairo: al-Hayʾa al-ʿAmma li-Qusur al-Thaqafa, 2014), pp. 78–9.

Faris, Muhammad, 'Qabl an Yughriq al-Nahr al-Jamiʿ', *al-Taliʿa*, 11, November 1969, pp. 109–11.

Fathi, Ibrahim, 'Malamih Mushtarika fi al-Intaj al-Qasasi al-Jadid', *Gallery 68*, April 1969, pp. 110–14.

Fayyad, Sulayman, 'Burtrih Malik Hazin', in Muhammad ʿUbayd Allah (ed.), *ʿAlam Bahaa Taher: Dayf Dar Majdalawi li-ʿAm 2005* (Amman: Dar Majdalawi li-l-Nashr wa-l-Tawziʿ, 2005), pp. 15–25.

Feiler, Gil, 'Migration and Recession: Arab Labor Mobility in the Middle East: 1982–89', *Population and Development Review*, 17:1, March 1991, pp. 134–55.

Foucault, Michel, *Discipline and Punish: The Birth of the Prison*, trans. Alan Sheridan (New York: Vintage, 1995).

———, *The History of Sexuality: An Introduction*, vol. 1, trans. Robert Hurley (New York: Vintage Books, 1990).

——, *Madness and Civilization: A History of Insanity in the Age of Reason*, trans. Richard Howard (New York: Pantheon, 1965).

——, 'Of Other Spaces', trans. Jay Miskowiec, *Diacritics*, 16:1, Spring 1986, pp. 22–7.

Frye, Northrop, 'From Fables of Identity: Studies in Poetic Mythology', in Michael McKeon (ed.), *Theory of the Novel: A Historical Approach* (Baltimore: The Johns Hopkins University Press), pp. 131–8.

Gardet, L, 'Dhikr', in P. J. Bearman, T. Banquis, C. E. Bowworth, E. van Donzel, W. P. Heinrichs Bowworth (eds), *Encyclopaedia of Islam*, 2nd edn, *Glossary and Index of Terms*, http://dx.doi.org/10.1163/1573-3912_ei2glos_SIM_gi_00846 (last accessed 5 June 2018).

Ghannam, Farha, *Remaking the Modern: Space, Relocation, and the Politics of Identity in a Global Cairo* (Berkeley: University of California Press, 2002).

al-Ghitani, Gamal, 'Hakadha Yatakallamu al-Udabaʾ al-Shabab', *al-Taliʿa*, 9, September 1969, pp. 53–4.

——, 'Jadaliyyat al-Tanass', *Alif: Journal of Comparative Poetics*, 4, Spring 1984, pp. 71–82.

——, *Khitat al-Ghitani* (Cairo: Dar al-Shuruq, 1981 [1980]).

——, *Mutun al-Ahram* (Cairo: Dar al-Shuruq, 2002 [1994]).

——, *Pyramid Texts*, trans. Humphery Davies (Cairo/New York: American University in Cairo Press, 2007).

——, *Shath al-Madina*, (Cairo: Dar al-Shuruq, 1992).

——, *Waqaʾiʿ Harat al-Zaʿfarani* (Cairo: Maktabat Matbuli, 1985 [1976]).

——, *The Zafarani Files*, trans. Farouk Abdel Wahab (Cairo/New York: American University in Cairo Press, 2009).

——, *al-Zayni Barakat* (Cairo: Dar al-Shuruq, 2009 [1974]).

——, *Zayni Barakat*, trans. Farouk Abdel Wahab (Cairo/New York: American University in Cairo Press, 2004).

——, *al-Zuwayl* (Cairo: Dar al-Shuruq, 2008 [1974]).

Goldschmidt Jnr, Arthur, 'Darwish, Sayyid', in Arthur Goldschmidt Jnr, *Biographical Dictionary of Modern Egypt* (Boulder/London: Lynne Rienner Publishers, 2000), p. 47.

Gordon, Joel, *Nasser's Blessed Movement: Egypt's Free Officers and the July Revolution* (Oxford: Oxford University Press, 1992).

Haag, Michael, *Alexandria: City of Memory* (New Haven: Yale University Press, 2004).

Hafez, Muhammad, Hatem al-Suri and Rasha Ramzi, 'Ibrahim Aslan: ʿAman ʿAla

Rahil al-Ghalban', *al-Bawaba*, 5 January 2004, http://www.albawabhnews.com/310830 (last accessed 6 June 2018).

Hafez, Sabry, 'The Egyptian Novel in the Sixties', in Issa Boullata (ed.), *Critical Perspectives on Modern Arabic Literature* (Washington, DC: Three Continents Press, 1980), pp. 171–87.

———, *The Genesis of Arabic Narrative Discourse* (London: Saqi Books, 1993).

———, 'Jamaliyyat al-Riwaya al-Jadida al-Qatiᶜa al-Maᶜrifiyya wa-l-Nazᶜa al-Mudadda li-l-Ghinaʾiyya', *Alif: The Journal of Comparative Poetics*, 21, 2001, pp. 184–246.

———, 'Majmuᶜat 1968 al-Qasasiyya', *al-Majalla*, 47, March 1969, pp. 62–71.

———, 'Majmuᶜat 1969 al-Qasasiyya', *al-Majalla*, 166, October 1970, pp. 66–77.

———, 'Mustaqbal al-Uqsusa al-Misriyya', *al-Majalla*, 116, August 1966, pp. 6–16.

———, 'The New Egyptian Novel', *New Left Review*, 64, July–August 2010, pp. 46–62.

———, 'The Novel, Politics and Islam: Haydar Haydar's Banquet for Seaweed', *New Left Review*, 5, September–October 2000, https://newleftreview.org/II/5/sabry-hafez-the-novel-politics-and-islam (last accessed 6 June 2018).

———, 'Qisas Yahya al-Taher Abdullah al-Tawila', *Fusul*, 2:2, 1982, pp. 195–205.

———, 'The Transformation of Reality and the Arabic Novel's Aesthetic Response', *Bulletin of the School of Oriental and African Studies*, 57:1, 1994, pp. 93–112.

———, 'al-Uqsussa al-Misriyya wa-l-Hadatha', *Gallery 68*, October 1969, pp. 83–90.

al-Hajmari, Abdel Fatah, *Takhayyul al-Hikaya: Bahth fi al-Ansaq al-Khitabiyya li-Riwayat Malik al-Hazin li-Ibrahim Aslan* (Cairo: al-Majlis al-ᶜAla li-l-Thaqafa, 1998).

'Hakadha Yatakallamu al-Udabaʾ al-Shabab', *al-Taliᶜa*, 9, September 1969, pp. 13–91.

al-Hakim, Tawfiq, *Maze of Justice: Diary of a Country Prosecutor. An Egyptian Novel*, trans. Abba Eban (Austin: University of Texas Press, 1989).

———, *Yawmiyyat Naʾib fi al-Aryaf* (Cairo: Dar al-Shuruq, 1999 [1937]).

Halasa, Ghalib, 'al-Adab al-Jadid: Malamih wa Ittijahat', *Gallery 68*, April 1969, pp. 115–25.

———, 'al-Kibar wa-l-Sighar', *Gallery 68*, 2, June 1968, pp. 243–51.

———, 'Malamih al-Adab al-Jadid', *al-Masaʾ*, 28 May 1969, p. 6.

Halim, Hala [Hala Youssef Halim Youssef], 'The Alexandrian Archive: An Archaeology of Alexandrian Cosmopolitanism', PhD dissertation (University of California, Los Angeles, 2004).

———, *Alexandrian Cosmopolitanism: An Archive* (Fordham University Press, New York, 2013).
———, 'Alexandria Re-inscribed', *al-Ahram Weekly*, 9–15 March 2000, http://weekly.ahram.org.eg/Archive/2000/472/bk1_472.htm (last accessed 4 June 2018).
———, 'Forster in Alexandria: Gender and Genre in Narrating Colonial Cosmopolitanism', *Hawaa*, 4:2–3, 2006, pp. 237–73.
———, 'On Being an Alexandrian', *al-Ahram Weekly*, 11–17 April 2002, http://weekly.ahram.org.eg/archive/2002/581/cu1.htm (last accessed 4 June 2018).
Hammad, Hasan, *Malik al-Hazin: Dirasa Bunyawiyya Takwiniyya* (Cairo: Modern Press, 1994).
Hammond, Marlé, 'Subsuming the Feminine Other: Gender and Narration in Idwar al-Kharrat's *Ya Banat Iskandariyya*', *Journal of Arabic Literature*, XXXI, 2000, pp. 38–58.
Hammuda, Husayn, *al-Riwaya wa-l-Madina: Namazij min Kuttab al-Sittinat fi Misr* (Cairo: al-Hayʾa al-ʿAmma li-Qasur al-Thaqafa, 2000).
Hanley, Will, 'Foreignness and Localness in Alexandria, 1880–1914', PhD dissertation (Princeton University, 2007).
Haqqi, Yahya, *Fajr al-Qissa al-Misriyya maʿa Sitt Dirasat Ukhra ʿan Nafs al-Marhala* (Cairo: al-Hayʾa al-Misriyya al-ʿAmma li-l-Kitab, 1975).
Harlow, Barbara, 'Egyptian Intellectuals and the Debate on the "Normalization of Cultural Relations"', *Cultural Critique*, 4, Autumn 1986, pp. 33–58.
Harvey, David, *The Condition of Postmodernity: An Enquiry into the Origins of Social Change* (Oxford: Blackwell, 1989).
Hassan, Mahir, 'Majala ʿUmruha 88 Aman Tarsim Surat Adham al-Sharqawi: Mujrim Akbar wa Taghiya wa Shaqiy', *al-Masry al-Youm*, 2 October 2009, http://today.almasryalyoum.com/article2.aspx?ArticleID=227713 (last accessed July 5 2017).
Hilmi, Ahmad, 'Riwayat *Faraj*: Ahadahum Tara Fawqa ma Tabaqqa Minna', *Idaʾat*, 10 February 2016, https://www.ida2at.com/novel-vulva-one-flew-over-the-rest-of-us/ (last accessed 4 June 2018).
Hishmat, Dina, *al Qahira fi al-Adab al-Misri al-Hadith wa-l-Muʿasir: min Hilm al-Madina al-Kabira ila ʿUzla al-Dawahi* (Cairo: al-Mashruʿ al-Qawmi li-l-Tarjama, 2006).
'Hiwar Hawl Azmat al-Qissa al-Qasira', *al-Hilal*, August 1969, pp. 122–38.
Hourani, Albert, *Arabic Thought in the Liberal Age: 1798–1939* (Cambridge: Cambridge University Press, 1983).

Ibrahim, Abdel Hamid, 'Adab al-Shabab fi Masarahu al-Sahih', *al-Masa⁾*, 4709, 22 October 1969, p. 6.

Ibrahim, Sonallah, *Beirut Beirut* (Cairo: Dar al-Mustaqbal al-ᶜArabi, 1984).

———, *Beirut Beirut*, trans. Chip Rossetti (Doha: Hamad Bin Khalifa Univerity Press, 2016).

———, *The Committee*, trans Mary St. Germain and Charlene Constable (Syracuse: Syracuse University Press, 2001).

———, *Dhat* (Beirut, Dar al-Mustaqbal al-ᶜArabi, 1993).

———, 'The Experience of a Generation', trans. Marilyn Booth, *Index on Censorship*, 16:9, 1987, pp. 19–22.

———, *al-Lajna*, (Cairo: Dar al-Thaqafa al-Jadida, 2012 [1981]).

———, *Najmat Ughustus* (Cairo: Maktabbat Mabuli, 1987 [1974]).

———, *The Smell of It and Other Stories*, trans. Denys Johnson-Davies (London: Heinemann, 1971).

———, *Stealth*, trans. Hosam M. Aboul-Ela (London: Aflame Books, 2009).

———, *That Smell and Notes from Prison*, ed. and trans. Robyn Creswell (New York: New Directions Books, 2013).

———, *Tilka-l-Ra⁾iha* (Cairo: Dar Shahdy, 1986 [1966]).

———, *Yawmiyyat al-Wahat* (Cairo: Dar al-Mustqabal al-ᶜArabi, 2004).

———, *Zaat*, trans. Anthony Calderbank (Cairo: American University in Cairo Press, 2001).

Idris, Samah, *al-Muthaqqaf al-ᶜArabi wa-l-Sulta: Bahth fi Riwayat al-Tajriba al-Nasiriyya* (Beirut: Dar al-Adab, 1991).

Imbabi, Fathi (ed.), *Siham Sabri Zahrat al-Haraka al-Tulabiyya: Jil al-Sabᶜinat* (Cairo: Dar Merit, 2004).

ᶜIsa, Salah, *Muthaqqafun wa ᶜAskar: Murajaᶜat wa Tajarib wa Shahadat ᶜan Halat al-Muthaqqafin fi Zill Hukm Abdel Nasser wa-l-Sadat* (Cairo: Maktabat Madbuli, 1986).

Jabra, Jabra I., 'Modern Arabic Literature and the West', *Journal of Arabic Literature*, 2, 1971, pp. 76–91.

Jackson, Rosemary, *Fantasy: The Literature of Subversion* (London: Meuthen, 1981).

Jacquemond, Richard, *Conscience of the Nation: Writers, State, and Society in Modern Egypt*, trans. David Tresilian (Cairo: American University in Cairo Press, 2008).

al-Kafuri, al-Saᶜdawi (ed.), *Yusuf al-Qaid: Sabᶜun ᶜAman min al-ᶜIshq li-l-Ard wa-l-Insan* (Cairo: al-Hay⁾a al-ᶜAmma li-Qusur al-Thaqafa, 2014).

Kendall, Elisabeth, *Literature, Journalism and the Avant-Garde: Intersection in Egypt* (New York: Routledge, 2006).

Khalaf, Sulayman, 'The Evolution of the Gulf City: Type, Oil, and Globalization', in John W. Fox, Nada Mourtada–Sabbahh and Mohammad al-Mutawa (eds), *Globalization and the Gulf* (New York: Routledge, 2006), pp. 244–66.

Khalaf, Sulayman, and Saad Alkobaisi, 'Migrants' Strategies of Coping and Patterns of Accommodation in the Oil-Rich Gulf Societies: Evidence from the UAE', *British Journal for Middle Eastern Studies*, 26:2, November 1999, pp. 271–98.

Khalifah, Omar, *Nasser in the Egyptian Imaginary* (Edinburgh: Edinburgh University Press, 2016).

al-Kharrat, Edwar, *City of Saffron*, trans. Frances Liardet (London/New York: Quartet Books Limited, 1989).

———, *Girls of Alexandria*, trans. Frances Liardet (London/New York, Quartet, 1993).

———, *al-Hassasiyya al-Jadida: Maqalat fi al-Zahira al-Qasasiyya* (Beirut: Dar al-Adab, 1993).

———, 'Ibrahim Aslan wa Qinaᶜ al-Rafd', *Gallery 68*, February 1971, pp. 78–83.

———, *Iskandariyyati: Madinati al-Qudsiyya al-Hushiyya: Kulaj Riwaʾi* (Cairo: Dar wa Matabiᶜ al-Mustaqbal, 1994).

———, *al-Kitaba ᶜAbr al-Nawᶜiyya: Maqallat fi Zahirat "al-Qissa-al-Qasida" wa Nusus Ukhra* (Cairo: Dar Sharqiyyat li-l-Nashr wa-l-Tawziᶜ, 1994).

———, 'Lawrence Durrell Sammim ᶜAlam al-Iskandariyya bi-Baraᶜa', in Edwar al-Kharrat, *Muwajahat al-Mustahil: Maqatiᶜ Ukhra min Sira Dhatiyya li-l-Kitaba* (Cairo: Dar al-Bustani li-l-Nashr wa-l-Tawziᶜ, 2005), pp. 255–60.

———, 'La Yujad Adab Qibti Muᶜasar', in Edwar al-Kharrat, *Muwajahat al-Mustahil: Maqatiᶜ Ukhra min Sira Dhatiyya li-l-Kitaba* (Cairo: Dar al-Bustani li-l-Nashr wa-l-Tawziᶜ, 2005), pp. 101–6.

———, *Turabuha Zaᶜfaran: Nusus Iskandaraniyya* (Cairo: Dar al-Mustaqbal al-ᶜArabi, 1986).

———, *Ya Banat Iskandariyya: Riwaya* (Beirut: Dar al-Adab, 1990).

———, 'Yahya al-Taher Abdullah wa-l-Rihla ila "ma Waraʾ al-Waqiᶜiyya"', in Yahya Taher Abduallah, *al-Daff wa-l-Sunduq* (np: Matbuᶜat Khatwa, 1981), pp. 5–32.

Khashaba, Sami, 'Jil al-Sittinat fi al-Riwaya al-Misriyya', *Fusul*, 2:2, 1982, pp. 117–25.

Kilpatrick, Hilary, 'ᶜAbd al-Hakim Qasim and the Search for Liberation', *Journal of Arabic Literature*, 26:1/2, March–June 1995, pp. 50–66.

Klemm, Verena, 'Different Notions of Commitment (*Iltizam*) and Committed Literature *(al-adab al-multazim)* in the Literary Circles of the Mashriq', *Arabic and Middle Eastern Literatures*, 3:1, 2000, pp. 51–62.

Knapp, Bettina L, 'Introduction', in Bettina L. Knapp (ed.), *Exile and the Writer: Exoteric and Esoteric Experiences: A Jungian Approach* (Pennsylvania: University of Pennsylvania Press, 1998), pp. 1–19.

Larkin, Margaret, 'A Brigand Hero of Egyptian Colloquial Literature', *Journal of Arabic Literature*, 23:1, March 1992, pp. 49–64.

La Towsky, Robert, 'Egyptian Labor Abroad: Mass Participation and Modest Returns', *MERIP Reports*, 123, May 1984, pp. 11–18.

Lefebvre, Henri, *The Production of Space*, trans. Donald Nicholson-Smith (Oxford: Blackwell Publishing, 1991).

Litvin, Margaret, 'Egypt's Uzbek Mirror: Muhammad al-Mansi Qandil's Post-Soviet Islamic Humanism', *Journal of Arabic Literature*, 42, 2011, pp. 101–19.

Mabro, Robert, 'Alexandria 1860–1960: The Cosmopolitan Identity', in Anthony Hirst and Michael Silk (eds), *Alexandria Real and Imagined* (London: Ashgate, 2004), pp. 247–62.

Mahfouz, Naguib, *Adrift on the Nile*, trans. Frances Liardet (New York: Doubleday, 1993).

———, *Awlad Haritna* (Beirut: Dar al-Adab, 1986 [1959]).

———, *Bayn al-Qasrayn* (Cairo: Maktabat Misr, 1959 [1956]).

———, *Children of Gebelawi*, trans. Philip Stewart (London: Heinemann/ Washington, DC: Three Continents, 1981).

———, 'Hiwar Hawl Azmat al-Qissa al-Qasira', *al-Hilal*, August 1969, pp. 124–5.

———, *Khan al-Khalili* (Cairo: Maktabat Misr, 1979 [1946]).

———, *Khan al-Khalili*, trans. Roger Allen (Cairo: American University in Cairo Press, 2008).

———, *al-Liss wa-l-Kilab* (Cairo: Maktabat Misr, 1962 [1961]).

———, *Midaq Alley*, trans. Trevor Le Gassick (New York: Anchor Books, 1992).

———, *Miramar*, 2nd edn (Beirut: Dar al-Qalam, 1974 [1967]).

———, *Miramar*, trans. Fatma Moussa Mahmour (London: Heinemann, 1978).

———, *Palace of Desire*, trans. William Maynard Hutchins, Lorne M. Kenny and Olive E. Kenny (New York: Doubleday, 1991).

———, *Palace Walk*, trans. William M. Hutchins and Olive E. Kenny (New York: Doubleday, 1990).

———, *Qasr al-Shawq* (Cairo: Maktabat Misr, 1957).

———, *Sugar Street*, trans. William Maynard Hutchins and Angele Botros Samaan (New York: Doubleday, 1992).

———, *al-Sukkariyya* (Cairo: Maktabat Misr, 1962 [1957]).

———, *Tharthara Fawq al-Nil* (Cairo: Maktabat Misr, 1985).

———, *The Thief and the Dogs*, trans. M. M. Badawi and Trevor Le Gassick (Cairo: American University in Cairo Press, 1984).

———, *Zuqaq al-Midaqq* (Cairo: Maktabat Misr, 1965 [1947]).

Mahmoud, Sayed, Mary Mourad and Mohamed Saad, 'Q&A with Gamel El-Ghitani: Politics Dominate Literature in Post-Revolution Egypt', *Ahram Online*, 11 September 2012, http://english.ahram.org.eg/NewsContent/18/0/52426/Books/0/QA-with-Gamal-ElGhitani-Politics-dominate-literatu.aspx (last accessed 6 June 2018).

Massad, Joseph, 'Art and Politics in the Cinema of Youssef Chahine', *Journal of Palestine Studies*, 28:2, 1999, pp. 77–93.

———, *Desiring Arabs* (Chicago: Chicago University Press, 2007).

Mazid, Baha al-Din Muhammad, 'Radwa Ashour fi *Athqal min Radwa*: Sardiyya Mughayara', in Faten Mursi (ed.), *al-Mandil al-Maᶜqud: Dirasat fi Aᶜmal Radwa Ashour* (Cairo: Dar al-Shuruq, 2016), pp. 38–55.

Mehrez, Samia, *Egyptian Writers Between History and Fiction: Essays on Naguib Mahfouz, Sonallah Ibrahim and Gamal al-Ghitani* (Cairo/New York: American University in Cairo Press, 1994).

———, *Egypt's Culture Wars: Politics and Practice* (Cairo: American University in Cairo Press, 2010).

———, 'From the Hara to the ᶜImara: Emerging Urban Metaphors in the Literary Production of Contemporary Cairo', in Diane Singerman (ed.), *Cairo Contested: Governance, Urban Space and Global Modernity* (Cairo/New York: American University in Cairo Press, 2009), pp. 145–76.

———, 'Introduction', in Abd al-Hakim Qasim, *Rites of Assent: Two Novellas*, trans. Peter Theroux (Philadelphia: Temple University Press, 1995), pp. vii–xx.

———, (ed.), *The Literary Atlas of Cairo: One Hundred Years on the Streets of the City* (Cairo/New York: American University in Cairo Press, 2010).

———, (ed.), *The Literary Life of Cairo: One Hundred Years in the Heart of the City* (Cairo/New York: American University in Cairo Press, 2011).

———, 'Re-Writing the City: The Case of Khitat al-Ghitani', in Issa J. Boullata (ed.), *The Arabic Novel Since 1950: Critical Essays, Interviews and a Bibliography*, Mundus Arabicus, vol. 5 (Cambridge: Dar Mahjar, 1992), pp. 143–67.

———, 'Sonallah Ibrahim and the (Hi)story of the Book', in Samia Mehrez, *Egyptian Writers Between History and Fiction: Essays on Naguib Mahfouz, Sonallah Ibrahim and Gamal al-Ghitani* (Cairo/New York: American University in Cairo Press, 1994), pp. 39–58.

———, 'Take Them Out of the Ballgame: Egypt's Cultural Players in Crisis', *MERIP*, 219:31, Summer 2001, pp. 10–15, http://www.merip.org/mer/mer219/take-them-out-ballgame (last accessed 6 June 2018).

Moore, James, 'Between Cosmopolitanism and Nationalism: The Strange Death of Liberal Alexandria', *Journal of Urban History*, 38:5, 2012, pp. 879–900.

Moretti, Franco, *Atlas of the European Novel: 1800–1900* (London: Verso, 1999).

Morsi, Faten, 'al-Jamiᶜa fi Riwayatay "*al-Bab-al-Maftuh*" wa "*Atyaf*"', *Alif: Journal of Comparative Poetics*, 2009, pp. 139–52.

Muhsib, Hasan, 'Hakadha Yatakallamu al-Udabaʾ al-Shabab', *al-Taliᶜa*, 9, September 1969, pp. 24–6.

Mursi, Ahmad, 'Tasdir', *Gallery 68*, April–May 1968, p. 2.

al-Musawi, Muhsin, *Arabic Poetry: Trajectories of Modernity and Tradition* (London/New York: Routledge, 2006).

———, 'Beyond the Modernity Complex: ᶜAbd al-Hakim Qasim's Re-Writing of the Nahdah Self-Narrative', *Journal of Arabic Literature*, 41, 2010, pp. 22–45.

———, *Infirat al-ᶜAqd al-Muqaddas: Munᶜatafat al-Riwaya al-ᶜArabiyya baᶜd Mahfouz* (Cairo: al-Hayʾa al-ᶜAmma li-l-Kitab, 1999).

———, *Islam on the Street: Religion in Modern Arabic Literature* (Lanham: Rowman & Littlefield, 2009).

———, *al-Nukhba al-Fikriyya wa-l-Inshiqaq: Qiraʾa fi Tahawwulat al-Safwa al-ᶜArifa fi al-Mujtamaᶜ al-ᶜArabi al-Hadith* (Beirut: Dar al-Adab, 2001).

———, *The Postcolonial Arabic Novel: Debating Ambivalence* (Leiden: Brill, 2003).

Naaman, Mara, 'Sonallah Ibrahim (1937–)', in Majd Yaser al-Mallah and Coeli Fitzpatrick (eds), *Twentieth-Century Arabic Writers: Dictionary of Literary Biography*, vol. 346 (Farmington Hills: Cengage Gale, 2009), pp. 84–90, http://link.galegroup.com/apps/doc/PREYHY633962737/DLBC?u=uiowa_main&sid=DLBC (last accessed 6 June 2018).

———, *Urban Space in Contemporary Egyptian Literature: Portraits of Cairo* (New York: Palgrave Macmillan, 2011).

Najib, ᶜIzz al-Din, 'Hakadha Yatakallamu al-Udabaʾ al-Shabab', *al-Taliᶜa*, 9, September 1969, pp. 43–4.

al-Nimr, Nahla, 'Edwar al-Kharrat ᶜAshiq al-Iskandariyya . . . Wadaᶜan', *al-Wafd*, 8 December 2015, https://alwafd.news (last accessed 4 June 2018).

al-Noweihi, Magda, 'Memory and Imagination in Edwar al-Kharrat's *Turabuha Zaʿfaran*', *Journal of Arabic Literature*, XXV, 1994, pp. 34–57.

O'Malley, Maureen, 'Scenes from Cairo's Camel Market', *Inscriptions*, 6, 1992, https://culturalstudies.ucsc.edu/inscriptions/volume-6/maureen-omalley/ (last accessed 1 June 2018).

Ostle, Robin C., 'From Intertext to Mixed Media: The Case of Edwar al-Kharrat', in Luc Deheuvels, Barabara Michalak-Pikulska and Paul Starkey (eds), *Intertextuality in Modern Arabic Literature since 1967* (Durham: University of Durham Modern Languages Series, 2006), pp. 133–48.

Phillips, Christina, '"Abd al-Hakim Qasim (1935–13 November 1990)', in Majd Yaser al-Mallah and Coeli Fitzpatrick (eds), *Twentieth-Century Arabic Writers: Dictionary of Literary Biography*, vol. 346 (Farmington Hills: Cengage Gale, 2009), pp. 198–202, http://link.galegroup.com/apps/doc/PRLUDL712816179/DLBC?u=uiowa_main&sid=DLBC (last accessed 30 May 2018).

al-Qaid, Yusuf, *Akhbar ʿIzbat al-Minisi* (Cairo: al-Hayʾa al-ʿAmma li-l-Taʾlif wa-l-Nashr, 1971).

———, *al-Bayat al-Shitwi* (Cairo al-Hayʾa al-ʿAmma al-Misriyya li-l-Kitab, 2002[1974]).

———, *al-Harb fi Barr Misr: Riwaya* (Cairo: Dar al-Shuruq, 2008 [1978]).

———, *al-Hidad*, 3rd edn (Cairo: al-Hayʾa al-ʿAmma li-l-Kitab, 1987 [1969]).

———, *War in the Land of Egypt* (London: al-Saqi Books, 1986).

———, *Yahduth fi Misr alʿAn: Riwaya* (Cairo: Dar al-Shuruq, 2008 [1976]).

al-Qalamawi, Suhayr, 'Muqadimma', in Yusuf al-Qaid, *Akhbar ʿIzbat al-Minisi* (Cairo: al-Hayʾa al-ʿAmma li-l-Taʾlif wa-l-Nashr, 1971), pp. 5–17.

———, 'Zahirat al-ʿAqqad lan Tatakarrar', *al-Taliʿa*, 9, September 1969, pp. 66–8.

al-Qasas, Jamal, and Sara Rabiʿ, 'Radwa Ashour: Jisr min ʿAta Ibdaʿi bayn al-Mutakhayyal wa-l-Waqiʿi', *al-Sharq al-Awsat*, 2 December 2014.

Qasim, Abd al-Hakim, *Ayyam al-Insan al-Sabʿa* (Cairo: Dar al-Kitab al-ʿArabi, 1969).

———, 'Hakadha Yatakallamu al-Udabaʾ al-Shabab', *al-Taliʿa*, 9, September 1969, pp. 20–2.

———, *al-Mahdi wa Turaf min Khabar al-Akhira* (Beirut: Dar al-Tanwir, 1984).

———, *Muhawala li-l-Khuruj* (Cairo: al-Hayʾa al-Misriyya al-ʿAmma li-l-Kitab, 1987 [1980]).

———, *Qadar al-Ghuruf al-Muqbida* (Cairo: Matbuʿat al-Qahira, 1982).

———, *Rites of Assent: Two Novellas*, trans. Peter Theroux (Philadelphia: Border Lines, 1995).

———, *The Seven Days of Man*, trans. Joseph Norment Bell (Evanston: Northwestern University Press, 1996).

Radwan, Noha, 'A Place for Fiction in the Historical Archive', *Critique: Critical Middle Eastern Studies*, 17:1, 2008, pp. 79–95.

———, '*Spectres* by Radwa Ashour and Barbara Romaine', *Journal of Palestine Studies*, 40:4, Summer 2011, pp. 97–8.

al-Raʿi, Ali, *al-Riwaya fi Nihayat al-Qarn* (Cairo: Dar al-Mustaqbal al-ʿArabi, 2000).

Rakha, Yousef, 'Empty Feeling', *The Review*, 1 May 2009, http://www.pressreader.com/uae/the-national-news-the-review/20090501/281565171707275 (last accessed 6 June 2018).

———, 'Floating Bureaus', *al-Ahram Weekly*, 18–21 January 2001, http://weekly.ahram.org.eg/Archive/2001/517/cu1.htm (last accessed 6 June 2018).

Ramadan, Yasmine, 'The Emergence of the Sixties Generation in Egypt and the Anxiety of Categorization', *Journal of Arabic Literature*, 43:2–3, 2012, pp. 409–30.

Rashwan, Nur, 'Bahaa Taher: Rafadt Mansib Wazir al-Thaqafa baʿd al-Thawra Mubasharatan', *al-Shorouk*, 1 June 2011, http://www.shorouknews.com/news/view.aspx?cdate=01062013&id=aee88a0c-d912-4af4-906e-1747aa3ae179 (last accessed 6 June 2018).

Raymond, André, *Cairo: City of History*, trans. Willard Wood (Cairo/New York: American University in Cairo Press, 2001).

Reynolds, Dwight Fletcher, *Heroic Poets, Poetic Heroes: The Ethnography of Performance in an Arabic Oral Epic Tradition* (Ithaca: Cornell University Press, 1995).

Rodenbeck, Max, *Cairo: A City Victorious* (New York: Alfred A. Knopf, 1999).

Rowlandson, Jane, and Andrew Harker, 'Roman Alexandria from the Perspective of the Papyri', in Anthony Hirst and Michael Silk (eds), *Alexandria: Real and Imagined* (Aldershot: Ashgate, 2004), pp. 79–111.

Roy, Delwin A., 'Egyptian Emigrant Labor: Domestic Consequences', *Middle Eastern Studies*, 27:4, October 1991, pp. 551–82.

Rushdi, Rashad, 'Hiwar Hawl Azmat al-Qissa al-Qasira', *al-Hilal*, August 1969, pp. 133–5.

Sagi, Abraham, *Albert Camus and the Philosophy of the Absurd* (Amsterdam: Rodopi BV, 2002).

Said, Edward, *Representations of the Intellectual: The 1993 Reith Lectures* (New York: Vintage Books, 1996).

al-Saʾigh, Muhammad Dhannun, *Thunaʾiyyat al-Makan: al-Ightirab fi Adab*

Yahya al-Taher Abdullah: al-Tawq wa-l-Iswira wa Hikaya ʿala Lissan al-Kalb: Namudhajan (al-Sharja: Daʾirat al-Thaqafa wa-l-Iʿlam, 2004).

Salameh, Duaa Mohamad, '*Nom de Lieu, Alexandria's Colonial Cosmopolitanism and Narratives of Identity and Alterity*', PhD dissertation (University of Wisconsin-Madison, 2012).

Salih, Arwa, *Mubtasarun: Dafatir Wahda min Jil al-Haraka al-Tulabiyya* (Cairo: Dar al-Nahar li-l-Nashr wa-l-Tawziʿ, 1996).

———, *The Stillborn: Notebooks of a Woman from the Student-Movement Generation*, trans. Samah Selim (Chicago: University of Chicago Press, 2018).

Salih, Sharif, 'Adham al-Sharqawi, Batal amm Mujrim?', *al-Nahar*, 21 October 2011, p. 35.

Salloum, Habeeb, 'Sayyed Darwish: The Father of Modern Arab Music', *al-Jadid*, 7:36, Summer 2001, http://www.aljadid.com/content/sayyed-darwish-father-modern-arab-music (last accessed 4 June 2018).

Sami, Karma, 'Balaghat al-Bayan fi Nasjiyyat Radwa Ashour', in Fatin Morsi (ed.), *al-Mandil al-Maʿqud: Dirasat fi Aʿmal Radwa Ashour* (Cairo: Dar al-Shorouq, 2016), pp. 23–37.

———, '*al-Hubb fi al-Manfa*: Butulat al-la Batal', in Muhammad ʿUbayd Allah (ed.), *ʿAlam Bahaa Taher: Dayf Dar Majdalawi li-ʿAm 2005* (Amman: Dar Majdalawi li-l-Nashr wa-l-Tawziʿ, 2005), pp. 143–5.

Sedghi, Hamed, and Najam Abbas, 'al-Būṣīrī', in Wilferd Madelung and Farhad Daftary (eds), *Encyclopaedia Islamica*, Brill Online, http://referenceworks.brillonline.com/entries/encyclopaedia-islamica/al-busiri-COM_05000049?s.num=6&s.q=busiri (last accessed 5 June 2018).

Selim, Samah, *The Novel and the Rural Imaginary in Egypt: 1880–1985* (New York/London: Routledge Curzon, 2004).

Sells, Ralph, 'Egyptian International Migration and Social Processes: Toward Regional Integration', *International Migration Review*, 22: 3, Autumn 1988, pp. 87–108.

Shaʿir, Muhammad (ed.), 'Abd al-Hakim Qasim: Katib al-Ahlam wa-l-Asa', *al-Akhbar*, 25 November 2012, http://www.al-akhbar.com/node/37763 (last accessed 6 June 2018).

———, *Kitabat Nubat al-Hirasa: Rasaʾil Abd al-Hakim Qasim* (Cairo: Dar Merit, 2010).

———, 'Muhammad al-Bisati: Hikayat Siriyya min al-Sira al-Dhatiyya', *Akhbar al-Adab*, 29 March 2009, http://akhbarelyom.org.eg:81/adab/articleDetail.php?x=adab20 (last accessed 9 March 2010).

al-Sharqawi, Abdel Rahman, *al-Ard*, 3rd edn (Cairo: Dar al-Katib al-ʿArabi, 1968 [1954]).
———, *Egyptian Earth*, trans. Desmond Steward (Austin: University of Texas Press, 1990).
al-Sharuni, Yusuf, 'Hiwar Hawl Azmat al-Qissa al-Qasira', *al-Hilal*, August 1969, pp. 131–3.
al-Shayib, Zuhayr, 'Hakadha Yatakallamu al-Udabaʾ al-Shabab', *al-Taliʿa*, 9, September 1969, pp. 46–8.
Shukri, Ghali, 'al-Adab al-Misri baʿd al-Khamis min Yunyu', *al-Taliʿa*, 5, May 1969, pp. 101–10.
———, 'al-Basma al-Akhira fi Adab al-Sittinat', in Ghali Shkuri, *Dhikrayat al-Jil al-Daʾiʿ* (Baghdad: Wizarat al-Aʿlam, Mudiriyat al-Thaqafa al-ʿAmma, 1972), pp. 233–50.
———, 'Jil Jadid am Ruʾya Jadida?', in Ghali Shukri, *Dhikrayat al-Jil al-Daʾiʿ* (Baghdad: Wizarat al-Aʿlam, Mudiriyat al-Thaqafa al-ʿAmma, 1972), pp. 59–62.
———, 'Jiluna wa-l-Riwaya', *Adab*, 2:2, Spring 1963, pp. 84–96.
———, *Siraʿ al-Ajyal fi al-Adab al-Muʿasir* (Cairo: Dar al-Maʿarif, 1971).
———, 'Thaqafat 68', *al-Taliʿa*, 12, December 1968, pp. 75–87.
Shukri, Jirjis, 'al-Riwaʾi al-Misri Muhammad al-Bisati: Abhath ʿan al-Makan Qabl al-Riwaya', *al-Mustaqbal*, 25 October 2005, http://almustaqbal.com/article/146311/ (last accessed 6 June 2018).
Siddiq, Muhammad, *Arab Culture and the Novel: Genre, Identity, and Agency in Egyptian Fiction* (New York: Routledge, 2007).
Singerman, Dianne, 'The Siege of Imbaba', in Dianne Singerman (ed.), *Cairo Contested: Governance, Urban Space and Global Modernity* (Cairo/New York: American University in Cairo Press, 2009), pp. 111–45.
Singerman, Diane, and Paul Ammar, 'Introduction', in Dianne Singerman and Paul Ammar (eds), *Cairo Cosmopolitan: Politics, Culture, and Urban Space, in the Globalized Middle East* (Cairo/New York: American University in Cairo Press, 2006), pp. 1–46.
Soja, Edward, *Thirdspace: Journeys to Los Angeles and Other Real-and-Imagined Places* (Oxford: Blackwell, 1996).
Soueif, Ahdaf, *Cairo: Memoir of a City Transformed* (New York: Pantheon Books, 2012).
Staff Writers, 'The Legacy of the Late Sheikh Imam, Creator of Modern Arabic Political Song', *al-Jadid*, 1:1, November 1995, http://almashriq.hiof.no/egypt/700/780/sheikh-imam/aljadid-sheikh.html (last accessed 4 June 2018).

Stagh, Marina, *The Limits of Freedom of Speech: Prose Literature and Prose Writers in Egypt Under Nasser and Sadat* (Stockholm: Almqvit & Wiksell International, 1993).

Starkey, Paul, 'Intertexuality and the Arabic Literary Tradition in Edwar al-Kharrat's *Stones of Bobello*', in Luc Deheuvels, Barabara Michalak-Pikulska and Paul Starkey (eds), *Intertextuality in Modern Arabic Literature since 1967* (Durham: University of Durham Modern Languages Series, 2006), pp. 149–59.

———, *Sonallah Ibrahim: Rebel with a Pen* (Edinburgh: Edinburgh University Press, 2016).

Starr, Deborah A., 'Recuperating Cosmopolitan Alexandria: Circulation of Narratives and Narratives of Circulation', *Cities*, 22:3, 2005, pp. 217–28.

———, *Remembering Cosmopolitan Egypt: Literature, Culture, and Empire* (London/New York: Routledge, 2009).

———, 'Why New York?: Youssef Chahine', in D. A. Starr, *Remembering Cosmopolitan Egypt: Literature, Culture and Empire* (London/New York: Routledge, 2009), pp. 75–105.

Stewart, Desmond, *Great Cairo: Mother of the World* (Cairo: American University in Cairo Press, 1981).

Surur, Hassan, 'Kashaf Majallat Gallery 68', *Gallery 68*, al-Juzʾ al-Thani (Cairo: Matbuʿat al-Kitaba al-Ukhra, 1997).

Taher, Bahaa, *Aunt Safiyya and the Monastery*, trans. Barbara Romaine (Berkeley: University of California Press, 1996).

———, *Bil-Ams Halumtu Biki* (Cairo: al-Hayʾa al-Misriyya al-ʿAmma li-l-Kitab, 1984).

———, *al-Hubb fi al-Manfa* (Cairo: Dar al-Hilal, 1995).

———, *Khalati Safiyya wa-l-Dayr* (Cairo: Dar al-Hilal, 1991).

———, *al-Khutuba wa Qisas Ukhra* (Cairo: al-Hayʾa al-Misriyya al-ʿAmma li-l-Kitab, 1972).

———, *Love in Exile*, trans. Farouk Abdel Wahab (Cairo: American University in Cairo Press, 2001).

———, 'Qariban min Baha Tahir: Hiwar maʿa al-Bahaʾ Husayn', in Muhammad ʿUbayd Allah (ed.), *ʿAlam Bahaa Taher: Dayf Dar Majdalawi li-ʿAm 2005* (Amman: Dar Majdalawi li-l-Nashr wa-l-Tawziʿ, 2005), pp. 161–87.

———, *al-Siraʿ fi al-Manfa: al-Qahira-Jinif, Jinif-al-Qahira* (Cairo: Bardiyya li-l-Nashr wa-l-Tawziʿ, 2017).

———, *Sunset Oasis*, trans. Humphrey T. Davies (London: Sceptre, 2009).

———, *Wahat al-Ghurub* (Beirut: Dar al-Adab, 2007).
Tewfiq, Nourhan, 'A Prize with a View', *al-Ahram Weekly*, 4 June 2015, http://weekly.ahram.org.eg/News/12421.aspx (last accessed 4 June 2018).
Tomlinson, Alan, and Christopher Young, 'Culture, Politics, and Spectacle in the Global Sports Event', in Alan Tomlinson and Christopher Young (eds), *National Identity and Global Sports Events: Culture, Politics and Spectacle in the Olympics and the Football World Cup* (Albany: State University of New York Press, 2006), pp. 1–13.
Tzalas, Harry, *Farewell to Alexandria*, trans. Susan E. Matouvalou (Cairo/New York: American University in Cairo Press, 2000).
van de Akker, W. J., and G. J. Dorleijin, 'Talkin' 'Bout Two Generations: The Concept of Generation in Literary Historiography', in Thomas F. Shannon and Johan P. Snapper (eds), *Janus at the Millennium: Perspectives on Time in the Culture of the Netherlands* (Lanham: University Press of America, 2004), pp. 11–25.
Warnes, Christopher, *Magical Realism and the Postcolonial Novel* (New York: Palgrave Macmillan, 2009).
Waterbury, John, *The Egypt of Nasser and Sadat: The Political Economy of Two Regimes* (New Jersey: Princeton University Press, 1983).
ᶜUbayd Allah, Muhammad (ed.), *ᶜAlam Bahaa Taher: Dayf Dar Majdalawi li-ᶜAm 2005* (Amman: Dar Majdalawi li-l-Nashr wa-l-Tawziᶜ, 2005).
Unattributed, 'Kalim min *al-Taliᶜa*', *al-Taliᶜa*, 10, October 1969, p. 95.
Unattributed, 'al-Kalima Alladhi alqaha Sonallah Ibrahim fi Khitam Muʾtamar al-Riwayah wa al-Madina', *al-Badil*, http://www.albadil.org/spip.php?article52 (last accessed 8 March 2012).
Unattributed, 'Yusuf al-Qaid', *The Egyptian Writers' Union*, http://egywriters.org/member (last accessed 6 June 2018).
Uthman, Nader K., 'A Storied Exile: Poetics of Displacement in Modern Arab/ic Novels', PhD Dissertation (Columbia University, 2009).
Yaqub, Nadia, 'The Tale of Those Who Did Not Travel: Reading Yaḥya al-Tahir ᶜAbdallah's 'The Neckband and the Bracelet as Sīrah', *Journal of Arabic Literature*, 36:2, 2005, pp. 111–34.
Zohry, Ayman, 'Egyptian Irregular Migration to Europe', *European Population Conference*, 2006, pp. 1–34.
Zohry, Ayman, and Barbara Harrell-Bond, 'Contemporary Egyptian Migration: An Overview of Voluntary and Forced Migration', *Development Research Centre on Migration, Globalization and Poverty*, December 2003, pp. 1–72.

Index

Abdel Meguid, Ibrahim, 184
   al-Balda al Ukhra (*The Other Place*), 167
   Alexandria Trilogy, 86–106
   al-Masafat (*Distances*), 90
   Burj al-ʿAthraʾ (*Virgo*), 90
   cinema and television adaptations, 186
   cultural/political roles, 187, 188
   literary awards, 186
Abdullah, Yahya Taher
   al-Tawq wa-l Iswira (*The Collar and the Bracelet*), 116, 136–45
   cinema and television adaptations, 186
   literary awards, 186
   short stories, 138, 143–4
aesthetic innovation, 3–4, 9–12, 19–21, 35, 39–41; *see also* narrative
agency, and sexuality, 41, 54, 82, 99, 175
agrarian reform, 117–18
Alexandria, 73–115
   exodus of foreign communities, 92–4, 96–7
   modern history, sources for, 102–6
   the religious and the national, 98–102
alienation, 12, 34, 37, 137–8, 159–60, 176
   nineties generation, 190–1
alley(s)
   as the nation, 32
   Zafarani Alley, 41–7
al-Masaʾ (newspaper), 40
Anderson, Benedict, 19–20
Appadurai, Arjun, 156, 177
Arab representations of the West, 154–5, 157
Arab–Israeli wars, 93, 96, 130–1
art, space of, 18
Ashour, Radwa, 184, 186
   Atyaf (*Spectres*), 56, 61
   autobiographical works, 61

Faraj (*Blue Lorries*), 55–63
literary awards, 186
political roles, 188
Qitʿa min Urubba (*A Piece of Europe*), 56, 61
Aslan, Ibrahim
   cinema and television adaptations, 186
   cultural/political roles, 187, 188
   The Heron (*Malik al-Hazin*), 47–55
   literary awards, 186
authenticity, 80–1
autobiography, 61, 75, 85, 154

Badawi, Muhammad, 3, 15–16, 143, 185
Bakhtin, M. M., 18–19
Bakr, Salwa, 11, 184–5
Beirut, 163–6
belonging, 80–1, 156; *see also* nationalism
biography
   and history, 56
   and mapping, 35, 128–9
Birds of Amber (Abdel Meguid), 91–8, 103, 104–5
al-Bisati, Muhammad
   al-Khaldiyya (*Over the Bridge*), 167, 171, 173
   cultural/political roles, 187, 188
   Daqq al-Tubul (*Drumbeat*), 155–6, 167–77
   Layali Ukhra (*Other Nights*), 167
   literary awards, 186
   political exile, 158
Blue Lorries (Ashour), 55–63
body, the, state control of, 38
Bonaparte, Napoleon, 51
Bourdieu, Pierre, 2, 7, 14, 185
Bread Riots, 53–4, 101
British colonialism *see* colonialism, British

cafés, 51–3, 55, 161
　as community/political spaces, 125–7
　as homosocial space, 53
Cairo, 31–72, 117
　alleys, portraits of, 41–7
　exile from, 162–3
　Heliopolis, 34–5
　Imbaba, 47–55
　Jamaliyya, 32, 41, 47
　nineties generation, 191
　prison themes/novels, 38, 41, 56–63
　University, 33–4
Camus, Albert, 39, 159
canals, as symbol of connection, 88–9
capitalism, 19, 98–9
censorship, 39, 40, 187, 188
Certeau, Michel de, 35
cinema *see* film genre
citizenship, and labour migrants, 173
City of Saffron (al-Kharrat), 77, 84–5, 86
class themes
　marginalised communities, Alexandria, 92, 94–6
　and the nationalist project, 99–100
　working class, Alexandria, 88
Clouds over Alexandria (Abdel Meguid), 98–102, 105
Colla, Elliot, 49–50
The Collar and the Bracelet (Abdullah), 136–45
colonialism, British, 80
　and anti-colonial struggle, 144
　cosmopolitanism, Alexandria, 78, 80, 86–7, 89
　and war, 87–8
communists, 15, 33–4, 100–1, 158
construction *see* housing/construction
consumerism, 162
Coptic Christians, 76, 78, 80, 84
cosmopolitanism, Alexandria
　colonial, 78, 80, 86–7, 89
　demise of, 87–8

Delta, Egyptian, 116
difference, 80, 104
discrimination, 174–7
diversity
　Alexandria Trilogies, 77–81
　cultural, Gulf States, 172–3
　see also cosmopolitanism; religion
Drumbeat (al-Bisati), 155–6, 167–77

economics, 48, 52–3, 98–100
　and exploitation, 24, 52, 155, 173, 175–7
Egyptian revolution (1952), 48, 80, 88, 137, 144
El Guabli, Brahim, 62
El-Enany, Rasheed, 155, 157
epic time, 143
epigraphs, 102–3
ethnoscapes, 156, 177
Europe/Europeans, 154–5, 157, 159; *see also* colonialism, British
exile, 154–83
existentialism, 159–60; *see also* alienation
exploitation *see* economics

fantastic narratives, 90, 96–7, 105, 132, 170–1
　the alley, 32, 42–7
　nineties generation, 190–1
female body *see* women
festival (*mawlid*), 120–1, 123–4
film genre, 36, 104, 186
flashbacks, 48, 61–2
folklore and songs, 102–3, 117, 133–5
football theme, 172–4
Foucault, Michel, 18, 38, 46, 59–60, 100

Gallery 68, 15
gender *see* masculinity; women
geographical description *see* map/mapping
Gheit el-Enab, Alexandria, 77, 79, 88
al-Ghitani, Gamal, 186
　cultural/political roles, 187, 188
　The Zafarani Files (*Waqaʾiʿ Harat al-Zaʿfarani*), 41–7, 60
Girls of Alexandria (al-Kharrat), 77, 78, 81–4, 85
Gulf States, 99, 167, 176; *see also Drumbeat*

Hafez, Sabry, 10, 12, 143–4, 188–9, 190–1
al-Hakim, Tawfiq
　ʿ*Usfur min al-Sharq* (*A Bird from the East*), 154
　Yawmiyyat Naʾib fi al-Aryaf (*Maze of Justice: Diary of a Country Prosecutor*), 127–8
Hanley, William, 77, 87
Haqqi, Yahya
　Qindil Umm Hashim (*The Lamp of Umm Hashim*), 32, 154
　and social realism, 40
ḥāra (alley) *see* alleys

Harvey, David, 19
Heliopolis, spatial biography of, 34–5
The Heron (Aslan), 47–55
housing/construction
    Gulf, labour migrants, 169–70
    Nasser's regime, 48
    Sadat's regime, 98
Hussein, Taha, 154

Ibrahim, Sonallah
    al-Lajna (*The Committee*), 39
    Bayrut Bayrut (*Beirut Beirut*), 39
    cinema and television adaptations, 186
    literary awards, 186
    other novels, 34
    The Smell of It (*Tilka-l-Raʾiha*), 33–41, 44
    and the state, 34, 187–8
Imbaba, portrait of, 47–55
impotency curse, 42–4, 46
inequality and discrimination, 174–7
international solidarity, failure of, 158–9, 165–6
Islamic identity/ideology, 89, 98, 99, 101, 121, 162; *see also* Sufism
itinerary, the, 35–6

Jackson, Rosemary, 43, 171
Jacquemond, Richard, 7, 13–14, 142, 184–5
Jamaliyya *see* Cairo
Jews, Jewishness, 81
journalism, and fiction, 164–6

Kendall, Elisabeth, 2, 7, 12
Khalaf, Sulayman, 170, 171, 172–3
al-Kharrat, Edwar, 122, 170, 185
    Alexandria Trilogy, 73–86
    al-Hassasiyya al-Jadida, 3, 10, 185
    on Ibrahim, 36
    literary awards, 186

labour migration *see* migration themes
land reform, 117–18
Lebanon
    prison, 59
    Sabra and Shatila massacres, 163–6
Lefebvre, Henri, 17, 46, 51, 161, 166
literary awards, 167, 185–6
Lorca, Federico García, 87
Love in Exile (Taher), 155, 156–67, 177

magic realism *see* fantastic narratives; mythic spaces
Mahfouz, Naguib
    Cairo novels, 32, 41
    Midaq Alley, 32
    Miramar, 74–5
map/mapping
    Alexandria Trilogies, 77, 79
    The Heron, 49–50
    rural narrative, 128–9
    and state surveillance, 36
Marzouki, Ahmed, 59, 63
masculinity, 43, 46, 99, 135; *see also* sexuality
Mehrez, Samia, 32, 33, 191
    on al-Ghitani's works, 44
    on alienation, 119
    on gender equality, 188
migration themes, 87, 98–9, 167, 176; *see also Drumbeat*
Miramar (Mahfouz), 74–5
mobility, 156
    symbols of, 77, 89–90
Morocco, prison literature, 59, 62–3
movement *see* mobility
movies, 36, 104, 186
Mubarak, Hosni
    labour migration, 168
    repressive regime, 57
    and the sixties writers, 33, 187–8
al-Musawi, Muhsin, 127, 164, 165
al-Muwaylihi, Muhammad, *Hadith ʿIsa Ibn Hisham* (*A Period of Time*), 31
My Alexandria (al-Kharrat), 77, 85–6
mythic spaces, 132, 136–43

Napoleon Bonaparte, 51
narrative(s)
    circular/repetitive, 38, 49, 62, 122, 134–5, 143–4
    multiple perspectives, 49, 52
Nasser, Gamal Abdel, 88, 117
    agrarian reform, 117–18
    and Cairo University, 33–4
    construction under, 48
    labour migration, 167–8
    nationalisation policies, 92, 94, 96
    repressive regime, 45, 54, 57
    and the Suez crisis, 93, 96
nation, imagined community, 19–20
nationalisation policies, 92, 94, 96

nationalism/national identity, 56, 173–4
  critique of, 24, 91–4, 97–8, 99, 177
  see also pan-Arabism
nature theme, 155, 160–1
neo-liberalism, 189
neo-realism, 11, 36
News from the Minisi Farm (al-Qaid), 116, 127–36
newspapers
  on Ibrahim's work, 40
  reports, 103–5
  see also journalism
nineties generation (writers), 188–91
No One Sleeps in Alexandria (Abdel Meguid), 87–91, 98, 102
novel, the, and Cairo, 31
al-Noweihi, Magda, 83, 86

officialdom, and folklore, 134–5
oil, and labour migrants, 167–9
oral traditions, 123, 134–5, 145
  Arabic and Islamic, 121
Over the Bridge see al-Bisati, Muhammad

Palestine, prison literature, 63
pan-Arabism, 167–8
A Piece of Europe see Ashour, Radwa
pilgrimage, 119, 122–3, 123, 125
poetry, 103, 105–6, 165
political activism, 166, 188; see also agency; students
political exile, 158–9
postcolonial aesthetics see aesthetic innovation
postcolonialism, critique of, 96–8
power, technologies of, 46
prison themes/novels, 56–63

Qasim, Abd al-Hakim
  Ayyam al-Insan al-Sabʿa (*The Seven Days of Man*), 116, 119–27
  novellas, 120
al-Qaid, Yusuf
  Akhbar ʿIzbat al-Minisi (*News from the Minisi Farm*), 116, 127–36
  cinema and television adaptations, 186
  literary award, 186
  other novels, 127, 129
  political roles, 188
Qurʾan, 121

realist literature, 12, 32, 40, 90, 118, 143, 168
religion
  diversity, 81, 84, 89–91, 94, 100
  see also Coptic Christians; Islamic identity/ideology
  resistance, 17
  Gulf city narrative, 171–2
  spaces of, 47, 49, 51, 53–4, 166
  writing as, 39, 62–3
  see also students
revenge, 128, 135, 140
revolution/change, 44, 46–7
riots, 53–4, 101
rural migration, 87
rural spaces/novels, 116–53
  marginalisation of, 117, 119–21, 126–7, 131, 136–7, 143
  mythic, 136–41
  and political transformation, 118–19, 136–7

al-Sadat, Anwar
  agrarian reform, 118
  'Open Door' economic policies, 48, 52–3, 57, 98–101, 162, 167–8
  and political exile, 162
  religious ideology under, 99
  repressive regime, 54, 57, 157–9, 187
Said, Edward, 33
Sartre, Jean-Paul, 13–14, 39, 159
Saudi Arabia, 169
Second World War, representations of, 73, 79–80, 87–90
security, state see censorship; surveillance
Selim, Samah, 122, 126–7, 136, 144
Sells, Ralph, 167–8
The Seven Days of Man (Qasim), 116, 119–27
sexual violence, 41
sexuality, and agency, 39–41, 46–7, 54, 82, 99, 175
shantytowns, 48
al-Sharqawi, Abdel Rahman, *al-Ard* (*The Land*), 118
short stories, 31, 138, 143–4
sirah, 143
sixties generation (*jīl al-sittīnāt*), 13–14
  aesthetic innovation, 3–4, 9–12, 19–21, 38
  cultural and political roles, 187–8
  influences and strategy, 12–16, 165
  youthfulness, 8–9

The Smell of It (Ibrahim), 33–41
social realism *see* realist literature
social space, 17–18; *see also* time
socialism, state, 5, 16; *see also* communists
Soueif, Ahdaf, 31
Spectres see Ashour, Radwa
Starr, Deborah, 88, 89, 96
state repression
   writing as resistance, 39
   see also censorship; surveillance
students
   political activism, 34, 57, 60, 98, 100–2
   see also resistance
Suez crisis, 91–2, 93, 96
Sufism, Sufi ritual, 117, 119, 121–2
   death of, 125–7
surveillance, 33, 36, 38
   Blue Lorries, 59–60
   Gulf States, 172
   The Smell of It, 39
   The Zafarani Files, 44–6

Taher, Bahaa
   literary award, 186
   Love in Exile (al-Huhh fi al-Manfa), 155, 156–67, 177
   political exile, 158–9, 187
television adaptations, 186

temple, the, and mythic violence, 141–3
time
   epic time, 143
   and space, representations of, 18–19
torture, 41, 63
trams, 77, 89–90

urban narratives, 64–5; *see also* Alexandria; Cairo; *individual titles of works*
utopian community, 122, 171

vengeance *see* revenge
villages *see* rural spaces/novels

walking, 77, 88, 90
war themes, 73, 87–90, 91, 96, 130–1
welfare state, dismantlement of, 48, 101
Western other, Arab representations of, 154–5, 157
women
   Alexandria Trilogies, 81–4
   and collective history, 60
   as land (metaphor), 141
   transgressions of, 139–41, 173
   writers, 184–5, 186
writing, complexities of, 61–3

The Zafarani Files (al-Ghitani), 41–7, 60

EU representative:
Easy Access System Europe
Mustamäe tee 50, 10621 Tallinn, Estonia
Gpsr.requests@easproject.com

www.ingramcontent.com/pod-product-compliance
Lightning Source LLC
Chambersburg PA
CBHW070346240426
43671CB00013BA/2423